**Kiplinger's**

# Retire *and* Thrive

## HOW MORE THAN 50 PEOPLE REDEFINED THEIR RETIREMENT LIFESTYLES

## Robert K. Otterbourg

 PUBLISHING

This publication is designed to provide accurate and authoritative information in regard to the subject matter covered. It is sold with the understanding that the publisher is not engaged in rendering legal, accounting, or other professional service. If legal advice or other expert assistance is required, the services of a competent professional should be sought.

President, Kaplan Publishing: Roy Lipner
Vice President and Publisher: Maureen McMahon
Acquisitions Editor: Karen Murphy
Development Editor: Trey Thoelcke
Senior Managing Editor: Jack Kiburz
Typesetting: the dotted i
Cover Design: Design Solutions

Published by Kaplan Publishing,
a division of Kaplan, Inc.

Printed in the United States of America

06 07 08   10 9 8 7 6 5 4 3 2 1

**Library of Congress Cataloging-in-Publication Data**

Otterbourg, Robert K.
  Kiplinger's retire & thrive : how more than 50 people redefined their retirement lifestyles / Robert K. Otterbourg. — 4th ed.
      p.      cm.
    Includes index.
    ISBN-13: 978-1-4195-3823-0
    ISBN-10: 1-4195-3823-3
    1. Retirement—United States—Planning.   2. Retirement—United States—Case studies.
  3. Retirees—United States—Attitudes.   I. Title.   II. Title: Kiplinger's retire and thrive.
  III. Title: Retire & thrive.   IV. Title: Retire and thrive.
  HQ1063.2.U6077 2006
  646.7'9—dc22
                                                                        2006014591

## Dedication

To Sue for sharing the earlier, and now our retire-and-thrive, years.

And to the men and women profiled in this book. Whether they continue to work full- or part-time, or they focus on other endeavors, they refuse to sit idly on the sidelines in what should be their retirement years.

# Contents

# Contents

## What's Next?

In the past few years, I attended two reunions. The first was Colgate University, where I found that I was definitely in the minority. Most of my classmates were fully retired with little or no intention to return to the workplace even on a part-time basis. What they were doing as full-time retirees seemed to me about as enjoyable as a month of Sundays. How, I wondered, do they fill the 2,000 to 2,500 hours or more annually that they once devoted to their careers?

Three years later, I attended a Columbia University Graduate School of Journalism reunion. I found a different scenario. These classmates continue to work either on a full-time or part-time basis as reporters, editors, columnists, book writers, and producers of television documentaries. They like their work and the income, factors they share with many other retirement-age Americans.

Why retire is a recurring theme of this book and one that concerns so many people nearing retirement. It's a question that confronted a neighbor in the apartment house where I grew up. Mrs. M. asked that question of her 70-year-old son, who wanted to retire from the family business. At 95 and chairman of the company where both worked, the mother denied her son's request, saying that he was too young to retire. I can understand her view.

With those musings, the die was cast. The result is *Retire & Thrive,* a source of ideas, reassurance, and inspiration for those who want to catch a second wind in retirement.

For some, retirement, or whatever you want to call it, comes in their early to mid-50s and for others in their 60s, but for a growing number of people, retirement in the usual sense never becomes part of their lifestyle.

## Early, Late, or Never

The first edition of this book was published in 1995. The initial intention was to focus on people age 60 plus, including those taking early retirement, as well as those who elected to work indefinitely and not retire.

I soon found that I was limiting my editorial horizons by excluding people in their 50s, many of whom were losing their jobs or prematurely retiring. As a result, I packaged everyone from ages 50 to 65 into what I called the 50-plus set. By using age 50 as the starting point, I deliberately set a trap for the older members of the baby boomer generation who turned 50 in 1996. Ten years later, many in this boomer age group have turned or are about to turn 60. Hopefully, they have already found the answer or at least begun asking the question, what's next? In February 2003, broadcaster Jane Pauley asked herself the same question when she announced that she was leaving NBC after 27 years with the TV network. Her comments in the *New York Times* caught my attention: "I kept walking by bookstores and seeing titles talking about second acts of life." She said that at age 52 she still found herself wondering "what's next, or even, what is it I really want to do? . . . I think women think a lot about cycles. This year another cycle came around: My contract was up. It seemed an opportunity to take a life audit." Within two years, Pauley returned with a daytime TV talk show.

Early retirement in the face of layoffs and downsizing is becoming a common occurrence. The message is now loud and clear for those severed from the workplace: To survive, they need to adopt different career and lifestyle objectives. Chances are they will not be able to duplicate the job that they just lost. Furthermore, in the employment marketplace there is little discernible difference between a 52-year-old and someone who is ten years older. The future is bright for those 50-plus job seekers who are resourceful, inventive, and willing to do things differently. Others have less reason to be cheery.

## Need a Better Crystal Ball

The fourth edition reflects the mood of the 21st century. I'm amazed how fast the world has moved in the past few years. I should have used a better brand of tea leaves to help me forecast many of the trends noted in the earlier editions. As such, this edition recognizes both the ongoing events and particularly the trends that presently or will soon affect the 50-plus set.

Up to the mid-1990s, e-mail and Internet users were primarily the technologically savvy. Things changed, and data communications rapidly became of age. As a result, we exchange e-mail addresses as readily—and sometimes more readily—than telephone numbers.

Similarly, Internet growth is impressive among the 50-plus set. According to a Pew Internet and American Life Project *(www.pewinternet.org)*, 22 percent of those over age 65 use the Internet, compared with a 15 percent rate in 2000. By contrast, 58 percent of those aged 50 to 65 are Internet users.

## Baby Boomers Grow Gray Whiskers

The first batch of baby boomers, about four million a year, once cute little kids in diapers and later young adults who vowed never to "trust anyone over 30," started to turn 60 as of January 2006.

Men and women in this "never-going-to-get-old" age group need to consider future workplace and lifestyle alternatives.

AARP *(www.aarp.org)* is also concerned about boomers after viewing the demographics of its 36 million members. As such, it restyled its monthly magazine into three distinct editions to appeal to readers in their 50s, 60s, and 70s. More than a ploy to attract advertisers, this strategy shows that the retirement years affect a broad spectrum of ages—and interests.

## What Lies Ahead?

The first chapter sets the stage by exploring attitudes about retirement and describing 50-plus-set trends. Chapter 2 discusses how to plan for these life events. The next three chapters concentrate on what I find are the three most vibrant nonwork activities: becoming a student, working as a volunteer, and pursuing a hobby. The concluding chapters focus on the dynamics in the workplace: staying on, though very likely with a change of pace or focus; changing careers or becoming self-employed; and escaping from retirement and returning to the workplace

The editorial guideline for *Retire & Thrive* is clear-cut. The introductory part of each chapter highlights societal and demographic information, and relevant how-to information; the balance of the chapter is given to human-interest profiles. This book isn't intended to be comprehensive. Rather, the groups and activities cited were selected because they would have particular appeal to a diverse 50-plus-set audience. *Retire & Thrive* is intended for anyone age 50 to 65, in or out of the workplace.

The anecdotal profiles support the theme of each chapter. They are organized so that you learn what 50-plus-set people are presently doing and, just as important, the different routes they took to reach their present lifestyle. A number of the men and women portrayed are in their late 60s and 70s, but in nearly every instance they adopted their present lifestyle formula years earlier, often when they were in their 50s. I've added 20 new profiles in this edition and dropped a similar number that appeared in the third edition.

Where do I find the folks to profile? Many of them presently live in North Carolina, a somewhat deceptive statistic because most lived and worked in other parts of the country before relocating to North Carolina to take a new job or to retire. And thanks to Colgate alumni and friends of friends in other parts of the United States, I was able to achieve geographical diversity in the men and women being profiled.

Most of the women that I interviewed deferred careers for a decade or two to raise their children. Their lives and careers typically followed this chronology: a year or so after graduating from college they married; they had children and stayed home until the children were at least in elementary school; they went to graduate or professional school; and then they entered the workplace. The dilemma many such women face is why become a full-time or part-time retiree at age 65 when their career started at midlife

A few of the people I interviewed agreed to share their stories but asked that I preserve their privacy by giving them pseudonyms or using an abbreviated form of their names. They did not want to jeopardize their jobs or relationships with employers or clients.

## No Formulas

The editorial placement of many of the profiles provided a particular challenge. Those profiled could have easily been featured in several different chapters because their range of interests typifies the diversity that underscores the 50-plus set.

It would be much simpler if we could fit everyone in the 50-plus set into neat little boxes à la the words of one of Pete Seeger's classic folk songs. Real people defy that type of classification. Rather, they are discovering and implementing different lifestyle plans. Some of the solutions might lead you to think that 50-plus-set members are dabblers. That is hardly the case. A retiree might work as a part-time professional three days a week, serve as a volunteer two mornings, and then spend an equal amount of time with a hobby. More often than not, the people profiled selected a lifestyle that includes a combination of interests. Though they would deride such a description, the people in *Retire & Thrive* are, in a special sense, adventurers. Regardless of their interests, they are active and energetic. None are "couch potatoes." They have created a 50-plus lifestyle uniquely their own. By doing so, they reinvented themselves. Some developed new skills, but others took existing talents and reshaped them to meet new objectives.

The only certainty for the 50-plus set is that one size definitely doesn't fit all. Unlike many other cycles in one's life, in this one there's no grading system to indicate whether one is excelling or failing in retirement. There are no rules on what's right and what's wrong, nor are there any report cards or year-end job reviews. You can try a hobby or part-time job, and if you don't like it, drop it and try something new. Thus, with differing views on retirement, the people profiled in *Retire & Thrive* adhere to the sentiments that Frank Sinatra lyrically depicted in *My Way:* "And more, much more than this, I did it my way."

# What's All the Fuss about Retirement?

*"And in the end, it's not the years in your life that count. It's the life in your years."*
—Abraham Lincoln

If you've been coasting along contentedly toward midlife, AARP *(www.aarp.org)* knows how to elevate your blood pressure: a membership invitation arrives on your 50th birthday. So much for immortality. For a $12.50 membership fee, you're entered into AARP's expanding database of 36 million members, and you have taken the first step as a participant in the great retirement game.

When we become 50 we are understandably ambivalent, if not indifferent, about retirement. Youth, we rightfully maintain, is still on our side. Retirement seems like an event in the distant future. Sooner than anticipated, retirement is on the doorstep. It may even be accelerated by the twin effects of downsizing and early-retirement buyout plans. Retirement-related questions begin to surface, and, at best, we have entered into uncharted waters. As the many profiles in this book will make clear, it's difficult to define *retirement*. We've euphemistically called retirement the "golden age" and the "leisure years." Contrary to the dictionary definition, retirement is no longer a "withdrawal from one's position or occupation, or from active working life."

Marcel Marceau doesn't know how to define retirement. In his early 80s, he still ranks as one of the world's best mimes. When asked about retirement during a National Public Radio interview, Marceau said that he never worries about his age, and that's what keeps him young.

To Victor Marshall, who directs the University of North Carolina's Institute on Aging (*www unc.edu*) "retirement is an ambiguous word. It refers to an event, that specific point in time when a person leaves paid employment, including anticipation and planning, leaving the job, and adapting to a new status in life. It refers to a status, that of a person who has been in paid employment, but is no longer. It refers to a role, the conduct of persons in the retirement status."

Looking at the current environment of corporate restructuring and those affected by it, AARP found that "those nearing retirement no longer seek it as a sharp break with the past." Rather, today's "preretired" seek continuity. Many anticipate "retiring" from their life-long career only to continue working, either in a new job in the field they've been in or in an unrelated area.

Much depends on how you feel about your career. As much as some people enjoy their work, they might be emotionally burned out and physically exhausted after 30 to 40 years; they're ready to take a break or do something different. Countering those emotions may be a feeling of guilt, especially among "Depression-age babies" who were born in the 1930s. They were

---

## WHICH ONE ARE YOU?

Lydia Brönte, in her book *The Longevity Factor* (Harper Colllins, 1993), describes retirees this way:

- **Homesteaders,** who stay in the same field all their lives and remain endlessly fascinated by the work they chose
- **Transformers,** who find their dream job only after a major career shift
- **Explorers,** who, in the pursuit of opportunity and growth, make periodic career changes throughout their lives
- **Long-growth-curver and late bloomers,** who reach the highest peak later in life
- **Retirees and returnees,** who thought they were leaving work permanently, but who returned to work having missed the activity and challenges

inoculated with a self-perpetuating work ethic that makes it difficult to accept retirement of any sort.

When counseling retirees, Boston gerontologist David Karp finds that "some feel that there are important things left unfinished in their work lives. As would be expected, people with unfinished agendas were relatively more engaged in work and least likely to look on retirement favorably."

## Where's the Equal Opportunity?

Of course, feelings and decisions about retirement may be complicated by a spouse's attitude toward it. Many husbands are ready to leave corporate America and perhaps enjoy some leisure time with their wives. Not so with working wives, who in their 50s and 60s are not ready to retire, after having entered or reentered the workplace in their late 30s or early 40s once their children were in school. "They are too busy making a mark," says David Karp. "In their 50s, many men feel an urgency to do things that their occupational lives had made difficult, whereas many women feel an urgency to do occupational things their family lives had made difficult." He notes, not surprisingly, that men and women of the same chronological age often talk very differently about their work. "Many women are 'turning on' at the same age that their male counterparts are 'turning off.'"

The good news for many male retirees, whatever their reason for retiring, is that their wives are furnishing an additional financial safety net. As many of the profiles in this book note, a wife's income and benefits package give the family options that it might not otherwise have.

A working wife also gives her retired mate a breather in making the transition from the workplace to a new lifestyle. She avoids the homebound wife's cliché, "I married you for better or worse but not for lunch." In this changeover period, perhaps it is best that each spouse has some space. Bill Stanley (profiled in Chapter 6) works several days a week from his

Ridgewood, New Jersey, home office as a career-coaching consultant. His wife, Viola, in her late 50s and 13 years younger, is a full-time teacher who expects to teach until she's 65. Their separate daytime schedules pose few problems. Bill shops for food and enjoys cooking and attending to household chores.

## The Generation Gap

Our closest role models may not be much help in thinking about retirement. Growing up, I knew very few people who had retired. My parents and their friends were self-employed professionals or owners of small businesses who worked, as was the custom a generation ago, until they died or were physically unable to work. Because my father had virtually no retirement savings or benefits, retirement was not a part of the household vocabulary.

The formula was rather simplistic for my parents' generation. People worked longer and died earlier. In 1990, people who survived to age 65 could expect to live another 12 years, and 80 percent of the men 65 and older were still working. The Centers for Disease Control (*www.cdc.gov*) tells us that life expectancy is inching upwards. When Social Security was enacted in 1935, life expectancy was approximately 63 years. Seventy years later, a 65-year-old man can expect to live nearly 17 more years, and women an additional 3.

Americans are leaving the workforce at an earlier age, says the Census Bureau *(www.census.gov)*. In the early 1950s, 41 percent of men and nearly 8 percent of women age 65-plus still worked, compared with a current rate of 19 percent for men and 11 percent for women.

So we're living longer and leaving the workforce earlier. Simple arithmetic proves that most retirees need to find ways to redirect the 2,000 to 2,500 hours or more a year that were once spent at work and on work-related activities, such as commuting and "homework."

| MEDIAN RETIREMENT AGE | | |
| --- | --- | --- |
| YEARS INCLUDING | MEN | WOMEN |
| 1950–55 | 66.9 | 67.7 |
| 1955–60 | 65.8 | 66.2 |
| 1960–65 | 65.2 | 64.6 |
| 1965–70 | 64.2 | 64.2 |
| 1970–75 | 63.4 | 63.0 |
| 1975–80 | 63.0 | 63.2 |
| 1980–85 | 62.8 | 62.7 |
| 1985–1990 | 62.6 | 62.8 |
| 1990–95[1] | 62.7 | 62.6 |
| 1995–2000[1] | 62.3 | 62.0 |
| 2000–05[2] | 61.7 | 61.2 |

1. Based on 1990 actual and 1995 projected data

2. Based on projected data

Source: *Monthly Labor Review*, U.S. Department of Labor.

## A Financial Change of Fortune

A generation or two ago, a retirement package, if one existed, consisted of a testimonial gift together with a relatively small pension and equally small Social Security benefits. A pension was not always an inherent right. Less than 60 years ago, the average American worker, unless handicapped or ill, never considered retirement—or could afford to. For most Americans in the mid-1930s, retirement with an assured pension was limited to the wealthy and to a few long-term corporate and government employees. In an era when life expectancy was around 63 years, Congress set 65 as the age of eligibility to collect $30 in monthly benefits. Over the next 55 years, Social Security coverage was broadened to include nearly all wage earners. New features were added in stages—in 1965, Medicare insurance coverage; in 1974, the pegging of retirement benefits to the consumer price index. The average retiree in 1973 received a $166 monthly Social Security check compared with approximately $963 in 2006.

Nowadays, says AARP, 60 percent of workers collect Social Security benefits beginning at age 62, the earliest age of eligibility, compared with 40 percent of workers in 1980 and 28 percent ten years earlier. Not only have government-mandated benefits improved, so also has discretionary income. Marketers have discovered that the golden years for Americans between 55 and 64 are indeed bright in terms of discretionary income. While their incomes on average are slightly lower than those of the older baby boomers, these folks over 55 often have a financial advantage because their children have completed college and are self-supporting. Starting at age 65, income begins to decline.

## How High Is Up?

How much money do I need to retire and live comfortably? That's the question that clouds much thinking about the otherwise fulfilling possibilities of retirement. While hardly of retirement age, Sherman McCoy, in Thomas Wolfe's book *The Bonfire of the Vanities,* pointed out that he was "going broke on a million dollars a year." In *Cashing In on the American Dream—How to Retire at 35* (Bantam Books, 1988), Paul Terhorst, a renegade from corporate accounting in the mid-1980s, advised readers on a variety of ways to live comfortably on $50 a day (in late-1980s dollars). Nearly 20 years later, Paul and his wife, Vicki, stay consistent with their dream and continue on their worldwide travels. You'll probably want to be nestled somewhere between these two extremes.

It is critical to develop some form of game plan, one tailored to meet specific needs and interests. Be flexible. It makes little sense to write a game plan in indelible ink, but keep these points in mind:

■ **Keep debt low.** Until you know your expenses, it makes little sense to pick up additional financial burdens, such as a boat or second home.

■ **Don't use money as your sole excuse for not doing something.** Instead, be creative. It can easily cost $12,000 per person for a luxury two-week tour to

Greece, or less than $4,000 through Elderhostel (*www.elderhostel.org*). Being creative means looking for alternatives that complement your pocketbook.

## My Own Story

Unlike my father and his peers, I came to grips years ago with certain aspects of my work-oriented retirement lifestyle. Without labeling it as such, I innocently took the first step in the late 1980s. Nearly 20 years of running my own public relations firm was enough. After a number of excellent years, I lost several accounts. Such setbacks in the past were usually only temporary; I would recharge my batteries and replace the lost business. At 58, I was no longer as resilient or as patient. "If this is a problem at this age, what will happen when I am 65 or older?" I asked myself. Up to then, I had never considered retraining for another career or retiring.

The first step was to phase out of public relations. I discharged my secretary and embarked on a new career as a freelance writer. Two years later, my office lease ended, and I moved a truncated business into a spare room at home. Without much fanfare, I had created a new business lifestyle bordering on semiretirement.

The transition was easier than I anticipated. A few factors were in my favor: I knew what it was like to be self-employed, and I enjoyed being a writer. I was also a hobbyist as well as an officer and trustee of several not-for-profit groups. My daytime calendar was usually full. I anticipated few problems in my career and lifestyle switch.

As part of my changeover, I gave myself a 60th birthday present, which I have renewed at five-year intervals: I set a goal to work as a writer for the duration. In looking back over the past decade and, more important, looking ahead, I'm pleased with that decision. I've blended writing, hobbies, volunteerism, and family life into a rewarding lifestyle. Fortunately, my wife and I share similar lifestyle goals and views toward retirement.

# Baby Boomers Come of Age

The demographers are having a field day interpreting what will happen to the 77 million baby boomers, the generation born between 1946 and 1964. An estimated four million boomers turn 60 in 2006, and a similar number will reach that age in each of the subsequent 18 years.

Many boomers have had retirement forced on them. As downsizing victims, many have found it difficult to get another job that matches the one they lost. Some—especially those who walked away with generous severance packages—don't care. They want to work only part-time or find a less pressured job.

In 2005, Merrill Lynch *(www.ml.com)* noted in its *New Retirement Survey* that approximately 75 percent of boomers intend to keep working in retirement. They expect to leave their current job or career and then launch into an entirely new one.

Other boomers are deeply concerned after the stock market decline of the early 2000s drastically reduced their net worth. Many have had to consider alternative plans. A late 2002 AARP survey of 1,013 investors between 50 and 70 found that 77 percent of them had lost money in the stock market over the previous two years; one in four had lost between 25 percent and 50 percent in the value of their investments. As a result, 20 percent of those with declining portfolios postponed retirement.

Here's what Rhodes Craver, a trust and estates lawyer with Kennon, Craver, Belo, Craig & McKee in Durham, North Carolina, says about declining portfolios and retirement: "Many of my clients worked past their 50s before they contemplated retirement. It may have been a hot idea back in the late '90s for folks in their 50s to think about early retirement, but the financial landscape has changed a great deal in the last five years. Retirement in one's 50s is more of a dream today than it may have been ten years ago."

The stock market dive a few years ago, says Rhodes, hurt investors in a number of ways. The precipitous drop in interest rates and investment yields put a real crunch on a potential retiree's cash flow. Added to this uncertainty is the fear that reduced or nonexistent Social Security coverage may increase their financial woes.

With life expectancy increasing, people in their 50s realize that they can easily live another 30 or 40 years. Rhodes questions whether they will have sufficient money to support themselves. Golden parachute contracts aside, even CEOs face a topsy-turvy and uncertain corporate life. There's a revolving door for too many CEOs, according to outplacement consultants Challenger, Gray & Christmas (*www. challengergray .com*). In 2005, there were 1,322 CEO departures, the largest number since 2000. The turnover rate over the past six years "can be traced to several factors, including planned retirements, performance records, post-Enron ethical issues, and changing priorities in corporate strategies."

Boomers represent about 45 percent of the workforce and are the biggest consumer-spending age group. Unlike their parents and older siblings, they don't intend to cease being workers and consumers as they age. Even for those who at one time expected to have an ample retirement nest egg, full-time or part-time work has become a critical issue. Boomers, AARP reports, are not about to become an idle generation. Eighty percent expect to work at least part-time for the extra income and to stay active.

Boomers need more money than their parents' generation to live comfortably and to satisfy their self-indulgence. Even with the current rate of inflation, a retirement income consisting of a pension, Social Security, and an investment portfolio will not pay the bills for many consumer-oriented boomers.

| **RETIREMENT INCENTIVES** |
|---|
| ■ Offered a good buyout package |
| ■ Wanted to do something different |
| ■ Bored with job, work, or employer |
| ■ Company downsized, acquired, or merged and job eliminated |
| ■ Wanted to relocate |
| ■ Had personal or family health problems |
| ■ Wanted to start a business |
| ■ Not interested in working full-time |
| ■ Had sufficient income to make even part-time work not necessary |

## Workplace Realities

Not everyone gets to pick the date for retiring, as Robert McCord discovered. He'll never forget the day the *Arkansas Gazette,* the oldest daily newspaper west of the Mississippi, was sold to the *Democrat,* its Little Rock rival. With the sale, Bob lost his job. Over the years, Bob had held nearly every editorial position on the *Gazette* and *Democrat.* When Gannett, the Gazette's owner, sold the paper, Bob's journalism career nearly ended at age 62.

Many of the other older *Gazette* reporters and editors retired before the sale because the *Democrat* was not interested in hiring the *Gazette*'s senior and better-paid staff members. Bob was fortunate. His financial stresses were few, his expenses were fixed, the mortgage was paid, and the three McCord children were self-supporting. His wife, Muriel, did not work. What Bob really needed was a professional challenge.

Among the local media, Bob was well known and regarded, so it was not surprising when he got a call from one of the local television stations asking him to write and broadcast three editorials a week. Though Bob's TV days ended, he's now in his 13th year of writing a weekly political column for the *Arkansas Times.* "I don't go downtown to work anymore," says Bob. "I'm better off than a lot of other guys who lost their jobs and careers when the *Gazette* folded."

## Will You Be Cut?

The result of the continuing round of corporate purges is a labor force of more than 20 million Americans between ages 50 and 65 who face the distinct possibility of working fewer hours, being laid off or pushed into some form of early retirement, and most likely never finding as good a job as the one they just lost.

One good yardstick on downsizing trends in corporate America has unfortunately disappeared, namely, the survey conducted for 15 years by the American Management Association. Even so, it's not too difficult on your own to fill in the blanks. Just read news reports on plant closings and employee downsizing. To anyone in the age 50-plus set, these announcements are disquieting.

Despite the pattern of continual downsizing in corporate America, the employment rate has actually increased for the 50-plus set, says AARP in its *State of 50 Plus America* study. Two-thirds of those between ages 50 and 64 work, as do 20 percent of those ages 65 to 74 and 6 percent over age 75.

Early-retirement buyout packages proved to be more popular than their corporate designers had imagined, often stripping companies of too many high achievers. Companies that once offered these packages have scaled them back or eliminated them. There is a sound reason why buyout packages are so

---

## TIPS FOR DOWNSIZING

New York outplacement consultant Anita Lands provides these tips, which are particularly applicable to those in their 50s who may be downsized:

- **Try the raise-hand approach.** "Take me and give me a package." This way you feel that you're master of your own fate. It avoids the feeling that you've been pinkslipped.
- **Some people feel liberated when they're downsized.** Get a good severance package and then get out.
- **Gray—as in gray hair—is no longer as good as it was a few years ago.** EEOC rulings aside, corporate America prefers younger personnel when they can get them.
- **Keep active.** Instead of sitting at home, become a volunteer. You might find some job possibilities with a nonprofit. There's less money, even though corporate skills are often transferable.
- **Uncertain times call for proactive career planning.** Do some defensive planning to prepare for the future. Take a certificate course to provide new job skills before being downsized.

popular: those who remain with the company gamble on doing equally well on a subsequent round of buyouts. However, they often discover this strategy does not pay off. They want to stay on full-time, continue working an alternative schedule, or retire. The bottom line is that companies need to retain a portion of the aging boomers in their organizations.

## Setting the Work Rules

If you survive cutbacks and ignore the inducements of early-retirement payouts, you can, in theory, work indefinitely. The Age Discrimination in Employment Act of 1967 made it illegal to discharge or fail to promote a worker between ages 40 and 65 due to age. Ten years later, the age was raised to 70, and in 1987 the age ceiling was eliminated.

Corporate officers and partners in professional service firms usually sign employment contracts that specify their date of retirement. Even here there are some admonitions. Federal regulations stipulate that employment may be terminated at age 65 only if the executive has been in a policy-making position considered critical to the mission of the organization for the past two years and earned a pension that will pay at least $44,000 a year. The act also addresses the issue of age discrimination as it relates to benefits. If it's more expensive for an employer to provide benefits for older employees, it may reduce the level of benefits but can't charge older employees more for benefits.

Some workers in hazardous jobs are governed by mandatory retirement. The Federal Aviation Administration *(www.faa.gov)* requires that pilots on larger regional and all national airlines retire at age 60. The Age Discrimination Employment Act permits cities to retire police and firefighters at age 55. Even when retirement was voluntary, most police and firefighters retired in their 50s after 20 to 30 years of service, frequently due to job burnout or work-related health problems.

The Equal Employment Opportunity Commission *(www.eeoc.gov)*, the custodian of the 1967 act, monitors

> ## STILL ON THE PAYROLL
>
> - Can't afford to retire
> - Children still in college
> - Pension plan not financially secure
> - Corporate health care benefits doubtful for retirees
> - Married late, started family even later
> - Not enough money to maintain lifestyle in retirement
> - Don't like retirement living
> - Above all, enjoy working so why quit

workplace conditions, including those that pressure employees age 40-plus to accept retirement as a way to reduce the workforce. In 2004, there were nearly 18,000 filings, a number that varies year to year with fluctuations in the economy.

## The Social Security Penalty

Recipients of Social Security who are age 62 through full retirement age (age 65 for those born before 1942, incremental age adjustments to age 67 for those born after; see the Appendix) and elect to work need to be aware of the penalties on excess work-related income. The government deducts $1 of benefits for each $2 received in salary or commissions (not including investment income) that exceeds $11,520. Thanks to the Senior Citizen's Freedom Act of 2000, the situation has become more favorable for people once they reach full retirement age. Their Social Security benefits are no longer reduced by work-related income.

Collecting Social Security while continuing to work is still a contentious issue, particularly if you're a double or triple dipper who collects salary, pension, and Social Security. The purists argue that if you work, you should not collect Social Security. Multiple pensioners have their supporters. "I paid into the system all these years, why not collect?" is a typical response from blue-collar workers as well as corporate executives.

# What's Happening in the Professions?

Professionals find it difficult to define *retirement*. In accounting, architecture, law, and medicine, for example, the practitioner who satisfies state licensing requirements and meets other professional obligations, such as continuing education, is still considered a member of the profession regardless of age and hours spent in active practice. There are practical limits, however.

During an annual medical examination, I asked my doctor what retirement rules applied to physicians. "None whatsoever," he said. Normally, the type of medical specialty dictates when a physician retires, as do the amount and nature of physical activity required. "Would you use a 74-year-old doctor for complex surgery?" my doctor asked.

Other than a few medical specialists, the median retirement age is 65. Emergency-room doctors retire from that demanding environment somewhat earlier, while psychiatrists often work well into their 70s. Psychiatrists might even enjoy age as a possible ally. Somewhat like older judges, artists, and musicians, psychiatrists' wisdom seems to grow with age in the public's eye, often allowing them to take on the persona of a sage.

From a practical standpoint, partnership agreements often help winnow older partners. Less productive partners are forced to leave firms whose partners are required to work a specific number of hours a year or bring in a sufficient volume of new business consistent with the terms of their partnership agreements. The paternalistic, "clubby" relationships, once the hallmark of many midsized to large partnerships, have nearly vanished, along with laissez-faire arrangements that once permitted older partners to work indefinitely, often on a reduced basis. Smaller firms have fewer rules, and, of course, solo practitioners can operate indefinitely.

Thomas Evans, who until his retirement was a New York corporate attorney, notes that a lawyer's professional career life cycle has changed at most firms: "Until recently, the law firm associate was young, underpaid, and overworked. It was a form of apprenticeship. The next step was promotion to a junior partner. The pay was better, but the partner was still required to work long hours. Eventually, a lawyer age 50-plus moved to senior partner status. Lifestyle changed once again. The older lawyer worked fewer hours and was very well paid. It was a rite of passage to pay one's dues for 20 to 25 years and then reap the rewards in later life." The partner's life tenure in all but a few midsized to large firms has virtually disappeared, and "bloodletting" has become more widespread.

The news is better for the nation's 411,000 tenured and tenure-track college and university professors, says the American Association of University Professors *(www.aaup.org)*. Beginning in 1994, the federal government eliminated the mandatory retirement age of 70 for college faculty members. More professors are delaying their retirement, reports the Teachers Insurance and Annuity Association/College Retirement Equities Fund *(www.tiaa/cref.org)*, the nation's largest provider of pensions to educators. In 1987, the proportion under age 70 was 89 percent, and the proportion age 70 or older was 11 percent. Ten years later, 84 percent of TIAA-CREF participants receiving annuity income that year were under age 70 and 16 percent were age 70 or older.

While TIAA-CREF no longer updates these figures, the *New York Times (www.nytimes.com)* noted a few years ago that "the great majority of faculty members are still retiring by their mid 60s . . . older faculty members are increasingly being offered retirement incentives." *The Chronicle of Higher Education (http://chronicle .com)* reports colleges and universities are trying various incentives, such as financial bonuses or the opportunity to shift to part-time teaching, to encourage older faculty to retire.

Intertwined is the move in academia toward phased retirement. The policy varies from state to state and differs among private and public colleges and universities. At the 15 campuses in the University of North Carolina system, 12 of the institutions offer a three-year phased retirement plan, 2 offer a two-year plan, and 1 covers five years, according to a study in the *Industrial & Labor Relations Review* by Linda Ghent, Steven Allen, and Robert Clark.

## The Corporate Lions

The attitudes of senior corporate executives toward retirement have attracted a number of observers. Author Jeffrey Sonnenfeld, now a Yale University School of Management administrator, started and heads Yale's Chief Executive Leadership Institute. Sonnenfeld was smitten with the topic when he was teaching at the Harvard Business School in the late 1980s. He tracked how 50 CEOs, all running billion-dollar companies, were able to handle the transfer of power and their subsequent departure from active corporate life.

In his still relevant book *The Hero's Farewell* (Oxford University Press, 1988), Sonnenfeld categorizes how CEOs retire—if at all. He divides executives and their attitudes toward retirement into four groups:

1. **The monarchs** leave involuntarily or die, in the best tradition of a Hollywood saga, with their boots on.
2. **The generals** also leave involuntarily. During their retirement years, they plot a return. The general enjoys playing the role of the returning savior and hopes to be around long enough to take the firm and himself toward even greater glory.
3. **The ambassadors,** by contrast, quit gracefully and frequently serve as postretirement mentors. They often remain on the company's board of directors, do not try to sabotage their successor, and provide continuity and counsel.
4. **The governors,** who serve a limited term, depart for other interests and maintain very few ongoing ties with their company once they leave.

"When the time comes to step aside for newer and almost always younger leaders, many high corporate officers are beset with fears. . . . Leaving office means a loss of heroic stature, a plunge into the abyss of insignificance, a kind of mortality," says Sonnenfeld.

Senior executives innately resist stepping down. "Violinists in retirement," says Sonnenfeld, "can still offer solo performances or play with small ensembles. A conductor, however, needs the full orchestra to be employed, and thus a conductor's skills are not usually portable in retirement. The lack of portability of their skills makes retirement threatening to chief executives . . . the transition for leaders means finding new, involving, and challenging tasks."

Don't dismiss the problems facing CEOs as totally different from your own. On the surface they may appear dissimilar, but most 50-plus managers and professionals view stepping down much the same way as Sonnenfeld's monarchs, generals, ambassadors, and governors.

## A BOOMER LEAVES CORPORATE MANAGEMENT
### Marilyn Mellis Longman
#### Discovers a More Relaxed Lifestyle

Marilyn Mellis Longman no longer needs an alarm clock to get her going in the morning. Unlike most people her age, Marilyn is retired. She retired along with her husband, Doug, when she was 49, and he was in his mid-50s. "In many ways," she says, "I'm the classic boomer."

After growing up in New York City, Marilyn went to the State University of New York at Stony Brook. The year after graduation she received a master's degree in education, which was followed by a brief career in the classroom. Five years later and after placing first in her Boston University class, she had an MBA degree and was ready to take the first step in her migration from classroom to corporate America.

**"I was really looking for a lifestyle change, so that I could have more control over my life and achieve better balance."**

In 1976, when Marilyn joined General Foods (subsequently acquired by Philip Morris and then merged with Kraft) she was part of the early wave of women who wanted line jobs (sales, engineering, or production) rather than staff corporate assignments (public relations, human resources, corporate law, and so on). At the time, the company had few women with MBAs. Over the next 23 years, Marilyn held marketing jobs for such brand-name food lines as Pet Foods, Maxwell House Coffee, and Kraft Cheese. In the years before she left the company, Marilyn was director of corporate business development.

By the late 1990s, Marilyn and Doug were ready to jump ship. Doug, who has a doctorate in business administration, taught at the University of Texas in Austin and had worked for Citibank and General Foods, where he met Marilyn. The Longmans were living in Chicago.

"I had a heavy-duty job," says Marilyn. "For the past nine years I had worked a 12-hour day, from 7 AM to 7 PM. Up to then I had never thought about retirement. My father retired at 65, and my mother died at 61. When my dad retired, he didn't do too much. He moved to Florida. Not much of a role model there.

"Our goal was financial independence so that we could do whatever we wanted, whether continuing to work at our current jobs, getting different jobs, or not working at all.

"I was really looking for a lifestyle change so that I could have more control over my life and achieve better balance. I did not want to continue working so hard in my 50s, just in case I died at an early age like my mother. Rather than a rational perspective, it was purely emotional. At the time, Doug had left Citibank and was working as a consultant for Omnitech. He felt that he could continue doing that from North Carolina. Doug also thought that he might want to return to teaching."

In planning her future lifestyle, Marilyn was guided by Gail Sheehy's book *New Passages* and its discussion of "the Second Adulthood": "Today there is not only life after youth, but life after empty nest. There is life after layoff and early retirement." Sound planning enabled the Longmans to walk away from well-paying corporate jobs. "We didn't think of ourselves as retiring in the traditional sense. We were just leaving the corporate world to do other things. Doug's children from his first marriage were grown and living on their own, the stock market was good, and we both had six-figure salaries. We could live very well, and we could maximize savings."

Long before the stock market meltdown, the Longmans had a balanced investment strategy. "It included both equities and fixed investments. We never had more than 5 percent of our portfolio in any one stock, which reduced our vulnerability. The bonds in our portfolio buffered the magnitude of the losses in equities, so we were not as vulnerable as others may have been. Despite suffering significant losses in the market, we still have a large enough investment base to support us comfortably. Now that we no longer have steady salaries to rely upon, it has been psychologically harder to stomach the big downturns in the stock market. But our philosophy has been to stay on the current course because we know that it will pay off in the long term."

Not asking for a lifetime health care package was the one mistake that Marilyn admits she made when she left Kraft. Because the Longmans are too young to qualify for Medicare, they must pay a large premium for independent health care insurance. What's more, Marilyn wasn't eligible to tap her pension until she was 55.

Looking to relocate, the Longmans' criteria included an academic community in the eastern part of the United States, with a four-season climate warmer than that of the Northeast or Midwest and a nearby international airport. Because they were comparatively young by usual retirement standards, the Longmans were not overly concerned about medical facilities.

Once relocated to Chapel Hill, North Carolina, Marilyn handled a few nonchallenging commercial

**"We didn't think of ourselves as retiring in the traditional sense. We were just leaving the corporate world to do other things."**

consulting projects for package goods companies; Doug had similar consulting experiences. Both were ready to move in new directions. Like a trained corporate planner, Marilyn set some goals: intellectual stimulation by taking college courses (on topics such as women in politics and the history of American women) and more physical exercise. "Another goal was to achieve emotional satisfaction," says Marilyn. "In the past I didn't have time for community work. Now I'm a mentor with the Blue Ribbon Mentor Advocate Program. I've been matched with the same young girl, a high school student, for six years. I spend three to four hours with her each week helping her however I can."

Like other former corporate managers, Marilyn has found an outlet for her management skills as a nonprofit activist. As an Executive Service Corps consultant, board member, and marketing committee chairperson, she introduced a one-on-one coaching program whereby an ESC consultant coaches a director of a nonprofit agency.

Marilyn discovered that she doesn't really miss the corporate workplace. She feels that she's now in charge of her life. The Longmans rarely set their alarm clock, and Marilyn avoids early morning meetings, something that was endemic in her former corporate lifestyle.

## DIVESTING HIS OWNERSHIP
### John McAdams
*His Managers Will Own the Company*

If John McAdams has his way, the company that bears his name will be owned by his managers over the next 14 years. During this period, John expects to divest himself of the nearly 75 percent of the stock that he still owns. Plans call for him to sell his stock to what are now 15 and most likely some additional key managers. "This approach has already inspired elevated performance. They feel it's their company."

John, now in his late 50s, is divesting voluntarily. Unlike many closely held companies, he doesn't worry that his three children will get involved. "They're not interested in the business. Anyway, I don't believe in nepotism. My present goal is to learn how to let others make decisions." In this transition, however, John has altered but not decreased his workload. Even so, there are other things that he would like to do, and as John puts it, "Now is the time to start doing them."

It's not surprising that John and his company, which now employs about 150 people, have been providing land development and design services for 25 years. As a youngster, he built sand highway interchanges at the beach. Growing up in Raleigh, John went to Duke. Graduating as a civil engineer in 1970, he worked the following year in Denver, returned to North Carolina, and for the next eight years was employed by a local consulting engineering firm.

John's goal as a Duke student was to run his own business. By the late 1970s, he was ready to act on this dream. First thing on the agenda was an MBA to take what John says is the "mystery out of business." A year into Duke's evening MBA program, he went into business. "At first, we were generalists, but we switched over into land development work for local companies and governmental agencies."

Over the years, the bulk of the firm's assignments are from North Carolina–based companies, or outsiders who would like to do business in this area. "We only do land development work. We're not architects; we don't build anything. What we do is master planning, zone administration, create site construction documents, and obtain construction permits." Clients include home and shopping center developers, colleges and universities, and governmental agencies.

In 2003, the company opened its first branch office in Charlotte, with others being considered in the southeast corridor from Washington to Atlanta.

John is no longer involved in project management that involves working with individual clients on a regu-

**"My present goal is to learn how to let others make decisions."**

**John is no longer involved in project management that involves working with individual clients on a regular basis.**

lar basis. Instead, he concentrates on such strategic planning issues as branch office expansion and acquisitions.

"I'd also like to travel. I've done too little of it. I've only been out of the country once in my life. I don't want to be the typical tourist. My interest is not so much Europe but Africa, Latin America, and countries like Egypt. I like to stay a month in a city and get to know more about the area's people and culture.

"I would like to sail and own a 45-foot sailboat. Before buying one, my wife, Janice, and I would first rent one in the Caribbean and see how we really liked it. The last time I did any sailing was in 1981.

"If we don't do some of these things now, then shame on us. By divesting, I can continue to work a little less yet be involved in the company."

Consistent with his aim to do new things, the McAdamses bought a beach house in Wrightsville Beach, a few miles east of Wilmington, North Carolina, and about 160 miles from home. "It's all part of my need for delayed gratification."

If the plan he's putting together works out, John plans to have completed the financial and managerial transition by the time he's in his very early 70s.

---

### SUGGESTED READING

- *The Power Years: A User's Guide to the Rest of Your Life,* by Ken Dychtwald and Daniel J. Kadlec (Wiley, 2005). Will help boomers gauge the future insofar as creating a balance between work and leisure.
- *Women Confronting Retirement—A Non-Traditional Guide,* by Nan Bauer and Alice Radish (Rutgers University Press, 2003) presents the thoughts of 38 women who've had different career and lifetime experiences.
- *Looking Forward: Retirement—An Optimist's Guide to Retirement,* by Ellen Freudenheim (Stewart, Tabori and Chang, 2004). As the title implies, readers get a peek at their future life.

## SPECIAL INTERESTS READIED HIM
## FOR NEW CAREER
### William Zimmerman
### *Writing and Publishing Provide Direction*

Over a 40-year period, William Zimmerman had only three employers, all daily newspapers. Come retirement, Bill took his longtime avocation, writing and publishing inspirational books, and packaged them into a retirement career.

Bill was born, educated, and spent his entire career in New York City. His first job as a copyeditor after graduating from Queens College was with the *American Banker,* a daily business newspaper covering the banking and financial services industry.

Twenty-six years later, he left the newspaper as its editor. After a short stint as a *Sunday New York Times* business section editor, he joined *Newsday* in 1990, once again as a business editor.

During the Gulf War, Bill changed editorial direction. As special project editor, he launched *Newsday*'s Briefing Page, which was written for high school students on wartime events. When the war ended, the Briefing Page continued as a special weekly teenage news section.

Bill retired from *Newsday* in June 2004. "I realized six months after leaving *Newsday* how much I was actually preparing for retirement by means of my special interests—my love for writing and publishing books and my work over the years teaching kids. These activities helped me to find my path more easily."

His interest in book writing and publishing developed by chance. In the mid-1970s following a back operation, Bill spent a long recuperative period by writing his first book, *How to Tape Instant Oral Biographies.* Since then, he has averaged an inspirational book every two years. His 2005 book, *100 Things That Guys Need to Know,* was written for boys 9 to 14. "My books in many ways are autobiographical. They represent

**Guarionex Press also gave him a life apart from his 9-to-5 job.**

what I've learned, observed, and achieved. They are an extension of my life and my thoughts."

A number of his books were published by Guarionex Press, which he started as an escape valve and a possible vehicle for his retirement years. Though trained in the intricacies of newspaper editing, Bill added to his know-how by taking courses on book publishing at New York University's Publishing Center.

When *American Banker* restructured and Bill was ousted as editor, he said that it was like losing an old friend. Sent to an outplacement firm, he was forced to focus on the next step in his career. In his late 40s, Bill wavered between finding another job in journalism, which he did, or giving his full attention to Guarionex Press.

The demands of being a small publisher were apparent. Early on, Bill, his wife, Teodorina, a court reporter and actress, and daughter Carlota, then a youngster, would spend weekends and evenings packaging and mailing books to customers

Guarionex Press also gave him a life apart from his 9-to-5 job. "Guarionex Press was really mine. Along with my job, I was often working seven days a week. It was important to be publisher since I was my own boss. Up to then, I was only a corporate employee. At least, I owned something."

In his mid-60s and officially retired, Bill hardly considers himself to be a retiree. "I don't think I'll ever consider myself retired. I have worked since I was a kid, and I would not know how to stop being productive." It's one reason that he has set a goal to write and, if need be, self-publish a new book every two years.

Bill's source of retirement income is based on a formula that will eventually include pensions from *American Banker* and *Newsday*, Social Security, and IRA and 401(k) funds, plus his wife's pension and benefits.

"The other part of my life includes teaching and tutoring adults and children in writing and language skills. It's been a lifelong commitment. Presently, I have more time to devote to it." Accordingly, he tutors adults ages 20 to 65 two afternoons a week at a neighborhood New York City branch library.

Based on his newspaper experience, he was asked by the College of Mount Saint Vincent Institute for Immigrant Concerns to provide its students with the tools to enable them to produce a newsletter. This work, says Bill, is "very much in keeping with my own experience and mission in all my books and newspaper work to help people find and express their voice."

The third leg in Bill's three-legged stool is devoted to personal interests and "expanding my mind and my view of the world." In practical terms, it means taking lessons once a week on the recorder and an art course.

In many ways, Bill's thoughts about retirement started to gel after losing his *American Banker* job. "At the time, I felt expendable. I'm trying to avoid this feeling again after leaving *Newsday*."

---

### POINTS TO REMEMBER

- **So-called retirement age comes faster than anyone thinks** it will—and faster yet for those who are ousted by downsizing or offered early retirement.
- **There's no one definition of retirement.** How you view it is strictly a personal thing.
- **Longer life expectancy means more years to spend in retirement.**
- **Your role models may not provide much help** in preparing for retirement.
- **Managers who are 50-plus will find it increasingly difficult** though not impossible to find another good job.
- **Women view retirement differently** than men.
- **The age of retirement differs** among professions and vocations.
- **CEOs, believe it or not, have retirement problems** much like your own.

# Planning for Retirement

*"When you're through changing, learning, working to stay involved—only then are you through. 'Never retire.'"*
—William Safire's final *New York Times* column

**M**any of us spend more time planning our next vacation than we do formulating a retirement strategy. That's no great surprise. You've been busy living your life. Who has the time to schedule every nuance of life far into the future? Then one day, you get the wake-up call—maybe an early-retirement buyout offer or an invitation to attend a retirement-planning session. You're confronted with retirement head on, especially the questions: What will I do next? How can I afford to do it?

When evaluating retirement-related issues, here's what Keith Brodie, a psychiatrist and former Duke University president, has to say: "Retirement is not like a switch. You don't turn it on and off. Better to approach retirement gradually. It helps to maintain an even keel." I asked a good friend, who prefers to remain nameless, how he views retirement. He says that ambivalence rules the day. "Frankly, my thinking on retirement varies from day to day. On good days when I make a sale or come across a new project that I 'love,' I say, 'Why should I ever give this up? It's too much fun.'

"When we (my friend and his wife) were corporate drones (and at that time also childless), we saved like crazy so we're not all that worried about the financial aspects of retirement. On days when cash flow is tight, or some customer is acting belligerent, ornery, cutting legal corners, or just doesn't get it, I say who needs this. For my wife, the balance started to shift toward the latter a couple of years ago. She would retire in a 'New York minute' if I would agree. If given half a chance, she'd spend every day at the tennis court—rotator cuff problems or not.

"For me, I'd say the balance of enjoyment versus drudgery has slipped from a ratio of 90/10 to 75/25 over the past several years; I'll probably be ready to call it quits, more or less, in five to six years.

"Now what I'd do with myself if I retired is a mystery; I'm a man without a hobby. Perhaps I'd bike a bit more, go to the gym three times a week, travel with my wife, read a lot, maybe do a bit of pro bono work, or maybe use my skill in a freelance capacity."

Don't take it for granted that employers will provide retirement planning. Only a handful of larger companies offer a comprehensive retirement-planning program, and then only to their high-echelon employees. What seems like disinterest in corporate-sponsored retirement planning parallels other trends.

Companies are providing few support services to their retiring employees, according to a still-relevant late 1990s survey of corporate severance practices by Coopers & Lybrand (now PricewaterhouseCoopers; *www.pwcglobal.com*). These services, says the auditing firm, are being axed as companies look for ways to cut the costs of decreasing their workforce. If offered at all, outplacement services are reserved for executives. Little has changed in outplacement practices, says Bill Stanley, a one-time human resource executive and outplacement consultant, and now an executive coach. He finds that companies are providing little person-to-person outplacement help. It's done more often in group sessions and usually for briefer periods of time.

Another issue is corporate paternalism. When will there be another Aaron Feurerstein of Lawrence, Massachusetts? He made national headlines in the mid-1990s when Malden Mills burned to the ground, an event that could have led to the loss of several hundred jobs at one of the few remaining New England textile mills. As Malden's owner, he could have taken the insurance money and run. Not Feurerstein. He rebuilt the plant and continued to pay employees during the transitional period. However, corporate paternalism is on the decline, says Bill Hendrickson, author of *You Can Survive the Corporate Culture* (Publish America, 2004). (Bill is profiled in Chapter 6.)

Almost everyone has been feeling the effects in some way from corporate cutbacks. Gone are the days when IBM offered a retirement education-assistance program to all employees. Eliminated to cut corporate expenses, the program reimbursed employees up to $2,500 for coursework they took in nearly any subject, ranging from computer training to golf lessons.

Simply put, there's a need to explore all corporate avenues for retirement planning, because as cutbacks continue, these benefits will likely be reduced in many companies. That means you will have to depend on yourself to solve the twin retirement dilemmas—or opportunities—managing time and money. Not everyone benefits from a favorable buyout or pension. Some people who have enjoyed successful careers have failed to accumulate sufficient retirement income. This occurred more frequently in the days before portable pension plans and IRAs. People worked for a number of companies, only to take a new job before being vested in the company's pension plan.

F. Marion Thomson knows the problem firsthand. His tenure at different companies was often less than ten years. Thus, his retirement income is minimal. In practical terms, it means that he continues to work. Marion, now in his late 60s, actually enjoys his current career as a financial advisor associated with Ameriprise Financial (previously called American Express Financial Advisors).

There's an advantage, Marion says, in being a somewhat older financial planner. Clients often feel more comfortable in dealing with an advisor who has a "been there, done that" approach.

Here are some other factors to consider:

■ Being able to meet future retirement expenses is a common concern for most Americans according to

**You will have to depend on yourself to solve the twin retirement dilemmas—or opportunities—managing time and money.**

a MetLife *(www.metlife.com)* study on retirement income, which spotlights the "silent generation," folks between ages 59 and 71. MetLife describes them as the older siblings of the current boomers. The study found that 83 percent of preretirees and 90 percent of retirees in this age group are confident that they'll have sufficient income to live comfortably until they're at least age 85. The silent generation, MetLife notes, "have or anticipate multiple sources of guaranteed income to carry them through retirement."

■ The number of personal bankruptcies has soared, AARP reports. The new federal personal bankruptcy law notwithstanding, there were 1.6 million filings, twice the number reported in the early 1990s. In fact, bankruptcy is growing faster among Americans 65 and older than any other age group.

■ In a bygone era, it seemed that corporate pension plans were above reproach. This is no longer the case. Witness such blue chips as Bethlehem Steel, US Airways, and United Airlines, among others, who defaulted on their corporate pension plans. They turned over the responsibility for compensating pensioners to the Pension Benefit Guaranty Corporation *(www.pbgc.gov)*. Created by the Employee Retirement Income Security Act of 1974, this federal agency provides a partial retirement cushion for employees of companies insured by this plan. The maximum dollar amount is adjusted annually. "For plans ended in 2005," says the PBGC, "workers who retire at age 65 can receive up to $3,801.14 monthly or $45,613.68 annually. The guarantee is lower for those who retire early or when there is a benefit for a survivor."

■ Phased retirement has become another 21st century buzzword. It extends beyond college faculty retirement as discussed in Chapter 1. A study by human resource consultant Watson Wyatt *(www.watsonwyatt.com)* points out that "two-thirds of full-time workers over age 50 anticipate reducing the hours of work before retiring completely."

■ The current crop of baby boomers need to work when they retire. Hewitt Associates *(www.hewitt.com)*, a benefits consulting firm, notes that individual median savings through 401(k) retirement plans is less than $45,000.

David L. is the CEO of a consortium of health care companies. I am not using his real name because neither he nor his employer wants to publicly announce his pending retirement at this time. Here's how David views phased retirement programs in general as well as the route he's about to take: "Phased retirement helps to bring about a transition and provides a degree of continuity, particularly when it involves a retiring senior executive. It can also serve as a fallback position in the event the new leadership does not work out.

"Phased retirement is an excellent alternative to the sometimes precipitous or traumatic scenario of waking up one morning with 'no place to go.' In addition to providing a way to keep an executive active professionally, it continues to serve as a vehicle for maintaining relationships with colleagues and business associates. For me, personally, besides all of the above, it is a gradual preparation for the next stage of life. I'm now able to gradually engage in the leisure activities, which were difficult to pursue while I was working full-time."

# Going Plural: A Model for Your Future

Call it what you may, but many in the 50-plus set believe that a portfolio, or patchwork, work-and-lifestyle formula represents smorgasbord living at its best. British consultant and author Charles Handy champions this cause in his book *The Age of Unreason* by showing how to combine various work and nonwork interests (hobbies, volunteerism, education) into "portfolio" careers. Handy, a futurist, maintains that people of all ages, not just retirees and the 50-plus set, will be living portfolio careers as a result of technological, societal, and corporate changes.

It is only natural that professionals and the self-employed put into play various flexible work and lifestyle game plans in preparation for retirement. By doing so, they have the option to reduce their work schedule yet stay put in the workplace. Corporate managers, by contrast, are guided by more rigid employment practices, but once they leave their jobs, they are free to create new lifestyles and structure different career patterns.

Going plural aptly describes the lifestyle approach taken by Edward Koch, former New York City mayor. "I never thought I would have a third career. To be honest, I never counted on a second, but there it was," he wrote in *Citizen Koch*. His current resume is still impressive: law firm partner, newspaper columnist, radio and television commentator, movie reviewer, and mystery book writer. In 2004, he and his sister wrote a children's book, *Eddie: Harold's Little Brother.* Though he does not reveal his income, he said it surpassed his former pay as mayor and a member of Congress.

Robert Stevens, a Durham-based health care marketing consultant, is already looking almost ten years ahead. Though he's only in his early 50s, the execution of his plan cannot take place until the third of his three children has completed college. By then, he'll be nearly 60. His wife, Elizabeth, the same age, is also a marketing consultant with a different specialty.

"Other than financial planning, most of my contemporaries, as far as I know, have not thought too seriously about retirement," says Bob. "My friends just live and work for today. A few have had retirement forced upon them due to corporate downsizing and retrenching."

Bob, however, is not waiting for another ten or more years to get started. As such, he's been an adjunct faculty member for the past few years teaching health care marketing at the University of North Carolina's School of Public Health and is also a coauthor of a book to be published in 2007 on health care marketing. When he's in his 60s, Bob, who has an MBA degree,

---

**SUGGESTED READING**

- *Boomer Nation, the Largest and Richest Ever and How It Changed America,* by Steve Giller (Free Press, 2004).
- *Prime Time: How Baby Boomers Will Revolutionize Retirement & Transform America,* by Marc Freedman (Public Affairs, 2002).
- *Retirement Places Rated,* 6th edition, by David Savageau (Wiley, 2004).
- *Retire Worry-Free,* by the editors of *Kiplinger's Personal Finance* magazine (Dearborn Trade, 2005).

---

hopes to be in a better position to make the transition from health care consultant to college instructor.

## Time to Say Goodbye to Computer Illiteracy

There probably are not many computer illiterate corporate managers and professionals left as computer-savvy boomers near retirement. Knowing how to operate a desktop or laptop computer is no longer an optional skill.

Computer know-how is nearly mandatory for those planning to reenter the job market, start a business, change careers, become a consultant, or even serve as a nonprofit board member.

It's easy to find basic and refresher computer training courses. Besides community college and high school adult education courses, there's SeniorNet *(www.seniornet.org),* a nonprofit that has specialized for the past 20 years in teaching basic computer skills to about one million folks in the 50-plus set. Its formula is based on 16 hours of classroom instruction in the basics of word processing, e-mail, and Internet access. Once the fundamentals are learned, students can sign up for courses in graphics, Web design, and Quicken financial software. Like other adult education programs, students learn in a classroom with folks their own age. The cost is about $25 a course plus a Senior-Net membership fee.

SeniorNet's world is also enhancing its basic program. Computer literate boomers want to upgrade their current computer skills and tackle digital imaging and cybersecurity techniques.

## Move or Stay Put?

When it comes to retirement migration, your guess is as good as mine as to the number of people who retire and relocate. Sociologist Charles Longino of Wake Forest University *(www.wfu.edu)* notes that "interstate migration has held very steady for migrants age 60 and above at 4 percent to 4.6 percent over a five-year period. Short-distance migration within states has declined over the past half-century for persons of all ages."

Longino points out that the Sunbelt is "generally the dominant regional destination, yet there is greater variety than commonly assumed. Ocean County in New Jersey, for example, has consistently received enough retirees from New York and Pennsylvania to keep it among the top 100 interstate destinations for several decades."

Numerically, the states receiving the most migrants are Florida, Arizona, California, Texas, North Carolina, Georgia, Nevada, Pennsylvania, New Jersey, and Virginia.

The United States, Longino says, has not adopted the European pattern of building retirement-related communities convenient to urban shopping. Instead, retirement enclaves are located in the outskirts of cities and towns, away from transportation and urban amenities.

But there's more to relocation than statistical analysis. Even though most retirees might never buy a retirement home, chances are they'll shop the marketplace for a city or town that complements the lifestyle they seek.

This concept is consistent with the findings in AARP's Beyond 50.05 report that over one-half of the 50-plus set feel attached to their communities. They overwhelmingly said yes when asked whether they would be living in the same community in another five years.

Staring at age 50 and continuing for the next 10 to 15 years, hordes of curious Americans are on the road searching for potential places to move. They tour the Sun Belt states, look at communities and homes, examine the lifestyle, and return home. Some buy and others decide to stay put.

## Why Move?

Family, friends, and nostalgic haunts keep them close to their home base. Yet home base need not be a four-bedroom home on a one-acre lot. The alternatives are plentiful. Some stay put in the same hometown but buy or rent a smaller home or apartment. Others hedge their bets by remodeling an existing home. And there are those folks who maintain both a winter and a summer home, ranging from a plush apartment on New York's Park Avenue and a home in Nantucket to a modest home in the Midwest and a recreational vehicle or a small condo in Florida.

The change in the tax law is a boon for retirees who want to buy a home more suitable to retirement and at the same time augment their nest egg and their monthly cash flow. Gone is the one-time $125,000 capital gains exclusion on the sale of a home. The 1997 Taxpayer Relief Act increased the ante for home-sellers regardless of age to $250,000 for a single tax-payer and $500,000 for a couple filing jointly. The new rules offer a form of financial downsizing that is especially attractive to the 50-plus set. What better incentive than to sell a home, replace it with a less expensive apartment or home, and pocket the difference?

Too often retirees rent a home or apartment on a part-time basis, often seasonally, to see if they like the community or region. In theory, this practice makes sense, but seasonal relocation hardly represents an

**To get a realistic point of view, retirees need to sever ties "back home" and make what was their rented or seasonal home their only home.**

accurate gauge of what life is like year-round. To get a realistic point of view, retirees need to sever ties "back home" and make what was their rented or seasonal home their only home.

## What About a Retirement Community?

Retirees face a dilemma when they ponder whether to move or stay put. If they decide to relocate, what type of community will they select after they have lived in the same home for 30 years or more? Do they favor a balanced urban or suburban residential area with neighbors of all ages, or would they prefer to move to Sun City, Arizona, by far the nation's largest retirement community where the average age is 73.

Del Webb *(www.delwebb.com)*, considered to be the largest developer of larger-scale retirement communities, is actively marketing to baby boomers. Besides the traditional Sun Belt communities, it has or will be building new communities in Illinois, Massachusetts, Michigan, and New Jersey, and is considering communities outside the United States. A Del Webb survey showed that 60 percent of baby boomers will most likely move to a new home when they retire. About 25 percent might buy a home in what Del Webb calls an age-qualified active adult community where the homes have been designed to include a room that doubles as an in-home office.

The National Association of Realtors *(www.realtor.org)* also recognizes the surge in second-home purchases. Hardly unexpected, baby boomers are buying more second homes than any other age group. Come retirement, it is estimated that 20 percent of these homes will convert to primary homes.

Perhaps the most important question to ask is whether you want to live in a community that's limited to one age group. Don't overlook the drawbacks, most notably an exclusion from the being in a mixed community with folks of all ages.

## Kinds of Places to Retire

The site selection possibilities should include this diverse menu of residential options:

- **A large city.** Surprisingly, a number of suburbanites relocate to the city to be nearer the array of activities that a large city has to offer.

- **A college community.** There's a lot to do in a college community in terms of sports, adult education, and cultural activities. It's even better when you're an alumnus.

- **A summer community.** Retirees are taking summer cottages and remodeling them for year-round rather than seasonal usage. That might sound like a great idea, but it's best to visit these towns in the off-season. The weather could be dismal and the community desolate. In short, it might be a wonderful summer lifestyle but impractical for year-round use.

- **Returning home.** When both husband and wife are from the same area, returning home is often rewarding even if the couple hasn't lived there for many years. This is particularly delightful when there are fond memories of hometown U.S.A.

- **Moving outside the United States.** Mexico and Costa Rica appeal to some retirees. Guadalajara, Mexico, is home to 30,000 Americans and Canadians. The living is definitely cheaper in Mexico; however, be aware that Medicare benefits are not available outside the United States.

- **Taking to the road in a recreational vehicle.** Interestingly, 1 in 12 U.S. households that owns a car also owns an RV, according to a University of Michigan study. What's more, nearly half of the RVs on the road are owned by people over age 55. Baby boomers represent the leading growth market. The question is, do you want to live in an RV year-round or use it seasonally? There are more than seven million RVs in use, says the Recreational Vehicle Industry Association *(www.rvia.org)*. Despite rising gas prices, 370,000 RVs were sold in 2004. Staying in touch, once a problem for RV travelers, has become easier due to cell phones and wireless computers. Many RV folks are snowbirds. They live in the north from April to October, and then they hop into their RV in the fall and travel south.

- **Rural America.** Lots of Americans are trying to escape from congested metro centers to the quieter, and usually less expensive, lifestyle of a smaller community. Be cautious about this type of move unless you know and understand how life in a small town works. Be prepared to find that there may be few, if any, coffee bars, ethnic restaurants, or other amenities associated with suburbia and large cities.
- **An airpark.** Some seasoned pilots live in communities known as airparks, where homes are built along a runway. Not surprisingly, the most popular locations for the country's nearly 500 airparks are in Sun Belt states like Florida, Texas, Georgia, and California.

## Lifestyle Factors to Consider

Now it's time to examine the merchandise. Take these factors into consideration when contemplating relocation:

- **Health care services.** How good is the local hospital and the medical community in general? This should be a prime consideration for anyone over age 60. Rural America might be scenic, but traveling 150 miles once a week to see a medical specialist makes little sense.
- **The job market.** Retirees often want to work part-time or full-time. Even if you think you might not want to work after you settle down, investigate whether there's a demand for your skills.
- **Taxes.** Check the state and the city income, property, and nuisance taxes. Otherwise, be prepared for a possible shock. Based on Tax Foundation *(www.taxfoundation.org)* findings, Maine with a 13 percent tax rate has the highest combined state and local tax rate; Alaska is a bargain at 6.4 percent. Thirty-seven states have combined state and local tax rates that range between 9 percent and 10 percent
- **Weather.** Sections of the Sun Belt might be great in January, but what about the hot and humid summer days?

- ■ **Sports.** Do you like to play tennis or golf, fish, or take walks? Is there a good country club or golf course, lake, or park nearby? If there is a private country club or golf course, is it affordable?
- ■ **Religion.** Are there churches, synagogues, or mosques in the community? If not, what's the level of tolerance in the community for other religions?
- ■ **Transportation.** How many miles is it to the closest airport? This is important for retirees who want to visit children and grandchildren, take vacations, or make business trips.
- ■ **General amenities.** Good restaurants, retail stores, libraries, and other activities are often taken for granted back home. Check to see if the area being considered has sufficient variety for your needs.
- ■ **Security.** Crime exists in the smallest hamlets. It's not just exclusive to metro centers. If this is a concern, get an alarm system or move to a gated community.
- ■ **Politics.** Don't move into a community where the prevailing political sentiment goes strongly against your grain.
- ■ **Adult education.** Is there a community or four-year college within easy reach?
- ■ **The emotional factor.** Is this the place where you'd like to live the rest of your life?

## A Little Life Planning

Chances are your employer doesn't offer a retirement-planning program, and if it does, the program likely will be devoted almost exclusively to financial planning. The alternative is to find a program on your own that's similar to a program sponsored in the past by New York University's Center for Career, Education & Life Planning (*www.scps.org*).

At the "Over 50? What's Next?" course, outplacement consultant Anita Lands told participants to focus on ways to clarify goals, manage change, and develop a personal plan based on self-assessment and exploration of realistic alternatives in both work and leisure areas. Information and inspiration similar to what Anita offers in her course is available through many other college-sponsored and independent counseling and self-help groups.

Anita's preamble at the first session set the tone for the seminar by describing it as a realistic primer for most soon-to-be retirees. "Whether you're thinking about changing jobs, working part-time, retiring, or simply remaining productive, you can make a better decision when you see where the road is heading. On-going life and career planning is a must if you want to create and sustain a desirable level of satisfaction from your job and life."

The participants at one workshop series included nine women and four men, all 50-plus, who had either recently retired or were considering it. Their objectives differed: change jobs or careers, reenter the job market, return to school, or start their own businesses. David, a building supply company's chief financial officer, said he felt "stuck in the mud trying to figure it out. I'd go into my own business, but I'm not sure I want to take the risk." Then there was Maureen, a just-retired bank officer, who said, "I'm bored out of my mind. What's the next step? Will I be 'bad' if I don't go back to work immediately?"

Don't retire. Instead, retread—or in current parlance, rewire. In guiding the class, Anita employed many of the tools that she uses with her corporate outplacement clients. She encouraged students to think creatively, to consider different career or retirement options, and, above all, to take a fresh look at themselves, evaluate their work and leisure skills, set goals, and implement an action plan.

Potential couch potatoes squirmed as Anita spoke:

"We have to learn how to transfer skills and develop new ones. We get locked into old skills, things that we do too easily.

"Remember, the way expenses are increasing we are all under some pressure to earn extra money.

One secret is to take an avocation and perhaps turn it into a vocation.

"Please rid your vocabulary of such baggage as *should have, would have,* and *could have.* Why turn 84 and still have the attitude of I *should have* done something else after I retired?

"Avoid being referred to as a former VP. You need a new identity, and it comes only by acquiring new skills, activities, and life values.

"Whether you work part-time or full-time, you're still part of the workforce. It is time to plan your life on your terms. Up till now there have been scripts for school, work, and family. The old scripts no longer apply. It's up to you to write a new one.

"Above all," Anita says, "don't retire—rather, retread."

Mike Thomas, a founding partner in the Intensive Life/Career Planning Workshop *(www.lifecareerplan.com),* aims to help workshop participants plan for the next five years by balancing work with their personal life. Owners of family businesses, says Mike, often have difficulty letting go when they reach the traditional retirement years. "There's a fear that something negative is going to happen to them by having nothing meaningful to do. The business is often their hobby and in many ways their life."

It's a catch-22 environment. Some aging business owners don't trust their heirs to carry on successfully without them, Mike notes. "They never really bothered to groom them, yet they need to let go because they lack the energy they once had."

## Say Hello to "Our Group"

When "Our Group" has lunch in a midtown New York City restaurant, it looks like any other luncheon meeting of six midlife business and professional women. Their conversation varies from work to lifestyle issues. But the group actually has a different purpose. These former New York

> **"Avoid being referred to as a former VP. You need a new identity and it only comes by acquiring new skills, activities, and life values."**

City teachers and administrators meet monthly as a postretirement support group.

Little did Mary R. and her friends realize that they were pathfinders when they started what they refer to as "Our Group," an organization that has no charter, official status, officers, or dues. Ever since their first meeting more than 30 months ago, they have provided each other with informal and ongoing support that goes well beyond the assistance offered by many structured organizations.

The first lunch meeting after their retirement set the tone for future meetings. Little time was spent reminiscing. As Mary puts it, "We have better things to discuss." They typically talk about part-time work, using free time and adjusting to a less hectic lifestyle that includes the freedom to have a leisurely breakfast, read the newspaper, and not leave for work at 7 AM. At one lunch, they chatted about a newspaper article they had read on Charles Handy's concept of "portfolio careers" and how his concept applies to them.

Our Group has found that six members is a practical number to meet and talk over lunch or dinner in a restaurant or to meet in someone's living room. They see no need to expand beyond their present number.

Our Group has created a basic formula that could easily serve as a template for many other retirees:

- **The group shares a strong common thread.** For example, members of the group have had the same employer or similar professional training or jobs.
- **Its members know and generally respect each other.**
- **The group is small.**
- **The meetings are informal but directed.**
- **The group avoids letting one or two of the members dominate** it or its agenda. Also, the members will not allow the group to become a stage for "show-and-tell" instead of mutual support and discussion.
- **The meetings, while informal, depend on the professional tone of the participants** for their continuity.
- **Above all, gossip is downplayed.**

# 30 YEARS WITH ONE EMPLOYER
## Dale Gaddis
### *Uses Library Skills in Parallel Ways*

After 30 years with the Durham (NC) County Library, Dale Gaddis, then in her late 50s, called it quits. In making the transition, Dale set new personal goals to alter her lifestyle.

Dale's career spanned a historical period in Durham. When she joined the library staff in 1967, the city was racially integrating its once-segregated libraries into a single county system. By the time she retired 35 years later, the system consisted of the main downtown library, four regional branches, and several satellite branches.

Her interest in being a librarian was somewhat of a fluke. Her father, a career naval officer, was posted in a number of bases in the United States and overseas.

At Duke University, her career goal was foreign service, a dream that was never realized. She found the foreign service exam to be "brutal." She attended Emory University in Atlanta for graduate school. One year later, Dale had a master's degree in librarianship. She reasoned that her library training could lead to a job overseas allowing her to mix business and pleasure. Then things changed. She got married, returned to Durham, and went to work as the head of adult services in the Durham Public Library.

Two children and several years later, she rejoined the library staff, and had a succession of assignments over the next few years in older adult and reference services. In 1975, she became the library's assistant director. Seven years later, Dale was named director. Fast forward another 20 years, and she was ready for the next move.

"I got tired of working. I had given most of my life to the library. I was tired of being involved with people trying to sue the library over one thing or another. In 2001 a bond issue was passed. I had been director

**Like other retirees who enjoyed their occupations, it is only natural to use those skills in another capacity.**

20 years, and with expansion I didn't really want to get involved in fundraising.

"Of the things I've done, I liked being a reference librarian. I was pleased to be involved in implementing the library's computer system, and I liked training the staff." One of her last tasks as director was developing a ten-year capital improvement plan, which included several new branches along with the expansion and refurbishing of others.

Retirement meant a time for exploring. Dale's children, now grown, had their own careers. "Before retiring, I took a short course at Duke, 'What Are You Going to Do with the Rest of Your Life.' I learned that my skills were architecture (her former husband's career), geography (her daughter's), and being a librarian."

Dale set some immediate postretirement goals. High on her list was to get in better shape. "I now walk about two miles five times a week with a friend at 6:30 in the morning, and I take an exercise course three mornings a week."

But there's more to retirement than exercise, taking care of her granddaughter one day a week, going on a few trips, and reading 22 books a year. "When I was working, I was lucky to read 3 or 4 books."

During the transitional postretirement period, she sold a larger home and bought a smaller one in the same area. Her two children live nearby. The profit on the house sale provides income, along with a state pension and income from a 457 plan, the government's equivalent of a 401(k). She receives additional income from consultant assignments and teaching a college course.

Like other retirees who enjoyed their occupations, it is only natural to use those skills in another capacity. Dale is no exception. "My contacts in the state's library family proved to be useful because I was recommended by other librarians to do several consulting assignments."

She prepared a three-year budget to implement the newly adopted strategic plan. Being experienced in the passage of Durham's 2001 bond issue, Chapel

Hill retained her to coordinate the passage of its $16.1 million library expansion bond issue, and she was involved in preparing a long-range Orange County (North Carolina) library plan.

Durham is also the home of North Carolina Central University and its School of Library and Information Science. Once again her professional contacts produced results. "I teach once a week. I find that my workplace experience helps to make the class interesting and practical." And what does she teach? A class on public library systems, of course.

## NO STRANGER TO SETTING HIS OWN COURSE
### Hank Baer
#### *Law Partner Turned Professor and Independent Attorney*

In this era of job and career uncertainty, it is critical to know when and how to take early retirement. At age 55, Henry "Hank" Baer felt it was time to make a change. He negotiated his way out of his law firm from a position of strength while he had something tangible to offer his partners at a time when they still needed him as much as he needed them. How Hank handled his planned departure could serve as an example to others.

Graduating from Brown University, Hank was commissioned in the Navy. Though he was not a lawyer, he was assigned on a number of occasions as a defense counsel. "From that point on, I wanted to be a lawyer. When I got out of the Navy, I applied to law school at Harvard but was turned down." Hank went to work as a sales representative and then worked as sales manager for ten years in his family's business, Imperial Knife Associated Companies.

"I still wanted to be a lawyer, but I was now married and had two small children. I applied once again to law school. The only person who knew about it was my wife, Ellen. When I was deliberating over my decision,

**"My brother-in-law's death forced me to face the fact that we're not going to last forever."**

she said, 'Either go to law school or shut up.'" This time Hank was accepted at Harvard.

The Baers moved to Cambridge. Hank financed his education with the GI Bill, student loans, some savings, and Ellen's salary as a hospital nurse. Hank completed law school when he was 36, and went to work for Skadden, Arps, Slate, Meagher & Flom, one of the few corporate law firms that hired middle-aged lawyers directly out of law school. It was then a small law firm with only 41 lawyers, all based in New York. Hank was named a partner in 1978. Four years later, as a labor relations specialist, he was named chairperson of the firm's labor and employment law practice committee.

Over the years, the firm changed. In 1971, it was "small and collegial, and run like a family business. As it grew, it became increasingly more businesslike and, for me, less fun." By 1990, its peak year, the firm employed more than 1,000 lawyers, including 225 partners and a support staff of approximately 2,500 people in its offices in the United States and overseas.

Hank began to consider alternatives, all using his skills as a lawyer and arbitrator. One of his close professional colleagues and his immediate supervisor at the firm was John Feerick, a year younger than Hank, who had left the firm as a partner while in his late 40s to become the dean of Fordham Law School. Hank, John, and a third lawyer, Jonathan Arfa, had jointly written a legal textbook and collaborated on a number of legal articles. Perhaps subliminally, John had set the stage for Hank's departure seven years later.

Two dissimilar events, which occurred almost at the same time, triggered Hank's decision to change his work habits. Ellen's brother died at 47, and Hank and Ellen won an American Express around-the-world sweepstakes. They traveled for 60 days in Australia, New Zealand, and Europe. "Until then, I had never been absent from the office for so long a time. I also decided to do things differently than my father, who was literally kicked out of Imperial Knife when he was 85. My brother-in-law's death forced me to face the fact that we're not going to last forever."

It was time to stop putting off things he wanted to do in law and in his personal life—things that could not be readily accomplished in a very demanding legal practice. He went to see John Feerick at Fordham and advised him of his plans to step down at the firm, Hank recalls. John told him that when a teaching position opened, he would consider Hank for the position.

In 1990, nearly 19 years after joining the firm, Hank resigned as a partner, withdrew his capital investment, and became "of counsel." In this new relationship, Hank maintains a professional relationship with the firm but no longer has a partner's vote or shares in the firm's profits. He does most of his work from an office that he maintains at his own expense in Florida. Some of-counsel lawyers receive a certain percentage of their legal fees, but Hank is a W-2 employee and is paid a salary. "I serve in a management position, as opposed to a legal position, dealing with human [resource] issues for the firm's several thousand employees worldwide.

"I have an understanding with the firm that continues to be renewed. My income is less than when I was a partner, but I accepted the change so I could mold my life to my liking—a combination of law, teaching, and other interests. I no longer want to bill the required thousands of hours a year and be accountable for the duties of a partner."

Hank was able to save and invest steadily during his years as a partner at what was probably the nation's most profitable law firm during the 1980s. Downshifting has not altered his lifestyle. With the money Hank received from his capital investment in the firm, he and Ellen bought an apartment in Florida and invested the remainder. They remain on the firm's health care and life insurance plans. Ellen, who retired as a professor of nursing at the University of Pennsylvania, now teaches nursing part-time at the University of Miami.

When Hank was asked to teach a labor law course at Fordham, he was once again a fledgling. "I had

**His objective remains constant— to create a balance in his professional life as a lawyer, teacher, and arbitrator.**

never taught before. It's different from giving an occasional lecture." Fortunately, Ellen and their son, who also had teaching experience, tutored him on classroom techniques. "Teaching is intellectually stimulating. Students keep me sharp.

"At first I would spend up to 18 hours preparing for a 3-hour lecture. As a result, I have become a better lawyer." After moving to Florida, he taught for several years at Nova Southeastern University in Ft. Lauderdale.

Hank's new lifestyle means living in Florida six months a year, with the balance of the year in New York or at his summer home on Long Island. He works as a lawyer in Florida and New York. His objective remains constant—to create a balance in his professional life as a lawyer, teacher, and arbitrator.

## LOOKING AHEAD IS A KEY FACTOR
### Don DeBolt
### *Trade Association Head Weighs His Options*

Don DeBolt was a Washington, D.C. trade association executive for more than 40 years. He's also displayed an entrepreneurial streak since his early 20s, when he was a part-owner of a men's clothing store in his home state, South Dakota. It was this same entrepreneurial spirit that guided Don's retirement strategy. Don planned to retire, as he did in late 2004, as president of the International Franchise Association. He expected his penchant for and experience with smaller businesses would stimulate his postretirement options.

The first of his family to go to college, Don left in his senior year without a degree. "I still have the lingering thought that that's something still unfinished, and it may get back on the radar screen again."

Besides his clothing store experience, Don was also a J.C. Penney management trainee and a commissioned salesman for a distributor representing a

South Dakota machinery manufacturer. "I worked for the distributor for a couple of months in its Washington office before moving my wife and three-month-old son out from Vermillion, South Dakota. I left my job, and I got 'keep body and soul together' type jobs—working in a restaurant at night and as a correspondence clerk by day and showing model homes on the weekend. I was broke. That was the time in my life when the decisions were between buying razor blades to shave with or a pound of hamburger to eat."

As a result of his downward financial spiral and the need for a job with steady income, Don took what would be the first of four trade association positions, starting with the Menswear Retailers of America. "When I left 18 years later, I was executive director. By then, I was burned out. I asked the board to release me from my contract, which had another year to go. I planned to devote my efforts to real estate."

Instead, one of Don's uncles inspired him to start what became Credit Card Acceptor Corp., a company with a niche specialty—enabling trade associations to offer credit cards at discount rates to their member companies. "At our peak, we had 40 clients. I was a one-man band operating from our apartment. Little maintenance was required once the marketing was done and the deal made." The CCAC concept frizzled out a few years later.

It was time to look for another job. "After MRA, I never intended to run another association; I didn't think the skills were transferable." But Don's association experience became a lifeline. Over the next few years in the late 1980s, Don worked as director of the National Spa and Pool Institute, and the International Swimming Hall of Fame.

Once again, Don was bitten by the entrepreneurial bug. In 1990, he started what evolved into *CEO Update,* a biweekly, 28-page newsletter for executives in the nonprofit management field. It was a one-man start-up operation. Don did everything from writing the newsletter copy to pasting labels on the envelopes. Little did he realize at the time that *CEO*

**"Retirement is an inaction word to me. My father said that retirement was the saddest mistake that he had ever made."**

*Update* would ease his transition into retirement 14 years later.

When he joined the International Franchise Association (as president in 1995), Don stepped down as publisher of *CEO Update* but became publisher emeritus and remained president of the company. Don's involvement was limited to Sunday mornings, when he did bookkeeping and what he called "financial things." "I saw this work as my Sunday morning golf game." Though only a few hours a week, he maintained a hands-on relationship with the newsletter.

Don also considered a range of retirement options, including the possibility of becoming a franchisor. "After this job, if I can't figure out which franchise is the right one for me, I will have been asleep at the switch."

He already eliminated the idea of a full-time retirement lifestyle. "*Retirement* is an inaction word to me. My father said that retirement was the saddest mistake that he had ever made."

Don's IFA retirement became a reality on December 31, 2004. "I showed up at *CEO Update* the next week. I found that the superteam of folks that have been running it in my absence had updated all the systems with new technology. It resulted in my becoming an entry-level employee in my own business, learning the ropes all over again."

## SPENDS HIS LIFE IN THREE- TO FIVE-YEAR UNITS
### Fred Cavalier
### *Prefers Relaxing in Rural America*

Fred Cavalier is a maverick. He worked 26 years in sales, marketing, and management jobs for a number of small to midsize technology companies, followed by five years as an instructor and administrator for a community college. He severed these ties and then relocated from Raleigh to a log cabin in the mountains of northwestern North Carolina. At 56, Fred was ready to live his dream.

Armed with a bachelor's degree and a master's degree in biology as well as an MBA, Fred sold pharmaceuticals for a few years and then joined a corporate conglomerate as a sales manager. By the mid-1980s, Fred shifted gears as he headed sales for an electronics company and two biotech companies, followed by four years as president and general manager of a West Coast office equipment firm.

Each job was consistent with Fred's financial plan. Over the years, he worked for start-up and turnaround companies. He took risks. Instead of relying totally on a salary, he accepted equity positions. During these years as Fred switched jobs, he lived in New England, North Carolina, and California. "When I was in my mid-20s and already working, I learned that we pay little attention on ways to accumulate money. I feel that having money makes me independent. I've learned how to manage money as one does other parts of one's life. I had to watch my assets and develop a plan, which ultimately had to include divorce, child support, and education of my two children. Even so, when I got divorced, I left Connecticut broke. I lived simply. I had few belongings—a TV set and a bridge table."

By the mid-1990s, Fred was ready for his next move. This time he returned to Raleigh, where he already owned a home. A coach and mentor suggested that he teach. Fred's goal was to teach high school business courses, but he found that he was ineligible to teach because he lacked the required "how-to" education courses. Instead, Fred became a part-time instructor at Wake Technical Community College, and a year later he was named director of Wake's Small Business Center.

Fred energized the center with a series of self-help programs for current and prospective business owners but found that he wanted to embark on another adventure. "When I lived in California, I had dreamed of owning a log cabin in the mountains. But that wasn't possible because homes there were too expensive. After returning to North Carolina, I started looking for such a place no more than a three-and-a-half-

**"I look at my current life as another chapter. I don't know when this chapter will end."**

hour drive from Raleigh. I thought it would be a weekend place." By mid-2000, Fred found a suitable mountain site and built a 1,500-square-foot log cabin that abuts the Blue Ridge Parkway.

Returning to Raleigh on Sundays, Fred asked himself the same question: Why live this dual lifestyle? Each Sunday night the answer was the same: He had a job in Raleigh. Fred solved that riddle in 2002 when he resigned. He cut his ties even further by selling his Raleigh house.

Fred's action was consistent with his approach to life. "I have a short attention span, and I get bored quickly. I look at my current life as another chapter. I don't know when this chapter will end."

What Fred is doing now represents a 180-degree change from his past corporate lifestyle. "I'm learning how to live in slow motion. It now takes me longer to do things I used to do quickly. I can spend an afternoon going into town for food."

Living by himself in the cabin costs less than it did in Raleigh or California. Too young for Social Security or pension income, Fred lives on income from investments. "I let my money work for me. I move things around to offset any drop in the market." Other than buying a four-wheel-drive car to handle the rough mountain terrain, Fred says that he's lucky that he doesn't need expensive adult toys.

"I love to walk in the woods with my two dogs who are in heaven here. My children and friends visit me. What I'm doing is not retirement. I feel that I'm still active, but not in the traditional sense. I might very well do something different in the next chapter of my life, but I don't know when it will begin. In many ways, what I'm doing beats how I used to live. I don't miss living in motels more than my home, waiting for airport limos, and driving rental cars."

His immediate aim was to complete four seasons. He's now in his fourth year with no immediate plans to leave what he calls his mountain home. "Right now I haven't gotten myself to think that far ahead. For the first time in years, I feel that I'm in control. The key is one's mindset by having fun, doing new things, and enjoying the challenges they bring."

## CONSIDERED RETIREMENT FOR SEVERAL YEARS
### James Leach
#### *Wants to Spend More Time as a Writer*

At 60, Jim Leach decided it was time to retire from his job as vice president for communications and public relations at Colgate University. "I was thinking of making a change for about five years, and seriously considering stepping down for about two of them."

Jim left Colgate in May 2005 after 25 years of fulfilling a range of assignments for several university presidents—editor of the alumni newspaper, vice president for communications and public relations, and secretary of the university.

In his resignation letter to Colgate's president, Rebecca Chopp, Jim said: "In September, I will have been here for 24 years without a break of more than two weeks at a time. I am finding myself less tolerant of the daily aggravations one should expect in a position such as mine. Where I have always been able to adapt to the pressures, if not thrive on them, I'm losing some of my resiliency.

"When I arrived in Hamilton (Colgate is located in New York) at 35, I was part of a 'new' Colgate. I increasingly feel at 59 that I am considered to be part of the 'old' Colgate. Not a comfortable feeling for someone whose aim is to die young at an advanced age."

Jim went on to say that he had a strong desire to return to the "storytelling that got me interested in this work initially."

Over a 35-year career in college communications, Jim said that he had little time to do non–work-related writing. "Retirement gives me the opportunity while I still have my health and my wits."

Another factor that precipitated his decision was the death of his father and several friends. It was time

> **"I don't miss living in motels more than my home, waiting for airport limos and driving rental cars."**

for Jim to consider some other work and lifestyle alternatives.

Other than the two years in the late 1960s that he spent in the Panama Canal Zone as an Army writer and photographer, Jim's entire life has been spent in upstate New York or as he put it, "I've lived my entire life at pretty much the same latitude, from Buffalo in the west to Plattsburgh in the east." He went to Utica College, spent a year as a radio newscaster, 10 years doing public relations at two upstate colleges, and the last 25 years at Colgate.

Where some soon-to-be retirees plan to take an exotic overseas vacation or play golf on a daily basis, Jim spent his first month decompressing. He owns what upstate New Yorkers call a camp (actually a summer cottage) on Lime Kiln Lake about 100 miles from Hamilton in the Adirondack Mountains.

"My aim was to get away. There's no phone, no Internet, no television, and I have to drive about 15 miles to get a cell phone signal. I took a bag of books, a bag of cameras, a bike, a canoe, and a dog, and I let each day evolve as it did. My only self-imposed obligation was to spend a couple of hours each day doing physical things and to keep a journal."

Financial concerns, although a recurring issue to most retirees, is presently not on his front burner. Jim has no intention to leave Hamilton. Besides involvement in civic and community activities, Linda, his wife, who is a few years younger, teaches middle school English in a nearby town. His pension comes via the College Retirement Equities Fund, and he also receives lifetime health care benefits from Colgate.

Jim expects to return to the workplace. He was asked by Rebecca Chopp to work about one day a week doing some writing for her. "I don't have an exact schedule, but I also expect to do some freelance writing and photography, and there's a good chance I'll be retained by some colleges as a communications consultant.

"I know that I want to keep busy yet do something different. Making a ton of money is not my concern. I got into writing in the first place because I could put a sentence together and I could take pictures, and that's what I want to do in the future."

---

## CHANGING GEARS IN COLLEGE MANAGEMENT
### Gwendolyn Bookman
### *Plans a Different Lifestyle*

If Gwendolyn Bookman has learned anything in life, she discovered at a comparatively young age how to roll with the punches, even when she appeared to have been knocked down.

At 29, Gwendolyn was married and the mother of a four-year-old son. She had recently entered law school when her husband, Joe, died. "Fortunately, Joe had a good benefits program where he worked, and I was able to continue law school and graduate."

Gwen, from Durham, North Carolina, attended the then-segregated local school system from kindergarten through high school. She graduated from Howard University in Washington, D.C., the first of five historically black colleges and universities where she's been both a student and a staff member. A psychology major at Howard, she got her first job as a researcher with the National Institute of Health in Bethesda.

The Bookmans moved to Houston, her husband's hometown, and Gwen did research for the Urban Resource Center at Texas Southern University. Two years later, Gwen became a Texas Southern law student. Law was never a career goal, but being a lawyer would open up doors for interesting work.

An honors law school graduate, Gwen was one of the first blacks to clerk for a Texas Supreme Court justice. The following year, she joined a small Houston law firm practicing general, family, and equal opportunity law. As a single mother, she found the hours too long and hectic. "This was the first and only time in my career that I left a job without already having another one. Since then, I've been lucky. All my jobs have come by word of mouth and from recommendations."

**"Since then, I've been lucky. All my jobs have come by word of mouth and from recommendations."**

In 1980, her job on the Texas Southern Law School staff represented the start of what has been to date a 25-year career in college teaching and administration. By the mid-1980s, she left Houston for an administrative post at Howard University.

In what seems like job wanderlust, Gwen once again moved, this time to Boston, where she had jobs at Harvard University and Wellesley College. For two years, she was also a student in international law and economic development at Tufts University. "It seems that I'm on a five- to ten-year job cycle. I've either gotten bored, or new and often more interesting jobs opened up."

Gwen worked on diversity issues at Wellesley and as a liaison between the college's administration and its outside legal counsel. When Nan Keohane, Wellesley's president, left in 1993 to become Duke University's president, Gwen also resigned. This time her destination was Atlanta.

At Spelman College, a school for black women, she was the college's secretary as well as assistant to the president. This led to another Atlanta job at Morris Brown College, where in addition to working in the provost's office, she taught a course in legal studies.

"I left Morris Brown to join Johnetta Cole, Spelman's president, who resigned to become president of Bennett College in Greensboro." Besides the challenge of the job, it was 50 miles from her family in Durham.

Cole's mandate was to improve Bennett's academic standing and to increase enrollment. Besides serving as Cole's executive assistant and the college's secretary, Gwen teaches political science and serves as the department's interim chairperson.

"I'd also like to run a class to teach students about the need to save and how to put money aside for retirement. I wish I had known about this when I was younger." She previously would leave a job, withdraw her retirement money, and spend it.

But Gwen is already looking ahead. In 2007, Cole will retire and this means that Gwen, who will be 60, needs to consider her next career or lifestyle move. Full-time retirement is not one of her choices. Her goals are to live in other parts of the United States or Africa, perhaps take another college job teaching, or do some consulting. The chance to travel and study overseas is one of her passions. In 2005 and 2006, she participated in seminars in Ghana, Cancun, and Brazil.

At this time, Gwen wants to keep her options open. Even with her son and his family in Boston, she has ruled out relocating there. "I find it too expensive to live there."

## HER RANGE OF SKILLS OPENS DOORS
### Susanne Nelson
#### *Retirement Not Part of Current Agenda*

Susanne Nelson is literally a coal miner's daughter. But this coal miner's daughter also has a PhD. Now in her late 50s, she does not plan to retire from her educational software job. Besides work, her other goal is to establish what she hopes is her legacy, a scholarship fund to enable West Virginia youngsters to attend college.

Susanne was raised in Wheeling, the eldest of four children. Her father was a coal miner with an eighth-grade education, and her mother dropped out of high school in her senior year.

Higher education was never discussed at home. College would become a unique family experience, considering that neither her parents nor her siblings would ever attend college. Years later, her mother finished high school and became a licensed practical nurse. "Up to the time I went to college, I had never seen a college or a dorm room, and I knew very few people who ever went to college."

As a high school class valedictorian, she received a scholarship to a two-year state college followed by another two years at the University of West Virginia. "I got my degree in family resources, which is a fancy way to describe home economics. I thought of myself

**Three years later, she received a PhD in special education with an emphasis on the gifted.**

as the next Betty Crocker or Ann Pillsbury." Little did she realize at the time that home economics would become another valuable asset in her skill set and lead to some future part-time jobs.

An academic interest in child development led to a master's degree in that subject from the University of West Virginia. As an educator, she continued to hold a skeptical view of the ways students were being taught. She admits that she disliked school even though she did well. Years later as an experienced teacher, Susanne introduced ways to avoid what she calls the repetition of daily lessons and the lack of variety in the classroom.

Married, she relocated to Caribou, Maine, in the northeast corner of the state where her husband worked as a clinical psychologist. It's here that she met a nun, Sister Theresa, who introduced her to a series of jobs—caseworker and then program director for Big Brothers/Big Sisters and office manager for the Catholic Social Service Agency. Eight years later, Susanne says she was ready to move.

Along with her son, she returned to Princeton in her home state of West Virginia and became certified to teach math and instruct gifted students. It's part of her belief that it's good to have a lot of different skills.

For the next 11 years, Susanne taught in Mercer County schools. "I wore many hats. I created new initiatives. I set up Saturday seminars for gifted junior and senior high school students."

Consistent with a goal to challenge students, she became challenged herself when a visiting William & Mary College professor asked her why she wasn't working on a doctorate.

It didn't take Susanne long to follow up on the challenge. In 1991, with a 13-year-old son and her husband, by now a part-time worker, she left West Virginia, moved to Chapel Hill, and enrolled as a doctoral student at the University of North Carolina's School of Education. Three years later, she received a PhD in special education with an emphasis on the gifted. Her financial support consisted of a $12,000 stipend, in-state tuition, and three part-time jobs—an assistantship at UNC, some consulting assignments, and a faculty member position at another local university.

Her various teaching skills, workplace experience, and doctorate led Susanne to her current job. In 1996, the two founders of SAS Institute launched Cary Academy, an independent school for sixth grade through high school students. "I saw an SAS newspaper ad, and I became one of several hundred people to apply for the job. I was hired and my job was to work in curriculum development." Though it offers a full array of academic courses, Cary Academy, located adjacent to SAS's headquarters, was also set up as a laboratory to test the company's educational-related software.

After a year in curriculum development, she joined the SAS in School staff, the corporate group responsible for educational software development and sales. "Over the years, I've carried at different times four business cards—curriculum development, professional development, marketing, and education liaison."

When Susanne was diagnosed as having stage three non-Hodgkin's lymphoma, it could have been a tragic end to her career. Instead, she split her workday between her home and her office during cancer treatment.

Near 60, she has no plans to retire anytime in the near future. Divorced in the late 1990s, Susanne is focusing on the years ahead. "I want to stay at SAS using my education skills to develop new software products. By then, I will have retirement income from teaching in West Virginia, SAS income, and money from my divorce settlement.

"I'm also putting money aside to set up a scholarship fund in West Virginia to help talented youngsters go to college." It's here that her home economic skills resurfaced. Susanne works on weekends as a demonstrator at several area gourmet food stores. The money that she earns goes toward the scholarship fund. Suzanne's goal is to finance the scholarship during her lifetime. The scholarship will be used either in the county where she went to school or in Princeton, where she taught.

## THIS BOOMER COUPLE PLANS
## IN TEN-YEAR CYCLES
### Doug and Arianne Tepper
*Running a B&B Complements Their Lifestyle*

Doug and Arianne Tepper enjoy planning. They've been doing it for 30 years.

Doug's premise is rather simple. Most people, he says, select a career and then try to mold a lifestyle around it. The reverse is true for the Teppers. They find the lifestyle and then shape their career.

The Teppers come from different backgrounds. Doug, a New York City native, graduated from the Bronx High School of Science and from Ithaca College in Ithaca, New York. He studied drama and theater arts, hardly a surprise because he appeared in the early 1950s as a child actor in the TV show *Van and the Genie*. His college education led to a 35-year career teaching drama at Geneva High School in Geneva, a city of 15,000 people about 50 miles northwest of Ithaca. In the 1970s, he supplemented his teacher's salary by directing and producing Hobart College's summer theater. He had a similar position running a dinner theater at a local inn where he met Arianne, who managed the restaurant.

Arianne is an upstate New Yorker. Her father was a Cornell University professor. She attended Cornell's School of Hotel Management for several years and married Doug in the mid-1970s.

Planning was integrated into the Tepper lifestyle. "Our approach to planning is to sit around the kitchen table and get our arms around a problem." Doug realized in ten years that his nine-year-old son and seven-year-old daughter by a previous marriage would be ready for college. Doug's salary paid for household expenses (the two children lived with them) while they banked Arianne's salary. By the 1980s, they had saved enough money to pay for two overlapping college educations.

Planning also enabled Arianne to become a nurse. In 1977, Arianne entered a three-year nursing program and became a registered nurse, which in turn led to a 13-year career as an operating room nurse at Geneva General Hospital.

"My life at Geneva High School was a bit like the music teacher's role in *Mr. Holland's Opus*. We had an ideal life in Geneva. Arianne and I could both walk to work, and the two kids could walk to school. In 1984, with college paid for, we started another ten-year savings program. The goal was to have the money to buy a vacation or second home in a warmer climate. Once again, we lived on my salary and banked Arianne's."

As salaried employees, the Teppers had few tax deductions. Their lawyer advised them to invest their savings in some property. They looked at Caribbean and southern state properties. In 1990, they bought a two-bedroom, two-bathroom condo in West Palm Beach, Florida. "We never slept there until I retired 11 years later. We rented it during those years. We paid taxes on the income from a rented apartment, but we benefited from the expenses to maintain it."

With both children no longer living at home, the Teppers once again engaged in another round of planning. "What lifestyle do we want, and to have that lifestyle what work is available?" As much as they enjoyed living in Geneva, they wanted to own a house on a lake. With the Finger Lakes being so geographically accessible, it was no problem finding a lake house in upstate New York. A house on Keuka Lake, 25 miles from Geneva, met their needs. The lake is 22 miles long and shaped like a finger. Prior to buying a lake home and moving from Geneva, the Teppers rented a place on the lake for six weeks to test the community and its lifestyle.

"In July 1994, we took over the Finton's Landing Bed & Breakfast Inn, and until I retired six years later, I commuted to work." Arianne had already left nurs-

**"What lifestyle do we want, and to have that lifestyle what work is available?"**

**"How do we exit this business? It's not immediate, but inn ownership can't go on forever."**

ing to work at the inn. The house was built in the mid-19th century and had many owners before its conversion to a B&B, but it was in bad shape. They closed the inn that year on Halloween and did extensive renovation, resulting in building a second-floor, 35-by-35-foot loft apartment for themselves over a newly built garage.

Before the Teppers bought Finton's Landing, they did their homework. "We read books on B&Bs in the library and bookstores, read a master's degree thesis on B&Bs, and even spent five days running a friend's B&B in Charlottesville, Virginia, to see if we liked it. I was still somewhat skeptical because running a B&B calls for nurturing skills. I asked myself whether I could be service oriented and be pleasant to guests."

For the first six years of B&B ownership, Finton's Landing ran year-round. Business during the winter months was expectedly slow. Come Doug's retirement, they changed to a seasonal B&B schedule from early April to the end of October. It takes about six weeks to get the place ready for winter and do building maintenance. Come the New Year, they vacation in Florida.

Since growing up in New York City, Doug has been a New York Giants fan for over 40 years. Living in upstate New York has not lessened his enthusiasm. "We go to every home football game. We get an inn sitter, leave Finton's Landing on Saturday morning, drive to New Jersey, stay over Saturday night, see the game on Sunday afternoon, and drive home that evening."

The Teppers are not becoming, nor did they expect to become, rich as B&B proprietors. Doug says it produces the difference between his retirement income and what he earned as a teacher. After expenses, it provides ownership in a proven business as well as a place to live.

As planners, what have these two boomers set as future goals? "How do we exit this business? It's not immediate, but inn ownership can't go on forever." In a recent *New York Times* interview, Tom Edmonston of Realty Executives on Cape Cod, notes that the rate of

B&B turnover nationally is seven years. To which Doug asks, "What lifestyle do we want in the years ahead? We do know one thing; we like where we now live."

---

## POINTS TO REMEMBER

- **Retirement planning is an individual responsibility.**
- **Corporate paternalism is diminishing,** and few employers offer help in retirement planning.
- **Retirement provides the chance to juggle many interests**—work and play—at once.
- **You can find plenty of opportunities** for ideas and support before and after retirement.
- **More than ever, this is the time to think flexibly and creatively,** and to become computer literate.
- **It's never too early to take stock** of your financial needs and resources in retirement.

# Back to School

*"The capacity to take a fresh look at things makes a young person out of an old person."*
—Comments by Dr. George Vaillant, Harvard University Medical School professor, in his book *Aging Well*

**M**embers of the 50-plus set are college bound, but for them education often means more than collecting a degree. No longer do they need to play academic "show and tell." Just visit two-year or four-year colleges. They teem with older students. A few are degree candidates, but most are auditing undergraduate courses or participating in a number of noncredit learning alternatives available to older students. Only a small minority of the 50-plus set seek professional or advanced degrees.

Unlike younger undergraduates, who scramble to decide what major to declare or career to pursue, or have their nose to the grindstone to earn a grade-point average that will someday look great on their resume, the 50-plus set are in school for their own reasons. For instance, they might want to:

- **Get a degree** because they previously didn't have time, couldn't afford to, or weren't interested in obtaining one.
- **Study something** they were interested in as youngsters but didn't pursue because it didn't seem practical at the time.
- **Study in depth** something that they became interested in over the years.
- **Challenge themselves intellectually** and broaden their scope of interests.
- **Become "renaissance" people.**

- **Further their understanding of a public issue.** They might even put their newfound knowledge to work on behalf of society or their community.
- **Enjoy the ambience** associated with a college environment.
- **Search for new meaning** in their lives.
- **Break the shackles** associated with a past career.

Adult-education programs geared to older or retired students often provide more than an intellectual experience. For many students, school is a social experience, a chance to make new friends, or an opportunity to learn solely for the sake of learning. Because curricula are so diversified, classes attract birds of a feather; that is, people have a chance to meet other people with similar interests. Husbands and wives frequently take the same courses. For many, it is the first time in their married lives that they have shared a non-family experience. Other students form new friendships to replace workplace relationships lost in retirement.

## Those Who Do Seek Degrees

Despite all the scrambling for more education, the 50-plus set still make up only 3 percent of the total number of students obtaining undergraduate, graduate, and professional degrees. And when they get their degrees, says the College Board (*www.collegeboard.com*), a monitor of adult education trends, they "seek degrees that have immediate utility. They deposit their learning into a checking account—not into a savings account—so they can draw on it without delay. To most adults, learning is a liquid resource, not a long-term capital investment."

Education for the 50-plus set rarely goes as far as the route taken by Erle Peacock, Jr., of Chapel Hill, North Carolina. Erle went to law school in his mid-60s, following a 40-year career as a physician. The changeover was part of a personal pledge to quit doing major surgery when he turned 65. Erle's legal specialty focuses on health care issues.

## Return to the Classroom

Most significant, the U.S. Department of Education (*www.ed.gov*) points out that nearly nine million men and women age 55 to 64 take adult education courses. They take courses to enrich their personal lives, learn new skills to qualify them for a different job, or fulfill a lifetime dream. It shouldn't be a surprise to learn that twice as many of these students over age 55 are women, because many women married, put their husbands through school, and in the process sacrificed their own undergraduate or graduate education. Now many of these women are deciding that the time has come to obtain a long-delayed degree. As empty nesters, they have the time and resources to start or complete their education, embark on a new and more demanding career, or learn for the sake of learning.

## Getting Started

Those interested in returning to school should start their search at a local community college. More than 1,700 public and private two-year community colleges are located within commuting distance of nearly 95 percent of the nation's population. Couple this with approximately 2,400 four-year colleges, and it is easy to see the availability of higher-education opportunities. To ease the financial burden for students who wish to audit courses, 43 states plus the District of Columbia presently waive nearly all or a large part of the tuition at public-sponsored colleges, according to *Retirement Places Rated*. Depending on the state, the waiver age ranges from 60 to 65. Even so, many in the 50-plus set feel uneasy in a traditional college setting—not due to the academic requirements but because they are apprehensive about attending classes with students one-half to one-third their age. For many, it is the first time they are in school in 30 or more years. And age is frequently an asset in the classroom, as many 50-plus students attest. "Don't worry if you have gray hairs. My general rule is the older the student, the better," says Don Higginbotham, history professor at the University of North Carolina in Chapel Hill. "I find that older students who audit my early American and colonial history courses are more serious minded and better read, and I don't get blank stares from them in class."

As an aside, I've audited undergraduate courses on the topics of American colonial history, Southern culture, American economic history, the U.S. Supreme Court, the U.S. Constitution, and North Carolina politics. As an auditor, I'm not required to take tests or write papers, but I do the required class readings. Besides attending college courses, I find it refreshing to observe how college students view issues relative to each course.

While some undergraduates wonder why older students, often the age of a grandparent, take college courses, May Chrisman, a recent UNC graduate, finds that they give a different perspective to class discussions. In a course on the family and society, she said, "It was refreshing to hear older students discuss pop culture. They speak up for their generation as we do for ours."

## A Different Kind of Master's Degree

Imagine taking a college course called "The Emancipation of Music," "The Biodiversity Crisis," or "Madness and Society in Historical Perspective." These are just some of the courses available to students attending the 125 colleges and universities that belong to the Association of Graduate Liberal Arts (*www.aglsp.org*).

In what some consider avant-garde education, the programs appeal to somewhat older students—men and women over 30 who want to pursue a nontraditional course of study and receive a liberal arts master's degree in an environment geared to their workday schedules. The great appeal of these programs is the curriculum, which differs from traditionally structured Master of Arts pro-

---

### SUGGESTED READING

- *Adults in College,* by Wanda Schindley (Dallas Publishing, 2002). This book is a survival guide for nontraditional students.
- *Traditional Degrees for Non-Traditional Students,* by Carole Fungaroli (Farrar Straus & Giroux, 2000). The subtitle says it all: *How to Earn a Top Diploma from America's Great Colleges at Any Age.*

grams. The curriculum is interdisciplinary, permitting students to design a personalized course of study. Georgetown University has gone even one step further. In 2005, it enrolled students in the nation's first Doctor of Liberal Studies. Typical of master's degree programs is the one at Duke University, in which nearly 20 percent of the 165 students in the program are over age 55. At DePaul University, 20 percent of the Master of Arts in Liberal Studies (MALS) students are over age 50. "Graduate liberal studies, such as MALS, remain the best place for adult learners to find intellectual growth and challenge in an academic setting," says David Gitomer, who directs DePaul's program.

Rather than base admission totally on past academic record or performance on the Graduate Record Examinations, school officials also consider the applicant's work experience. Donna Zapf, the director of Duke's program and currently president of the Association of Graduate Liberal Arts, points out that added maturity, recent accomplishments, and a determination to succeed may help offset a weak or outdated college transcript.

Students enter the program for intellectual reasons (see the profile of Mike Collins later in this chapter). They are graded, they are challenged by academic discipline, and, above all, they are making a commitment—at least three years to acquire a degree for part-time students and usually a year for full-time students. While no thesis is required, students submit an essay based on original research.

The tuition varies in MALS programs, ranging from lower fees at public institutions to more costly tuition at private universities. Some students are reimbursed by employers or qualify for financial aid.

## Alternative Learning

Walk across the Duke campus and you'll find an academic alternative to the MALS program. The Duke Institute for Learning in

> **"Added maturity, recent accomplishments, and a determination to succeed may help offset a weak or outdated college transcript."**

Retirement (DILR, *www.duke.edu*) is one of nearly 400 similar college-sponsored adult education programs. About 100,000 students are enrolled in Learning in Retirement programs. Duke students, like those at institutes on other campuses, prefer art, music, literature, history, and related social science courses. Other than computer-related courses, don't expect too many how-to courses; those are offered at community colleges or in high school adult education programs.

The concept of peer learning is a pivotal part of an institute's program at most campuses. As Elderhostel puts it, people "love to learn in the company of their peers." Students often serve as the faculty, create the curriculum, and help operate the institute. Typically, students have little interest in taking courses for credit or being graded on their academic efforts. The tuition and registration fees on most campuses average about $100 to $400 a semester.

Though anyone 50-plus is eligible for Institute for Learning courses, chances are you will find the students attending them to be somewhat older. At New University for Social Research in New York *(www.nsu .newschool.edu),* students range in age from their mid-50s to early 90s.

Sara Craven, Duke's director, is candid when talking about her program. "Most of the nearly 1,300 people who take at least one Duke Institute of Learning in Retirement class a year do not want to attend class with younger students." DILR students include both high school dropouts and Fulbright scholars. Typically, students participate in the DILR program for five years.

Duke, like other colleges, is getting ready for baby boomers. Sara says they have needs different from current and previous members. "They want more techie stuff that relates to digital cameras or PowerPoint presentations. And at the same time, they want to take a course on World War II to learn more about their father's war."

Institute programs offer more than educational opportunities. They have evolved into a social hub. In

Durham, where many of the retirees are newcomers to the area, DILR provides the setting to make new friends. It sponsors duplicate bridge sessions, Sunday afternoon walks, brown-bag lunches, and an annual two-day retreat in the mountains of North Carolina.

Molloy College *(www.molloy.edu)* in Rockville Center, New York, has added another dimension to its program by permitting its 80 or so students to mix Molloy Institute for Lifetime Learning (MILL) courses with those taught in the college. "They can audit one course each semester. Nursing, education, and a few other courses are out-of-bounds," says MILL director Marion Lowenthal.

## Elderhostel Mixes Travel with Education

Just reading Elderhostel's several-hundred-page "Discover North America" catalog and its companion "Discover the World" catalog is an educational adventure. Elderhostel *(www.elderhostel.org)* offers something for everyone.

The thrust of the Elderhostel program is nontraditional and noncredit education, which is designed to appeal to diverse cultural, academic, active, outdoor, and creative tastes. At the Oregon Shakespeare Festival in Ashland, students attend performances and backstage tutorials with the performers (at a cost of $850 a person). There's a course in Colorado on painting Rocky Mountain landscapes ($650) and one in St. Louis where students spend five nights visiting museums, gardens, and ethnic neighborhoods ($700). For the more physically fit, one can spend five days hiking the Great Smoky Mountains ($547). Overseas, students can spend 16 nights in Greece exploring ancient sites ($3,375), two weeks learning what is described as the Cultures along the Pyrenees ($3,600), or two weeks in India visiting temples and ancient cities ($3,000). Prices for overseas courses include air travel; fares vary depending on the U.S. departure city.

**The thrust of the Elderhostel program is nontraditional and noncredit education.**

Elderhostel members must be at least age 55. A companion can attend as long as he or she is at least 50.

## COMBINES COLLEGE COURSES AND ELDERHOSTEL

### Frederick Levitt

*Manufacturer Turned Student*

Even in his 80s, Frederick Levitt considers himself a college student. He's not out to obtain another degree or become an academic expert in any field. Rather, Fred finds it challenging to be on a college campus and take courses with students usually one-third his age. When he's not auditing courses or running his part-time business, he's vacationing with his wife, Claire, on an Elderhostel trip.

Fred's current campus is the University of North Carolina in Chapel Hill. But before he moved to North Carolina, he had taken courses for a number of years at several different colleges near his former home on Long Island, New York. He received his only degree in political science and economics from Brooklyn College.

As a current college student, Fred is fortunate. Being over 65, he has only to pay a registration fee and get permission of the instructor to audit courses, usually two courses each semester. "Unless the course is filled, I usually get in. The courses that interest me rarely have a waiting list."

Unlike some retirees who attend Institute for Learning in Retirement courses at nearby Duke University, Fred prefers going to class with younger students. "I like the mix; it's half the fun. I avoid taking survey courses when the attendance is too large and there's little interaction with the instructor and the other students. I've yet to find a situation where the students haven't been friendly." Fred brings to class a perspective on issues that comes with age, which many of his instructors and fellow students welcome.

Fred concentrates mainly on courses in the humanities and other topics that interest him. He's audited courses on the Buddhist tradition in Tibet and India, the comparative economics of the East and West, the history of Rome from 154 BC to AD 14, the history of the Reformation, Moses and the Exodus, and the New and Old Testaments.

Even though audit students of any age are not required to take tests or write essays, Fred at times elects, strictly for his own satisfaction, to write a paper or take an exam. Even as an audit student, he's expected to keep up with a demanding reading list. He spends several hours each week reading the required books.

Fred's life since moving to North Carolina—and what was supposedly retirement with his wife, Claire—has not been limited to academia. A manufacturer of corrugated paper boxes for many years, he sold his business in the 1980s. Now he works from a home office the equivalent of two days a week as a broker in the same field. "Most of my customers have been with me for years and are located in the Northeast. Within the past few years, some of these companies have moved south." He services his current customers but rarely seeks new ones. Every few months, he makes a trip to the New York area to visit key customers and suppliers. The rest of the time, a telephone and fax machine are his primary means of communication.

Claire and Fred live eight miles from Chapel Hill in a three-bedroom home in Fearrington Village, a community with a high percentage of retirees. A positive factor in the Levitts' decision to relocate was the proximity to the University of North Carolina and its academic, cultural, and health care facilities.

The Levitts' lifestyle is supported by Fred's income as a box broker, his Social Security, investments, and savings.

Fred's busy academic routine is not limited to UNC courses. The Levitts have gone on at least one Elderhostel trip a year. They spent three weeks traveling and studying in Turkey, and closer to home at Mars Hill College in western North Carolina, they

**Fred brings to class a perspective on issues that comes with age, which many of his instructors and fellow students welcome.**

studied the politics of Latin America and China. On a lighter note, they took an introductory jazz course at Peninsula State College in Washington State, and at Fort Lewis College in Durango, Colorado, they observed what takes place behind the scenes at a music festival. As such, they attended rehearsals, met with the conductor and members of the orchestra, and were briefed on festival life. Attending Elderhostel trips is a way of life for the Levitts. It gives them the opportunity to visit other parts of the country and, in a number of instances, to attend nonconventional courses.

Fred's advice to others on adult education: "Age is no barrier to learning." He purchased a computer so he can cruise the information highway. And in Fred's thirst for knowledge, he looks forward each semester to scanning the UNC online course listings to determine what courses he'll audit.

## BROADENS HIS HORIZONS AND SETS AN EXAMPLE
### Gilles Turcotte
*Machinist Returns to College After a 40-Year Break*

Most folks start and graduate from college within ten years of finishing high school. Not so with Gilles Turcotte, who took a nearly 40-year break.

Born in Canada, Gil has lived most of his life in western Massachusetts, within 15 miles of Springfield. High school diploma in hand, Gil briefly attended college part-time in the late 1950s while he worked as an auto mechanic at Sears Roebuck. Marriage to his wife, Anne, the arrival of the first of their seven children (all now in their mid-20s to mid-30s), and a job with Pratt & Whitney in East Hartford, Connecticut, spelled the end of college for Gil.

Gil worked for Pratt & Whitney as a machinist for 33 years. He started at $98 a week, and by the time he retired, his salary had increased nearly tenfold. "I retired rather quickly. I wasn't expecting it at the time," said Gil. "Pratt & Whitney had an early-out program. I was told about it on a Friday and had until Monday to make up my mind." Making less money as a retiree presented few problems as the Turcottes already knew how to live frugally.

After accepting Pratt & Whitney's offer, Gil decided to return to college and get a degree. He wanted to satisfy his own intellectual curiosity and, by setting the example, wanted to encourage several of his children who hadn't attended college to do so.

Westfield State College, about 25 miles from home, was the nearest college where, as a 60-year-old, he would qualify for half-price tuition. He majored in liberal studies. "Westfield accepted most of my past credits except for one course in calculus and analytic geometry where I didn't do too well. I went to college as many as four nights a week. The last two years I went full-time. I even made the dean's list.

"I was fortunate to have a good advisor. She told me what courses and instructors to take or avoid. This was good, as I discovered not everyone is good at teaching older students. When I asked two instructors for help, they refused and said that they were there just to teach. Gil's advisor discussed the issue at a staff meeting, and the college went one step further. A plan was designed to direct older students to more accommodating instructors.

"I wasn't at school for the social life. Other than being polite, I ignored the other students; they weren't interested in me. I was there because I wanted to be in class, not because mommy and daddy were pushing and paying for it."

Gil received his degree in May 2002 about the same time his son, now a nurse, received his. "Next to getting married, finishing college was the best feeling in my life. College opened my mind. I found that there was more to life than the job. When I retired, I left the company behind while other retirees couldn't make the break; they live in the past. When I go to Pratt &

**"Next to getting married, finishing college was the best feeling in my life."**

**"For some reason or another, I think seniors are afraid of not making the grade."**

Whitney retiree lunches, the other guys just discuss 'shop.'

"College broadened me in other ways. After one course in which we studied Turkey, Anne and I visited Turkey."

A part-time job that Gil had taken many years before his retirement from Pratt & Whitney supplements Gil's pension income. He and Anne share the job of animal control officer, serving their hometown of Wilbraham and a neighboring town, Ludlow. "We're always on call to remove dead dogs, cats, raccoons, and skunks. Other than this work, Anne didn't have any other job. Anne works about the same number of hours as I do. We share the job and we go together on as many calls as we can. We earn about $20,000 from both towns. The job requires a lot of social interaction; the classes I took in ethics and sociology have really helped here."

Because of the income he earns from the animal control job, Gil expects to wait until he's 65 to receive Social Security. His Pratt & Whitney retirement package includes a health care package. Through his job as an animal control officer, however, he gets medical coverage. When he leaves that job, he'll be eligible for Medicare.

"Of the 20 people who retired from Pratt & Whitney when I did, most of them didn't know what they would do. I'm proud to say that I'm the only one who chose to finish my education and get a degree. For some reason or another, I think seniors are afraid of not making the grade."

But Gil changed directions in late 2004 when he retired as an animal control officer. Health was a prime reason. His interest, however, in education has not dimmed. "I'm back taking college courses that last three to four weeks, or in some instances a one-day seminar. The $99 price is quite reasonable. And once I get some health problems under control, I intend to proceed toward a master's degree."

## MASTER'S DEGREE PROVIDES LEVERAGE
### Mike Collins
### *Graduate Studies Opens Up New Vistas*

Mike Collins, in his early 50s, has been an independent contractor for more than 15 years, and thoughts of retirement have no place on his agenda. Even so, Mike has taken some steps over the past several years—earning a graduate degree and becoming self-employed—that could be adopted as strategies by many of his contemporaries who are evaluating whether to retire early or are preparing for retirement.

Mike is from Lumberton in southeastern North Carolina, and early on learned an important lesson from his parents. "My mother worked for a local car dealer, and my father was the transportation manager for an agricultural company. Neither seemed to enjoy their work. They looked forward to retirement. Work was a case of putting in their time." In contrast, starting in high school, Mike read books about "success." The concept that one had the power to shape one's life became his guiding light.

Mike should have graduated as a radio, television, and motion pictures major from the University of North Carolina in Chapel Hill in 1974, but because he was a student who did well only in the courses he liked, he flunked out. He worked for several years, returned to UNC and graduated in 1979. By then, Mike had demonstrated a maverick spirit that would guide his professional life thereafter.

After working for Bell South, 3M, and the Standard Register Company, a publisher of airline magazines, Mike decided to switch from corporate employment to self-employment.

"It began when I wrote a book, *The North Carolina Jobhunter's Handbook.* I needed other work to support myself so I started a lawn-mowing service. Next, I convinced the North Carolina Association of CPAs that I could sell advertising in their directories. My commission was 25 percent. After those experiences,

**"I didn't want to be the guy in his late 50s who looks at himself and says that I should have done this or that."**

I realized that I could be self-employed and make money."

Additional doors opened up to Mike after he wrote a series of articles that ran in several local business publications. An administrator at Wake Technical Community College's Small Business Center saw one of Mike's articles and asked him to conduct a workshop, which was named "Dynamite Marketing on a Firecracker Budget." This occasional workshop led to Mike's forming a new company, The Perfect Workday, for which he gives about 120 seminars a year, many at industry and association meetings. "I'm now doing bigger gigs before folks like PriceWaterhouse and Glaxo-SmithKline. Just as long as I stay current, I can do these workshops forever. I change them regularly based on current events, trends, and audience interest."

Even after establishing a steady source of income and gaining the freedom of self-employment, Mike looked for additional challenges. "In the early 1990s, I was told to get an advanced degree. I needed something to open more doors for me—a credential to work myself into larger programs. I didn't want to be the guy in his late 50s who looks at himself and says that I should have done this or that." Mike considered attending Duke's MALS program.

Mike delayed his decision to get the master's degree until 1999, partly from procrastination but also due to family events, including his father's illness in 1994. However, that experience opened Mike's eyes to a new opportunity that would, in a few years, provide the thrust of his master's degree studies. "When my father got ill, he needed a caregiver. In this case it was my mother. But I saw an important vacuum that needed to be filled—understanding the role of caregivers."

When he enrolled at Duke, Mike still was not sure what courses to take. Serendipity stepped in. In 2000, Mike spent several weeks with other MALS students studying at Oxford University, where he heard how welfare programs in Europe respond to the experiences of human development, especially aging. This exposure helped to solidify Mike's academic goals.

Combining what he had witnessed during his father's illness with what he had learned at Duke, Mike chose to concentrate on topics related to caregiving. One of his papers depicted how feature films portray caregivers, and his master's thesis explored the various ways that caregiving can be handled.

As a result of his Duke studies, which culminated with his graduation in 2003, Mike also produced a 28-minute video, "Care for the Caregiver." His new company, Caregivers 101, Inc., is marketing to people like his mother, who years earlier needed to find ways to take care of herself while attending to his father.

"If nothing more, my Duke studies kept me from getting stale in my small business lectures. Even better, I can tell my students that I, too, have started a business, Caregiver 101." And for a change of pace he finished his first novel, a mystery that was set in Chapel Hill.

## AN EVENING COURSE STARTS A DECADE OF EXPLORATION

### Jay Feldman

#### *From Corporate Lawyer to Music Student and Docent*

When Jay Feldman met with his financial advisor to determine whether he could afford to retire at age 57, he told his advisor that two budget items were not negotiable—season tickets to the New York Giants' home football games and a Saturday evening subscription to the Metropolitan Opera.

Following graduation from Harvard Law School, Jay worked for 20 years as a corporate lawyer before joining Nynex (now Verizon), one of the "Baby Bell" companies created by the breakup of the Bell system in the early 1980s. He spent the next 11 years heading up Nynex's corporate and securities law department. In 1994, Nynex was trimming its executive staff, and Jay realized his days there were limited.

**"My approach was experimental. If I liked it, I would take another one."**

"I was not ready for retirement at the time, but I knew I couldn't survive with the company until I was 65. In some ways, I was ready to retire. The job no longer offered the same challenges as it once had, and I was spending a lot of time just administering the legal department and supervising other lawyers. Nynex provided free access to a financial consultant so I would be prepared to respond to an offer. Before the financial plan was finished, Nynex made its offer. It was June 1, 1994, and I had 30 days to make a decision."

The incentive to retire was a pension and benefits package based on a number of years of service that exceeded those that he had actually worked for Nynex. It made retirement affordable. At the time, his wife, Nancy, worked in an alternative high school program; she would retire three years later.

When he left Nynex, Jay didn't have a plan. He considered but turned down some temporary consulting assignments. "I wasn't ready to go back into the workplace; I never looked back after that. Until then, I had never stopped to think about life in retirement. I knew I wouldn't be golfing every day, something my father did when he retired as a dentist at 60. Fortunately, Nancy and I had a vacation trip planned for July so it gave me time to think. I knew my plans had to have a volunteer element—payback for my good fortune to retire with reasonable economic security, and I also knew that I wanted to learn more about classical music and opera. But I had no idea what opportunities were available."

Jay's answer came via a *New York Times* Sunday advertisement promoting the Juilliard School's evening program. "I loved music and had been attending concerts and opera regularly since the late 1950s." Other than a required music course at Colgate and the annual campus concert series, Jay had no formal musical education. "Most of what I knew about music, I derived from concert programs and CD notes. I decided to take a course at Juilliard. My approach was experimental. If I liked it, I would take another one."

And, indeed he did. For 11 years, Jay has been a once-a-week, not-for-credit student, commuting about 25 miles to class from Port Washington on Long Island to Juilliard at Lincoln Center in New York. His course selection has varied: Mozart operas, Beethoven symphonies, the Wagner Ring Cycle, Mahler symphonies, and, most recently, 20th century string quartets. "I have tried to alternate between music that I know yet wanted to know more about and less familiar genres or composers. One course on Handel's operas led me to attend concert and opera performances that I might otherwise have missed."

Jay's fellow students at Juilliard range in age from those in their 40s to elderly senior citizens. About half of them are retired, and the others come to Juilliard at the end of their workday. The cost for 13 class sessions—the typical number per course—of 90 minutes each is over $400 minus a 15 percent discount for being a New York Philharmonic subscriber.

In keeping with Jay's experimental attitude, he also attended seven semesters in a Judaic studies program sponsored by the United Synagogue of Conservative Judaism in New York.

In the mid-1990s, Jay learned that the Nassau County Holocaust Memorial and Educational Center in Glen Cove, New York, a few miles east of his home, needed help from two groups—those who would give money and those who would volunteer their time. "I fit the latter type," said Jay. "I always liked history. It was my college major at Colgate. If I hadn't gone to law school, I would have gotten a doctorate and taught history. When I started with the center, it had about 5,000 visitors a year. Now, we're up to 35,000. Besides school children—and not just Jewish ones—we get visitors from college alumni organizations, senior centers, and tour groups. We also do interactive telecasting to schools." The center's job, Jay says, is to help visitors understand what holocausts, including the genocide in Rwanda, Kosovo, and Darfur, can do to a society.

**"If I hadn't gone to law school, I would have gotten a doctorate and taught history."**

When he first got involved with the museum, one of Jay's friends said that the relationship as a docent would last only a few years. Not so. He has averaged four hours a week for the past ten years, almost as long as his relationship with Juilliard. "I enjoy teaching—the face-to-face relationships with the students and answering their questions. I'm also involved in training new volunteers, and I conduct workshops for teachers on how they should teach their students about the Holocaust." Jay was invited to join the museum's board of directors but turned down the offer. "I wanted to avoid the politics and administrative work. I had had enough of that when I worked."

But Jay's retirement repertoire continues to expand. For the past several years, he has been writing letters on political topics that appear in the *New York Times* and *Wall Street Journal*. "I've become a voracious letter-to-the editor writer. Again, retirement provides the time to express one's thoughts."

## A RETIRED PHYSICAN RETURNS TO COLLEGE
### Tom Sawyer
*Ophthalmologist Renews Passion for Learning*

Tom Sawyer retired as an ophthalmologist in 2000. But retirement didn't mean that Tom planned to reduce his workload. It simply meant shifting gears from practicing medicine to pursuing his longtime passion of being a perennial college student.

A University of Michigan undergraduate and medical school student, Tom practiced for nearly 30 years in Milwaukee until the mid-1980s, when he moved to Pinehurst, North Carolina. "I was in my late 50s, and my office lease was not going to be renewed. I could easily have found a new office, but I didn't want to start investing in leasehold improvements. I made an offer to my associate to buy me out, which he accepted."

Even so, Tom wasn't ready to retire. He still enjoyed practicing medicine and had experienced no loss of manual dexterity, which is critical in ophthalmology. Serendipity stepped in. Tom saw a classified advertisement in the *Journal of the American Medical Association*. A multioffice ophthalmology practice in south central North Carolina was looking for a board-certified specialist to join its staff. It was the first time in his professional career that Tom responded to an employment ad. He applied, was hired, and became a Carolina Eye Associates staff member.

Tom and his wife, Marilyn, relocated to Pinehurst, bought a house, and he went to work. By the early 1990s, Tom was ready for another change. He would continue to work but at a slower rate—two days rather than four days a week. His views met the approval of Carolina Eye Associates, which reassigned him to a smaller office that it staffed twice a week. By that time, Tom had already decided to restrict himself to eye examinations and other routine medical work, an approach taken by older surgeons.

While Tom was starting to cut back on his medical practice, he found a new outlet, namely, auditing college courses. Being a lifetime learner is not new to him. Years earlier while practicing medicine in Milwaukee, he took *Sunrise Semester* courses, an early morning educational public television program. He enjoyed learning things aside from his medical specialty. "I worked in a narrow professional field where the only thing I did other than spend time with my family was to stay abreast of what was happening in ophthalmology."

After moving from Pinehurst to the Chapel Hill area in 1994, Tom returned to college as a University of North Carolina audit student. He started to take advantage of the rule that permits residents over age 65 in North Carolina to enroll in courses at state universities and community colleges at no charge.

Tom audits courses, which meet several times each week during the fall and spring semester, and a single summer school course that meets five days a week during a shortened yet more intensive six-week semester. When he took science courses, Tom would take the tests, do laboratory work when required, and

**On campus, his dress is similar to most undergraduates— jeans, sneakers, and the omnipresent backpack.**

write papers—an unusual approach for audit students of any age. "Why not? I want to do the full course and 'duke' it out with the kids."

On campus, his dress is similar to most undergraduates—jeans, sneakers, and the omnipresent backpack. "When I was taking biology courses, most of the students in my class at UNC had no idea that I was a doctor. I don't volunteer this information. To most, I'm just another old guy in class with them." Tom likes attending class with younger students and listening to them talk about careers in science and medicine. When this occurs, he breaks silence and serves as an unofficial mentor to students interested in a medical career.

Tom notes that he has more passion for the variety of courses that he's now taking than when he was a college student. Over the past ten years, he has roamed the UNC liberal arts curriculum, auditing a diverse selection of courses ranging from molecular biology, ecology, and population genetics to astronomy, music, art, sociology, history, the U.S. Constitution, and geography. Interestingly, a number of the current biology courses weren't given when he was an undergraduate, and some of the equipment being used had not been invented.

Tom says that doctors of his generation weren't trained to use computers. "When I moved to North Carolina, I wanted to learn about computers, so I took some courses at a local community college. But my computer needs are simple. I use the computer as a word processor to prepare spreadsheets for my reports. I sometimes log on to Medline, but I'd rather go to the UNC medical library and read the papers. I guess it's the way I was trained."

## POINTS TO REMEMBER

- **College extension programs are the prime educational route** for the 50-plus set.
- **Extension programs are not for everyone;** some in the 50-plus set like the discipline of being a matriculated student.
- **Master of Arts in Liberal Studies programs appeal to some retirees.**
- **With Elderhostel, education means a vacation,** too.
- **Many older students feel more comfortable attending school with their peers** than with younger students.
- **Older students enjoy the college campus environment.**
- **Adult education brings families together.**

# Volunteerism: More Than a Workplace Substitute

*"Some people think if you are 55 or 65 you ought to be retired. I'm still going strong at 81."*
—Former Senator Robert Dole

When Marvin Leffler exited his plumbing supply business, he was not concerned about how he would occupy his time. He substituted volunteerism for corporate management. What's more, he had already identified the vehicle that could use his talents.

Having spent more than 50 years in sales and an equal number of years as an active New York University alumnus, Marvin naturally became involved in the restoration and operation of NYU's Town Hall as one of the city's premier public auditoriums. When Town Hall was spun off from the university as a separate nonprofit organization, Marvin was named president. Though it's a nonpaying job, Marvin works a nearly full-time schedule attending to the things he likes and does best—sales, marketing, and getting diverse groups to work together.

Many early retirees, like Marvin, return to their roots when they choose to volunteer. Simply put, a former manager or professional has skills and experience needed by nonprofit groups. A doctor assists in a health clinic, an accountant advises start-up businesses, and an educator teaches nonreaders. One thing is certain: Whatever the assignment, 50-plus managers and professionals usually describe their volunteer work as "payback" time, a form of thanks for a rewarding career.

However, after 30 to 40 years of corporate life, the last thing many managers want to do is serve on a nonprofit organization's board of directors. If they are inclined to be volunteers, they often look for assignments where they can use their skills by working directly with people rather than as members of committees or boards of directors. Not that board work is less important, but many 50-plus managers and professionals want to break from their former corporate lifestyle.

Some in the 50-plus set prefer working in a hands-on capacity teaching handicapped children, delivering meals to the elderly at home, or assisting in a health or legal-aid clinic. But even with a desire for one-on-one work, can you imagine being as adaptable as Mary Pat Toups (profiled in this chapter), who provides legal assistance to the needy in California and is one of the leaders of the American Bar Association's Senior Lawyers Division?

John Gabor is a new convert to volunteerism. Other than a brief stint in Larchmont, New York, as a member of a school board election committee, John's earlier life focused on family, career, and personal interests. Retirement from a marketing career followed by relocation in 1993 to Fearrington Village in North Carolina meant some lifestyle changes. Nonprofit work to some extent would replace corporate employment. For the first three years in North Carolina, John was a Senior Corps of Retired Executives (SCORE) consultant. He left SCORE in favor of the Executive Service Corps (ECS), thereby trading consulting with upstart businesses for a chance to help small to midsize nonprofit groups.

To date, John has conducted about 20 board retreats and strategic planning sessions for ESC clients. "I really like hands-on work more than sitting in board meetings. It feels good helping people directly."

John, however, is somewhat reluctant to join nonprofit boards. The exception is the board of the Family Violence & Rape Crisis Center. "I guess I spend at least eight to ten hours a month in nonprofit work. As much as I enjoy it, I promised myself that I would not become president of a nonprofit organization. I don't want to get that involved; I want to do other things in my retirement."

In their book *Everything to Gain,* Rosalynn and Jimmy Carter write, "Helping others can be surprisingly easy, since there is much that needs to be done. The hard part comes in choosing what to do and getting started, making the first effort at something different. Once the initiative is taken, we often find that we can do things we never thought we could."

At 57, President Carter was out of work, and like other retirees he was looking for new relationships. "For us, an involvement in promoting good for others has made a tremendous difference in our lives in recent years. There are serious needs everywhere for volunteers who want to help those who are hungry, homeless, blind, crippled, addicted to drugs or alcohol, illiterate, mentally ill, elderly, imprisoned, or just friendless and lonely. For most of us, learning about these people, who are often our immediate neighbors, can add a profound new dimension to what might otherwise be a time of too much worrying about our own selves."

## The Facts Speak for Themselves

Take a look at the demographics of volunteerism. A recent AARP *(www.aarp.org)* survey found that about 80 percent of those age 50-plus belong to at least one nonprofit group. Those ages 56 to 64 spend about 60 hours annually as volunteers, and it increases another 28 hours a year for those over 66. As expected, nearly one-half the 50-plus set volunteer in church-related work, followed in order of preference by work with social service, civic or political, health care, education, and sports or recreational organizations.

You might think that an even greater percentage of the nation's 50-plus set would be volunteering.

**AARP finds that retirees with "higher education and those with upper incomes are more likely to volunteer out of a feeling of societal responsibility than older Americans in general."**

The reasons more people do not volunteer vary. The primary factors, other than sheer disinterest, include lack of available time, physical and health limitations, and family concerns. AARP finds that retirees with "higher education and those with upper incomes are more likely to volunteer out of a feeling of societal responsibility than older Americans in general."

## Help Fill the Volunteer Gap

Nonprofit organizations have an insatiable need for volunteers, one that's more difficult to meet than ever before. That's because the leadership and hands-on work in many volunteer organizations historically was provided by women who are now engaged in the workforce. The management skills required to direct a nonprofit group or head a committee were comparable to those used by their husbands in corporate jobs. But the scenario has changed. Women have entered the workforce, and volunteerism, once a substitute for the job market, has become of secondary importance. In response, some

---

### WAYS YOU CAN HELP

- Help the poor, homeless, or needy.
- Improve your community or neighborhood, or the environment.
- Provide services to older people through senior centers or other means.
- Help people cope with their problems.
- Tutor schoolchildren or do other work involving children or youth groups.
- Help out at a hospital or engage in other health-related work.
- Educate people on specific topics.
- Foster art, music, or other cultural activities.
- Promote the political process.

Source: AARP.

---

nonprofits have adjusted their operations, offering more flexible options so they can continue to attract working women as volunteers. The League of Women Voters and Junior League, as an accommodation to their boomer membership, now hold evening meetings in a number of communities.

### Will Boomers Come to the Rescue?

As the baby boomers age, a surge of more than 20 percent in new retirees in the next 15 years should mean more volunteers, right? Not so fast. According to a Civic Ventures *(www.civicventures.org)* study funded by the MetLife Foundation *(www.metlife.com),* boomers might have an interest working for a nonprofit group rather than quitting the workforce. "They are especially interested in careers in public service, with 60 percent saying it is important that work in retirement serve the community and those in need. . . . It's very important that the job gives them a sense of purpose." The nonprofit fields that interest them include helping the poor and needy, health care, teaching, and youth programs.

# A Nonprofit Sampler

Every base appears to be covered. Some volunteer groups are national organizations with membership in the millions; others are regional with more specific missions. Nearly all need more volunteer help. If you're concerned with homelessness, then Habitat for Humanity *(www.habitat.org)* offers practical solutions. Want to use your management skills? Try either the Service Corps of Retired Executives Association *(www.score.org)* or the Executive Service Corps Affiliate Network *(www.escus.org).* If you have a particular skill and don't know how to become a volunteer, scan the Yellow Pages for the names of volunteer organizations, or contact local volunteer clearinghouses like the Retired Senior and Volunteer Corps *(www.seniorcorps.org)* program, which specializes in providing volunteers age 55-plus to dozens of community organizations and agencies. Local newspapers and magazines sometimes publish lists of agencies currently in need of volunteers, and public television and radio stations occasionally conduct volunteer sign-up drives. Here are just several local or national groups to consider:

- The Environmental Alliance for Senior Involvement *(www.easi.org)* has assembled a network of 12,000 local, state, and national environmental groups. In Delaware, for example, a local group studied the impact of the West Nile virus in the state, and Oklahoma volunteers monitored streams and worked toward educating the public on ways to prevent pollution.

- Princeton's class of 1955 initiated the Princeton Project 55 *(www.project55.org)* to provide funds and manpower on civic leadership and public interest projects. The concept has now spread to 27 other colleges.

- The Experience Corps *(www.experiencecorps.org)* has nearly 2,000 volunteers in 14 cities. Volunteers, all over age 55, serve as tutors and mentors in city schools and after-school programs. About one-half the tutors receive up to a $200 monthly honorarium. In return, they are required to work 15 hours a week.

## Elderhostel Offers Community Service

In 1992, Elderhostel *(www.elderhostel.org)* introduced a number of U.S. and overseas programs in partnership with Global Volunteers, the Oceanic Society, and Habitat for Humanity.

Interested in Appalachia? Elderhostel sponsors a weeklong project involving restoration work at several "lost" communities in southwest Virginia. A typical volunteer project might involve maintenance at several of the area's museums and historic sites. In Yellowstone National Park, volunteers focus on the importance of seed banks and how they are set up. Volunteers then go into the field to identify plants and to collect and catalog seeds for storage in seed banks.

Global Volunteers *(www.globalvolunteers.org)* work primarily in rural communities throughout the world, including Ghana, India, Mexico, and parts of the United States. They concentrate on teaching English as well as doing maintenance work in poor, rural schools.

The Oceanic Society *(www.oceanic-society.org)* engages in a range of environmentally related research assignments such as studying river dolphins in the Amazon or collecting data on coral reefs in Belize.

The all-inclusive fees to participate in Elderhostel Service Programs can be up to $700 for a U.S. project, and range from $2,000 to nearly $3,000, including round-trip airfare, on overseas assignments. Volunteers live in the community, generally in quarters comparable in quality to a college dormitory. Before being accepted in some of the programs, prospective volunteers are asked to sign a form indicating their awareness of the physical nature of the program.

## Helping Small Business

The Service Corps of Retired Executives, better known as SCORE, provides management and professional know-how to potential, start-up, and existing small companies. Funded nearly entirely by the Small Business Administration, which is also a source of a large part of its client base, SCORE offers clients a menu of one-on-one and team counseling, and workshops in sales and marketing, manufacturing, distribution, and record keeping. In 2004, approximately 10,500 volunteer consultants in 389 local SCORE chapters and 800 offices counseled about 470,000 small business owners. SCORE seeks volunteers from all levels of corporate life ranging from managers and professionals to people who ran their own retail, service, and manufacturing businesses. Volunteers also conducted nearly 7,000 workshops and seminars for SCORE's clients.

In responding to client needs, SCORE also offers online consulting services. In 2004, 1,200 online consultants conducted about 110,000 counseling sessions,

"I've been an e-mail counselor since November 2001," says John Wyman (profiled in this chapter). "This means I go into a 'members only' SCORE Web site. I indicate my availability for receiving e-mails as well as how many e-mails per day or week I want to tackle. My maximum is one e-mail assignment a day. I receive about 15 new clients a month, and I respond to about 35 new e-mails and follow-ups. SCORE requires us to respond to each inquiry within 48 hours, but I generally do so within 24 hours." In February 2005, John had over 43 e-mail contacts, and he spent nearly 40 hours advising one client.

In contrast to traditional one-on-one consulting, John selects the time when he will respond to queries, usually in the evening. When he plans to be away, he removes himself from the SCORE availability list.

"One of the reasons I like e-mail counseling is that I can go into the SCORE database and give my qualifications and the geographic areas where I would like to work. I've picked people living in central Virginia, North Carolina, and South Carolina." In some instances, where clients are "local," John personally meets them.

The majority of John's clients ask fairly basic questions that require routine replies. The remainder he calls the "fun contacts"; that is, those who desire a mentor to help them through a crisis or those who need ongoing help to launch a new business. For example, John worked online with a dermatologist regarding ways to set up and staff a new office.

## Using Business Skills Overseas

Since 1964, the International Executive Service Corps (IESC, *www.iesc.org*) has provided a platform for retired managers and professionals to use their skills on overseas assignments.

IESC draws upon a skills bank of more than 11,000 retired and senior-level managers. One-half of the volunteers are retired. The IESC seeks volunteers who are willing to spend up to 35 days overseas. IESC pays the consultants' travel expenses and gives them a per diem for food and housing. (Spouses can accompany volunteers at their own expense.) IESC operates in nearly 60 different countries. In recent years, IESC has been seeking consultants with skills in tourism and hospitality, textiles and apparel, trade policy, and the agribusiness.

The Financial Services Volunteer Corps (FSVC, *www.fsvc.org*) concentrates on overseas investment banking, financial services, and economic policy assignments.

Another agency, the Citizens Development Corps *(www.cdc.org),* like IESC and FSVC, has an international orientation. The CDC typically trains entrepreneurs on ways to forge partnerships with U.S. companies. In 2005, it launched an additional service, the Tourism Development Corps. One of its first assignments was to develop a Bulgarian tourism industry.

## Management Assistance for Nonprofits

In the 1970s, an organization called the National Executive Service Corps (NESC), a New York City–based group, was established to provide management assistance at comparatively low fees to nonprofit organizations. It also assembled a network of affiliate offices under the NESC umbrella.

Recently, NESC has been restructured and folded into a national group with an almost identical objective, the Executive Service Corps Affiliate Network (ESCAN, *www.escus.org*). ESCAN has offices in 34 communities. Even though it is now part of the ESCAN affiliate, the New York–area operation continues to be called NESC. No different than its predecessor, ESCAN uses retired and semiretired executives and professionals as volunteer consultants. In practical terms, 6,000 volunteers in 2004 contributed 80,000 hours of time.

I've been a consultant with the Greater Triangle ESC since 1993. In 2004, about 30 consultants completed about 45 projects ranging from midsize nonprofits to a number of mom-and-pop-size social service agencies. Projects vary from organizing and staging a one-day board and management retreat to marketing, management, or financial assignments

**One of the by-products is a chance to become associated with different organizations.**

that last nine months or longer. Client fees are comparatively modest, from a low of $50 for a small, start-up nonprofit agency with limited financial resources to several thousand dollars for larger organizations. ESC can afford to keep a lid on fees because its consultants are all volunteers and its overhead expenses are minimal. Over the past 13 years, I've advised an AIDS residence group, a state-run historical site, a mental illness facility, a theatrical group, and the Durham County Library. One of the by-products is a chance to become associated with different organizations. As a result of one assignment, I became a library trustee and, subsequently, chairman of the board.

### What About the Peace Corps?

Peace Corps *(www.peacecorps.gov)* service is not just for recent college graduates or 35-year-old career changers. Of its nearly 7,800 volunteers and trainees (58 percent women; 42 percent men), about 460 are 50-plus and in some instances considerably older. Perhaps its most famous older volunteer was Jimmy Carter's mother, Lillian, who in the mid-1960s at age 68, a decade before her son became president, was a volunteer in India. Volunteers have varied backgrounds—business, health care, environment, and education. Overseas assignments in 72 countries are for two years; volunteers receive a bonus upon completion of their overseas tour. The Peace Corps provides free medical, dental, and prescription coverage. If you choose this form of service, expect to live in modest quarters often like the locals.

### A Need for Health Care Services

You may think of Hilton Head Island, South Carolina, as a paradise for the island's 35,000 permanent residents and the annual 1.5 million vacationers who visit there. But a real-life problem exists, namely, the working poor, the estimated 12,000 residents and people working on Hilton Head, who receive few if any primary health care services. What's more, a significant number of the island's schoolchildren have never been examined by a physician.

Dr. Jack McConnell, a physician and, until his retirement, Johnson & Johnson's corporate director of advanced technology, sparked the movement. He and a number of other retired health care professionals living on Hilton Head recognized the area's health care deficiencies and, in 1992, started the Volunteers in Medicine Clinic (VIM, *www.vim.org*). The clinic's volunteer staff, now numbering well over 200 retired physicians, nurses, dentists, and chiropractors, provides free vaccinations, physical examinations, and primary health care, as well as care in the areas of pediatrics, gynecology, cardiology, ophthalmology, and dentistry for upward of 22,000 patient visits a year. Since its founding, the clinic has serviced about 120,000 patients. As a result of its work, the clinic enables retired health care professionals to stay professionally productive.

Before it opened, the clinic managed to get the South Carolina General Assembly to legislate a "special volunteer license" for physicians who agreed to practice medicine free of charge in a nonprofit clinic and to dispense drugs. In practical terms, the physicians, dentists, and other retired health care practitioners are licensed to practice only at the Volunteers in Medicine Clinic. The clinic also obtained unlimited malpractice coverage for $5,000 from the South Carolina Underwriters Association for its staff of health care and lay volunteers.

The retired physicians need to apply individually to the State Board of Medical Examiners for the special license. The board then thoroughly searches the applicant's credentials. The protocol adopted in South Carolina, of course, would vary from state to state for similar types of volunteer clinics.

Some of the retired professionals in Hilton Head have an opportunity to continue in their medical specialties such as gynecology, ophthalmology, pediatrics, and dermatology while others are assigned as primary care physicians. A continuing education program is conducted at the clinic on a weekly basis. To many of the participating physicians, the clinic provides a

**While the Hilton Head clinic has 200 volunteer health care professionals, Dr. McConnell says that a volunteer clinic could operate with only one physician and a nurse.**

chance to work directly with patients, use their skills, and be an active participant in a medical facility.

According to the Volunteers in Medicine formula, the proper utilization of retired health care professionals should help to control health care costs by relieving hospital emergency rooms of the need to furnish high-cost, primary care medical services. While the Hilton Head clinic has 200 volunteer health care professionals, Dr. McConnell says that a volunteer clinic could operate with only one physician and a nurse.

Hilton Head is the only U.S. town in which every resident has access to health care, says Dr. McConnell. To date, more than 1,250 communities have either visited or contacted the Volunteers in Medicine Clinic, requesting information or help in replicating a clinic in their community. The Volunteers in Medicine Institute *(www.vimi.org)* was established to respond to these requests. Twenty-seven other clinics in both rural and urban communities are up and running in 13 states, and most likely an equal number are in various stages of development. And what is Dr. McConnell's dream? "There is sufficient retired medical personnel (about 550,000 physicians, dentists, and nurses) who, if prompted to come out of retirement on a part-time basis, could deliver most of the health care services needed by the 45 million Americans who have been left with little or no access to health care."

### What About Free Legal Services?

Name any community, and there's a need for skilled lawyers at affordable fees. What's more, plenty of folks can't pay for even reasonably priced legal fees. A growing number of retired lawyers, many of them among the 7,000 members of the Senior Lawyers Division *(www.abanet.org/srlawyers)*, provide free legal services to low-income people with everyday legal problems. Arizona, California, Florida, New York, and Texas have already adopted pro bono participation programs whereby state bar association dues are waived as long as the attorney receives no compensation for volunteer legal services. Other states are debating similar types of legislation for retired lawyers. Unlike the open policy in the other states, California does not grant emeritus status to lawyers previously not admitted to practice in the state.

Typically, members of the Senior Lawyers Division, who are age 55-plus and have been admitted to the bar for 25 years, are involved in representing indigent clients in such areas as landlord-tenant and consumer matters, family law, senior citizen issues, public benefits, and immigration law. The amount of time devoted to pro bono work varies greatly. As in all professions, there are some lawyers who never do volunteer work while others devote blocks of time to represent those in need. The division sponsors educational programs dealing with the legal and personal issues of Alzheimer's, Social Security, and comprehensive health care plans.

The division also develops, publishes, and presents educational programs and material to guide lawyers in making the transition from full-time to part-time jobs, changing careers, or retiring.

But retirement-age lawyers, who want to use their legal skills, are not restricted to ABA-related projects, especially if they want to volunteer on overseas projects. The International Senior Lawyers Projects *(www.islp.org)*, which is not affiliated with the ABA, assigns lawyers, both retired and active practitioners, to pro bono jobs involving economic development or finding legal means to implement legal reforms in Africa. One ISLP lawyer spent a week overseeing a course on corporate governance in Uganda.

### Harnessing Corporate Leaders

Finding a volunteer program may be as simple as finding out what programs your company already sponsors. It can be a great way to stay in touch with your fellow retirees and at the same time serve the community. If you haven't been involved before, this may be the time to start. Your company may be able to help you get involved, and if it can't, you may be

**A growing number of retired lawyers . . . provide free legal services to low-income people with everyday legal problems.**

able to help it get involved. The following details the approach taken by telecommunications company employees and Honeywell.

The Telephone Pioneers of America *(www .telecompioneers.org)*, as the name indicates, is a pioneer in volunteering. The nationwide group started in 1910; its membership consists of more than 625,000 retired and long-term employees in the U.S. and Canadian telecommunications industry.

The Pioneers, mostly employees of former AT&T and regional Bell operating companies, donate nearly 30 million hours a year to volunteer work. Special attention has been given to projects that help the lonely, disadvantaged, and disabled, such as building a 900-foot boardwalk that gives disabled and elderly people easier access to the wooded areas in Flat Rock Brook Nature Center in Englewood, New Jersey. More recently, the Pioneers have focused nationally on illiteracy, homelessness, and substance abuse.

Honeywell *(www.honeywell.com)* retirees have over the past 20 years contributed several million hours of service handling a range of projects calling for different management, technical, administrative, professional, and blue-collar skills. Typical of Honeywell's contribution is a design team of retired Honeywell engineers and scientists who created and assembled a hands-on electricity and magnetism kit, and a machine kit for use with third and fourth graders in Minneapolis-area schools. Students learn about series and parallel circuits, and see how motors work. The role of the retirees is not to lecture or do the work but to support, mentor, and provide good adult role models.

## Building for the Future

Amateur and skilled carpenters, plumbers, and electricians alike are welcome at Habitat for Humanity International *(www.habitat.org)*. Using a volunteer labor force of youngsters through oldsters in more than 1,500 affiliates throughout the United States and overseas in 83 other countries, Habitat for Humanity has built or rehabilitated more than 175,000 homes for people who otherwise couldn't afford decent housing. Because not every Habitat volunteer has the stamina or skill to build a house, an alternative is to work at the thrift stores operated by a number of affiliates.

Visit downtown Paterson, New Jersey, and see Habitat for Humanity volunteers in action. The area looks like any other construction site—workers in coveralls, hammers pounding and saws buzzing. Come Wednesdays, the scene is somewhat different. The volunteers, mainly 50-plus retirees, have helped build over 200 duplex and triplex homes in Paterson over the past 20 years. Some of the weekday volunteers made their living as plumbers and carpenters, others are skilled hobbyists, and some are novices like one retired physician, who said, "When I first went to work I just bent nails; now I can 'finish' them and work on my own."

## Help to Find Your Niche

AARP sponsors a number of community service programs for its 35 million members. The AARP Driver Safety Program (previously 55 Alive/Mature Driving) is the first nationwide driving refresher course designed exclusively for people over age 50. Taken annually by about 700,000 drivers, it spins off a tangible benefit—insurers give discounts on auto insurance rates in 34 states and the District of Columbia. Costing $10, the refresher program consists of an eight-hour classroom course divided into two four-hour sessions.

---

### SUGGESTED READING

- *Dynamic Boards,* by James Hardy (Essex Press, 1990). This book is hardly dated. As a board member, I continue to use it.
- *Make a Difference: America's Guide to Volunteering and Community Service,* by Arthur Blaustein (Jossey-Bass, 2003).
- *The State of Nonprofit America,* edited by Lester Salmon (Brookings Institution Press, 2003). An overview of the trends in the nonprofit field.

---

AARP Tax-Aide *(www.aarp.org/taxaide)* places over 30,000 volunteers in local offices to help low-income and moderate-income persons prepare their federal and state tax returns.

## A Giant Volunteer Agency

Recognizing that corporate downsizing and early retirement have increased the pool of potential volunteers, the Retired and Senior Volunteer Program (RSVP, *www.seniorcorps.org*) lowered its membership age from 60 to 55 as a way to snag baby boomers. RSVP, a part of the Corporation for National and Community Service, the federal domestic volunteer agency, is a massive broker of people, linking volunteers with organizations and agencies in need of volunteers.

An estimated 500,000 RSVP volunteers average four hours a week helping approximately 65,000 local organizations such as childcare centers, libraries, parks, museums, outreach programs, and hospitals. RSVP offers nonprofit agencies a base of volunteers with an array of business, education, administrative, and blue-collar skills. Its mission is to enhance the lives of the volunteers and the communities in which they live. While RSVP has little difficulty placing accountants and marketing people, skills often in demand at nonprofit agencies, the organization finds it a greater challenge to place volunteers whose workplace skills are not in demand in childcare centers, libraries, parks, museums, outreach programs, and hospitals.

Helen Featherson, who until her 2005 retirement directed the 30-year-old Durham RSVP program, finds that many volunteers are newcomers to volunteering. "There's a social relationship that attracts some volunteers, and a feeling of 'give back' time." As in all volunteering, she says that one of the biggest challenges is to get people to make a commitment and then show up at work.

Durham's RSVP has about 100 volunteers assigned to Reading Buddies. The job is to improve reading skills in 26 elementary schools. Another volunteer agency, Rock A Baby, cares for critically ill children at Duke Hospital.

## SHE SPEAKS FOR THOSE WHO NEED HELP
### Mary Pat Toups
*Trial Lawyer Turned Advocate for the Poor*

Many women in the 50-plus set have much in common with Mary Pat Toups and her midlife career as a lawyer. Now as a retiree, she has parlayed her legal know-how into a nearly full-time volunteer commitment. She specializes in serving the elderly poor and actively recruits other senior lawyers to the effort. For this work, she has been recognized nationally.

Mary Pat was married by the time she graduated from the University of California in Los Angeles, and then for 20 years she was a homemaker, a civic volunteer, and an elected school board member. Seeing the influence of lawyers in the governmental process, Mary Pat decided when she was in her early 40s to become a lawyer. She was one of 10 women in a class of 100 at Pepperdine University School of Law.

"My work as an elected school board official prepared me for law school by making me conscious of issues facing children, parents, the poor, and the elderly. When I passed the California bar examination, I became a sole practitioner, taking any case that walked in the door." She also liked the independence of being her own boss.

When her husband, a civil engineer from whom she was divorced in the early 1980s, was transferred to Washington, D.C., in 1978, Mary Pat decided to concentrate on a few legal specialties that personally interested her. "I first specialized in representing abused and neglected children, and then in 1984, I started to specialize in elder law." By then, Mary Pat had recognized that poorer elderly people received inadequate legal assistance.

**"I want to empower senior citizens so they better understand the laws that impact on their lives."**

As a practicing Washington attorney, Mary Pat never had a formal business office. "For $50 a year, my office was the courthouse library. All my child-abuse cases were assigned by the District of Columbia Superior Court. It was mostly trial work, which is like the theater. Both require acting and dramatic skill."

When Mary Pat turned 63, she decided to return to Southern California to be nearer her sons and daughters and grandchildren, though she fully intended to continue practicing law.

Leaving Washington meant selling her Watergate apartment and severing her local ties, especially the Kennedy Center for the Performing Arts. As a drama and music fan, she had performed as supernumerary and had had nonsinging, walk-on roles in several operas—*Tosca, La Boheme, Manon,* and the Royal Ballet's performance of *The Prince of the Pagodas.* "I'd be in court all day, then rehearse until midnight. We were paid a $70 honorarium and had to agree that we would only 'mouth' words, never sing them."

In California, she bought a two-bedroom home in an adult community in Laguna Hills, near Los Angeles. Mary Pat financed her move and her "retirement" with profits from the sale of her home and income from investments, Social Security, and payments from writing and teaching.

"In short, I'll never go hungry."

She practices multifaceted advocacy. Her legal practice is now totally voluntary. "I wouldn't consider it a good week unless I spend two days at the Legal Aid Society office in Santa Ana. I no longer accept fees. I only take clients on a consultation basis, referring them to other lawyers if necessary for additional legal help. Mary Pat estimates that she has helped an average of about 200 pro bono clients (defined by the American Bar Association as those who receive legal services at no fee or for a greatly reduced fee equivalent to the minimum wage) a year for each of the past ten years."

"I want to empower senior citizens so they better understand the laws that impact on their lives." This she accomplishes through her writing, teaching, and active participation in the ABA's Senior Lawyers Division. Mary Pat taught a how-to law course for the elderly at a local community college; wrote a column, "Legal Issues for Seniors," for the *Laguna Woods News;* and wrote a book, *Senior Lawyers Organizing & Volunteering: A National Profile,* which the ABA published.

Mary Pat is an advocate in the broadest sense, recruiting older and retired lawyers to work as volunteers with the elderly poor. Her goal is to convince them that as retired lawyers, they can use their skills to help the elderly understand their legal rights. It might be difficult for some lawyers who formerly had large, well-paying practices to work at this level, but volunteering with groups like the Legal Aid Society represents one way for them to continue being active, practicing lawyers. Mary Pat serves as a model. For her efforts, she received the ABA's "Pro Bono Publico Award" at its 2003 annual meeting in San Francisco. She was honored because her entire legal practice has been pro bono. Mary Pat made the awards ceremony into a family affair, with her four children, their spouses, and six grandchildren, then ages 3 to 16, attending.

## A PASSION FOR HISTORY
## AND THE ENVIRONMENT
### Kurt Loesch
*Treats Nonprofit Work as a Full-Time Job*

When Kurt Loesch retired in his late 50s, he didn't have a plan. "I didn't know what I would do, but I knew that things would take care of themselves." And so they did, because Kurt discovered his passion as a volunteer historian, organizer, and spokesperson for Point Lobos Reserve, a California state park that overlooks the Pacific Ocean south of Monterey.

A native New Yorker, Kurt migrated to California in 1948 after graduating from Colgate University. By the mid-1950s, after several jobs as a department store buyer, he left retailing and got a job as a manufacturer's representative. Liking the work, he became a self-employed representative, specializing in the sale of fabrics to wholesale distributors. Years later, new fashion trends changed the fabrics industry. "Women were wearing pants at home and work, and they had little time for home sewing. So I retired in 1984. I didn't know what I would do, yet I knew that things would take care of themselves. At the time, I played golf, but playing golf all the time soon gets old."

Until then, Kurt had had little time for hobbies or volunteerism. Being self-employed and living on commissions meant that business was his primary focus. But this all changed when Kurt and his wife, Betty, moved from Menlo Park to Carmel and again in 2001 to a retirement community in Pacific Groves.

Looking for something to keep him busy, Kurt encountered the green-jacketed volunteer docents who guide visitors through the Point Lobos State Reserve. Kurt was fascinated by their work, which was surprising because Kurt is neither a tree hugger nor an environmentalist, according to a story featuring him in *The Colgate Scene.*

Kurt learned the ropes at Point Lobos through a mandatory docent training program. At the outset of his training, Kurt experienced a learning curve. "I knew nothing about whales, abalone, or other local animals." And despite his indifference to environmental matters, Kurt found himself intrigued with the natural history of the area and with the people who lived there.

"But what closed the deal for me was connecting the faces of the present-day descendants to the names and stories of their ancestors who once lived in the area. In the process of reconstructing their stories, I became part of their families." For more than ten years, much of Kurt's energies were absorbed by helping to create a museum to house the artifacts left by past residents—of Chinese, Japanese, Portuguese, and American origin—who had lived and worked over the past several hundred years in the Point Lobos area.

"From the beginning, Betty was of enormous help. She saw that what I was doing was important, and she made me keep it up."

While restoring a mid–19th century cabin as a museum, Kurt researched at libraries and on microfilms and interviewed descendants of the earlier settlers. His work uncovered a personal interest in history that he had previously denied. Kurt said he disliked history when he was a student.

The opening of the Whalers Cabin in the 1990s stimulated Kurt to do more volunteer work on behalf of Point Lobos. He prepared a list of nearly 50 feature films that included scenes of Point Lobos starting with a 1914 silent film, *Valley of the Moon,* as well as *A Summer Place* and *The Graduate.* Based on this list, a local television station produced a 30-minute documentary on films that took place at Point Lobos.

Kurt's contribution to Point Lobos continued with his participation in the production of a one-hour documentary film. "For several years when the film was being produced, I was the go-between for the film people, researchers, Point Lobos group, and the state government. Even though we didn't receive state money, we still needed their approval for the project." Despite its limited distribution, 900 copies of the film were sold within the first year. Kurt's most recent project is a 400-page book on Point Lobos and the Whalers Cabin and exhibit, researched by Kurt and written by a local college professor. Kurt is counting on its being published by late 2006.

My goal is to get others involved in Point Lobos and the Whalers Cabin. I can't do all the work myself. I find that many volunteers are not motivated and have little commitment or passion. They need that to succeed in their endeavors and to make nonprofit groups work. I treat my work as a full-time job."

Kurt's involvement has not gone unnoticed. In 1993, he was recognized as the Docent of the Year among California's 20,000 park volunteers. Nor have his efforts been ignored in Point Lobos; the Whalers Cabin attracts 40,000 visitors a year.

> "I find that many volunteers are not motivated and have little commitment or passion. They need that to succeed in their endeavors . . ."

In January 2005, he began the process of applying for National Historic Landmark Status for the Whalers Cabin, which, based on Kurt's research, was built in 1851 and is possibly the oldest wooden cabin built by Chinese immigrants in the United States. "Landmark status will enable us to apply for grants to do major cabin repairs," says Kurt.

"Looking back, I guess I'm what you would call an expediter. I'm the guy who gets things done. I have never been afraid to make 'cold' sales calls. It's something I did as a manufacturer's representative. I pick up the telephone and get people to volunteer."

## VOLUNTEERISM ESTABLISHES
## NEW COMMUNITY ROOTS
### Hugh Morrison
### *A Recent Retiree Uses Past Professional Skills*

Other than the five-year period prior to retiring in late 2003, Hugh Morrison grew up, went to college, and spent the bulk of his career in and around Philadelphia.

A graduate of Lafayette College in Easton, Pennsylvania, and the University of Michigan School of Law, Hugh practiced law or was an in-house corporate counsel for 34 years in Bethlehem, about 40 miles north of Philadelphia.

Law school in Ann Arbor, Michigan, notwithstanding, he strayed geographically only one other time, when his employer, Braun Medical, reassigned him in 1999 to Southern California, where as a senior vice president and general counsel, his responsibility was Braun's West Coast holdings.

Come retirement time, Hugh and his wife, Mary, severed their ties with California and looked for a suitable East Coast community. "We had different lifestyle values than many Southern Californians. And we could sell our house in Irvine and make a profit."

He describes himself as an optimist, a trait he most likely inherited from his mother who in her early 90s wrote *Let Evening Come,* which was published in 1998, a few years before she died. Says Mary Morrison: "A standard complaint about writings on old age is that the books are either too bright and determinedly cheerful or too dark and gloomy."

Both Morrisons are married for the second time. Combined, they have six adult children approximately the same age with four of them living in the East. They eliminated certain eastern locations because Mary, though a New England native, doesn't like the cold weather.

"We started our search with *Retirement Places Rated* as our guide. We wanted to be in a college town with good medical facilities and a strong cultural life." That's how the Morrisons settled on Chapel Hill. What's more, they spurned the idea of moving into a retirement community. Unlike many who relocate upon retirement and immediately buy a house, the Morrisons rented a home for the first year. They built a house once they became more familiar with the different neighborhoods.

It's one thing to relocate upon retirement, but it's another matter to settle into a community where one has few, if any, roots, in terms of family, friends, or even familiarity based on attending college in the area.

The move presented Hugh with a challenge— how to become acclimated to a new community. Hugh once again became a joiner, a trait dating back to college where he worked on the newspaper and the yearbook and as a fraternity officer.

He applied this trait when he lived in Bethlehem and more recently as an Irvine transplant. Besides bar association membership, he was a board member of Leadership Lehigh Valley, chancellor of the Episcopal Diocese of Bethlehem, and board member of the Kemmerer Museum of the Decorative Arts and the Sayre Child Care Center.

When he relocated to Chapel Hill, he already knew, based on his past volunteer experience, how to burrow into a new community. "I went to the Chapel Hill RSVP chapter. They suggested that I get involved with both SCORE and the Executive Service Corps (both groups discussed earlier in this chapter). Then I joined the chamber of commerce, which assigned me to the environment and government relations committees. I've gotten so involved there have been times that I couldn't sleep, and my calendar was filled for several weeks. It seems I do all the things I did when I was working without actually going to work."

The Morrisons also joined Newcomers. Through this group, he met some golf partners. "We also met people at church and through the Chapel Hill Tennis Club, where Mary plays tennis. I try to keep my volunteer work apart from our social life."

Hugh's lifestyle is consistent with the advice that he received at a college alumni meeting. "Stay active and start each day with a to-do list." It's become his formula for relocation.

## HE'S NOW A FREE AGENT
### John Wyman
*Finds New Lifestyle as an Early Retiree*

"My wife, Nancy, taught me that you do what you have fun doing," says John Wyman. John credits his wife for setting him in the right direction since he took early retirement from AT&T in 1990 at age 50. Her advice prepared the groundwork for his transition from a business career to being a volunteer.

AT&T's buyout program was in many ways too good to turn down. Following graduation from Bowdoin College and military service in Vietnam as a lieutenant in a tank platoon, John worked for AT&T for the next 28 years. As a retirement incentive, the company offered a lifetime health care package and added five years of service, including credit for military service, to his pension.

The only hitch was that John had 30 days in which to make a decision. Even with the incentive to take early retirement, John's income would drop. He talked the matter over with Nancy and their two daughters, one an 18-year-old about to start college and the other a 14-year-old. "It was a tough decision to leave a secure job with a benevolent employer and start out on my own. My family supported me to the fullest, never asking, 'Did you get another job yet?'"

John was too young to sit on the sidelines. During his AT&T career, he moved 13 times and had 22 different assignments, though he didn't want another job with frequent relocations. As an alternative, John became a consultant specializing in what he describes as quality improvement techniques.

John set certain consulting goals. One was to serve no more than five clients at a time. Engelhard Industries, a worldwide precious metal fabricator, became his first and ultimately his only client. Engelhard offered him a deal, asking that John put his consulting business on hold and instead become a full-time contract consultant. This way he could work from his home office and be free of corporate bureaucracy. What's more, John didn't need health care benefits, because they were already part of his AT&T retirement package.

Over the next nine years he traveled extensively in the United States and overseas. Business travel offered certain advantages. "Nancy would come with me on trips if she wanted. When I visited jewelry manufacturers in Europe, she went along, and we combined business with a vacation. However, if I went to grubby mines in Georgia, somehow she had something better to do."

But international business travel also has its problems. "I am 6'4". Traveling in tourist class with my knees scrunched against my chin for up to 12 hours wasn't to my liking. I was supposed to be retired, and here I was traveling five to six days a week."

Moving from New Jersey to North Carolina, John severed his ties with Engelhard and subsequently Koz.com, a North Carolina–based dot-com start-up, as head of its professional services division.

**Even with the incentive to take early retirement, John's income would drop.**

**John no longer does any paid consulting. However, he finds volunteerism both interesting and important.**

Two years later in 2001, Koz.com went bankrupt, taking with it John's job and the dream of cashing in on his stock options. This might have caused panic for other 60-year-olds. Not so with John. Being frugal, he was able to adjust to less income.

As an AT&T employee, he had contributed the allotted amount to his pension fund while personally saving an additional 10 percent of his salary. He doubled his savings to 20 percent of gross income when he became an Engelhard consultant. He and Nancy live on his AT&T pension, and as of 2004 on their combined Social Security income. Touching savings is off-limits. "Nancy and I live below our means. We're cash poor, and we live on less. Nancy might have a new car, but I drive used ones. We take few vacations or expensive trips. A few years ago we traveled to the Amazon, but we don't expect to take another vacation like that one for a long while."

After Koz.com's downfall, John switched his focus to being a volunteer. Besides his ongoing work with SCORE, John has been pursuing a long-time interest in water lilies as a volunteer at the Sarah P. Duke Gardens in Durham. "I'm in charge of obtaining, growing, planting, and maintaining over 30 varieties of water lilies that we grow in three 40,000-gallon ponds. To improve our supply, we trade tubers in the winter with other botanical gardens around the world."

Based on what he calls the success and fun of teaching a course on entrepreneurial management at Durham Technical Community College, he developed a similar ten-week course, "Surviving This Economy—Building a Successful Nonprofit," for Duke's Certificate Program in Nonprofit Management. "This course," says John, "is for students who are motivated by a cause, not money."

John no longer does any paid consulting. However, he finds volunteerism both interesting and important. "I only do what pleases me—nothing else. I also wish to follow Nancy's example of the past 15 years by donating time to help nonprofits to survive."

## WORKS FOR INTERESTS, NOT MONEY
### Tom Young
*Human Resources Manager Becomes*
*Nonprofit Business Consultant*

Ever since Tom Young retired 13 years ago from GTE as a human resources manager and in every community in which he's lived since then, he has volunteered for the Executive Service Corps. When Tom returned to the workplace, ESC became his employer.

Tom, and his wife, Pat, were Dickinson College classmates. After two years of military service, Tom's first job was with Union Carbide. He then returned to Dickinson as the paid head of the alumni association, held several other corporate jobs, and in 1966 joined GTE. Though he remained with the same employer for nearly 25 years, he was regularly transferred to different GTE offices in the United States. His career odyssey consisted of 13 moves in 35 years.

Tom's specialty was human resources. One of his last assignments focused on identifying up-and-comers within the company, whom he recommended for promotion to higher-level jobs. "By 1990, I decided to leave GTE; I was 58 and I felt that I had no more worlds to conquer. Frankly, the job wasn't fun anymore. To make things easier, college and marriage expenses for our four daughters were behind us.

"I told my boss that I wanted to leave. My boss accepted my decision, but he asked me to stay on for one more year to help in moving the corporate offices from Connecticut to Texas." Tom found that the extra year enabled him to better plan for a more orderly transition from workplace to retirement.

During his transitional year, Tom was introduced to the Executive Service Corps and, unlike nearly all other ESC consultants who typically are retired, took on a volunteer assignment while he was still a corporate employee. This project began what has now become a nearly 16-year relationship with ESC. Over the next three years, Tom served in a volunteer capacity

> Tom found that the extra year enabled him to better plan for a more orderly transition from workplace to retirement.

as an ESC vice president and resident manager in its Connecticut operation.

The first priority on Tom and Pat's retirement-planning list was deciding whether to remain in Westport, Connecticut, where they had lived for 15 years, or to relocate. Their daughters lived in four different parts of the United States. The decision was to leave Westport. "We felt that we had outgrown the community, and that it had become too expensive a place to live, particularly on a retirement income." Pat, who had taught high school for many years, had been unable to accumulate a decent pension due to Tom's frequent moves. Planning for their retirement, Tom knew that they could count on income from his pension, Pat's small pension, Social Security, and savings.

The couple elected to relocate to Modesto, California, about 50 miles east of San Francisco. One daughter and her family lived there. As soon as they settled in, Tom joined ESC's San Francisco operation, became an active consultant, and was elected to its board. ESC wanted to expand its operation in the Bay Area, and Tom became the unpaid director of ESC's newly opened office in Modesto.

"After five years, we decided to move back East. One daughter lived in Las Vegas and another in New York City. As much as we like New York, we couldn't afford the cost. Our fourth daughter lived in Raleigh, and we decided to buy a house there." ESC soon returned as part of Tom's retirement lifestyle.

From his experience with ESC in New York, Connecticut, California, and North Carolina, Tom knew many of the organization's national leaders. One of their priorities was to make the Executive Service Corps Affiliate Network (ESCAN), which consists of two-thirds of the ESC's 34 affiliates, into a more viable group. It subsequently was renamed ESCAN. They recruited Tom, this time for a paid management position. The only possible hitch was its New York location. "I had no intention of moving to New York, so the deal calls for me to be in New York one week a month.

"My assignment was for two years. I saw it as a full-time job although I was paid for a 30-hour workweek. But I really put in more time than that. Except for the monthly trip to New York, I spent the balance of my time in my office at home. My job was to formalize the network and to make it work. Fortunately, I didn't have to travel a lot.

"I was paid more than an honorarium. It was a financial cushion on top of my other retirement income. I've even set up a 401(k) to capture some of it. I'm sure of one thing. I wouldn't have taken this job without the pay."

The question is what would happen in 2004 when Tom's two-year contract ended. Family members differed in their opinions of what Tom would do. At the time, Tom said that he'd quit, but Pat doubted that he'd give up.

Tom and Pat were each correct. Tom switched from a full-time paid position to being a part-time volunteer. "I'll stay with it a while longer. We're doing some more restructuring of ESCAN. Following some fundraising, ESCAN should be able to hire a paid director, and I would bow out. But there's no time frame yet."

> **At the time, Tom said that he'd quit, but Pat doubted that he'd give up.**

## THE MAKING OF A COMMUNITY ACTIVIST
### Gerard Stoddard
*Public Relations Executive Turned Homeowners' Association Leader*

When Gerard Stoddard walks down Fifth Avenue in New York, he could be easily tagged as a successful corporate executive. And for many years he was one. But a corporate merger and an abiding interest in his home-away-from-home put him on his present career path. Jerry made the transition from corporate executive to volunteer president of the Fire Island Association (New York) and then to paid president. Defying retirement, Jerry converted the position into a demanding

**Defying retirement, Jerry converted the position into a demanding career using much of his professional experience and skills.**

career using much of his professional experience and skills.

For 20 years, Jerry's career was closely associated with SCM Corporation, once the nation's premier typewriter manufacturer. When SCM was acquired by Hanson Trust, a British conglomerate, Jerry's job as vice president for corporate communications became redundant.

Jerry was protected financially by a contract, a fully vested pension, and savings and investments resulting from an excellent salary. In addition, he executed his stock options at a very favorable price. What's more, his expenses were contained. He owned and lived in a town house in New York's Chelsea section.

In the public relations field, an occupation noted for high job turnover, Jerry had had only two employers over 25 years. When he graduated from Cornell University, he was interested in public affairs and public policy and took a job with the American Petroleum Institute (API), the oil industry's prime lobbyist. While an API employee, he obtained a law degree at night from New York University. He passed the state bar exam but never practiced law. In future years, he was able to leverage his legal training.

He joined SCM as director of shareholder relations and six years later was named a corporate vice president. While responsible for the company's full range of public relations activities, Jerry personally handled its lobbying activities in Washington and New York, a job that required knowledge of public relations and the law.

When he left SCM, Jerry was much too young to consider retiring. Until the acquisition, he felt he had a secure and satisfying job. In many ways, he was unprepared for his departure from SCM. Unemployed, he looked for jobs through traditional search methods and even received a few offers, including one that, in effect, represented a career demotion. "At the time, I realized that this might very well be my last job offer. I would most likely never find a job equal to the one I had at SCM."

Jerry was not idle professionally as he looked for a full-time job. He started a public relations consultancy firm in his home. Law firms were then just beginning to market their services, and as a lawyer and public relations practitioner, Jerry received assignments from several large New York law firms. Lawyers, he soon concluded, are fine if they work for you—and not so fine if you work for them.

Jerry and his family, like many other New Yorkers, had two residences. During the school year, they lived in New York City. In the summer, the Stoddards moved to their Fire Island cottage, 55 miles from midtown New York. Jerry spent weekends on Fire Island with his family.

As is typical of many weekend retreats, Fire Island's population soars in the summer to 25,000 residents and declines in the off-season to several hundred residents who stay year-round. The swing in seasonal population places pressure on the island's environment and its relaxed lifestyle. This has led to a division among residents—those who want to see more commercial development and those who are opposed to it. Automotive vehicles are banned from the island. Walking and biking are the only modes of transportation. "I began to get interested in community life when someone wanted to build a hotel, something I didn't feel was in keeping with community living," Jerry says. "This activated me, and I got the local property owners to buy the land and make it into a park."

About the time he was leaving SCM, Jerry was elected president of the Fire Island Association, which represents the island's several thousand homeowners. "As a professional lobbyist, I knew that our association was too small to have any impact in either Washington or Albany." To build a bigger political power base, he helped to form the Long Island Coastal Alliance, consisting of similar beach communities on Long Island's South Shore. The alliance gave him the incentive to start *Coastal Reports,* a bimonthly, subscription newsletter devoted to coastal property owners. As such, Jerry had taken another step away from retirement.

**Lawyers, he soon concluded, are fine if they work for you—and not so fine if you work for them.**

**Jerry finds his present work is a much better alternative than retirement even though there are drawbacks.**

Jerry initially served on a volunteer basis as the association's president. Growing responsibilities and the expanding time commitment led the association's board of directors to pay him a $25,000 honorarium. Since receiving the honorarium, Jerry has sidelined his public relations consultancy and instead concentrates on his paid work with the Fire Island Association and on his volunteer leadership of the Long Island Coastal Alliance. The work uses his varied professional skills, including writing, knowledge of government operations, and lobbying in Washington and Albany.

"There are many psychic pleasures with my job. I testified several times before the U.S. Senate on the need for greater shore protection on Long Island and helped to win a major victory to enable coastal property owners to obtain flood insurance. Jerry finds his present work is a much better alternative than retirement even though there are drawbacks. "Volunteer groups can be as demanding as any client or corporate president, for that matter. But the issues are fascinating. I guess I'll stay on as president until the board gets tired of me and kicks me out."

## HE OPTED FOR NONPROFITS
### Leo Rogers Jr.
#### *Bank President Turned College Administrator*

Leo Rogers Jr. found himself unemployed for the first time in 27 years. Subsequently, his career search was guided not by advice from an outplacement firm but a passage from the New Testament: "From everyone to whom much has been given, much will be required; and from the one to whom much has been entrusted, even more will be demanded. For unto whomsoever much is given, of him shall be required: and to whom men have committed much, of him they will ask more." This verse from the book of Luke inspired the search that led to Leo's job as a college administrator with Fairleigh Dickinson University.

Leo's resume is impressive, summarizing a record of high achievement in business and community life. But in his mid-50s, Leo's bubble was deflated. The bank where he was president fell victim to the collapsed metropolitan New York real estate market.

His marketing know-how had helped to build the bank to a network of 74 branch offices. "I went into banking as a marketer. My job as president resulted largely from my work in marketing, advertising, and public relations. I was part of the changeover when banks decided to alter their image and the ways they did business."

When the bank went into receivership, Leo's credentials attracted the interest of other banks, but he wanted to change fields and careers.

Throughout his banking career, Leo also served on a number of boards of trustees, including a hospital and Blue Cross and Blue Shield of New Jersey. Those experiences later propelled him to look for a job in the nonprofit field. "I realized that nonprofit work is just as challenging as business, but there is more of an opportunity to serve others."

Fortunately, Leo qualified for early retirement from the bank, which gave him options in seeking a new job. "I didn't want a job just to say I got one. I wanted to be selective at this stage in my life," Leo says. "As a starter, I determined those things I like to do, do well, and would like to continue doing in the future."

As an executive, Leo had been somewhat pampered by the corporate lifestyle. Without employment, these perks were no longer available. He had to learn some basic office skills just to hunt for a job. "I was computer illiterate. Others had done that type of work for me." His wife, Carole, is a freelance writer who does her own word processing, and she encouraged him to develop computer skills. As a result, he became computer literate. "This was important because I would most likely be joining an organization where these skills would be necessary. I had to learn how to make ordinary things happen because nobody else will do them for you." Nearly eight months of

> Leo's credentials attracted the interest of other banks, but he wanted to change fields and careers.

**"I had to learn how to make ordinary things happen because nobody else will do them for you."**

networking and interviewing started to produce results. Leo was offered a job with one of the nation's larger outplacement firms to counsel other downsized senior-level executives. Though the business wasn't nonprofit, he liked outplacement because he would be helping others. But after living and working in New Jersey most of his life, he was reluctant to commute to New York. "I took several practice commuting runs to the firm's offices. If they had offered me the same job in their New Jersey office, I would have taken it, but I had little interest in commuting three hours each day."

During the time that he was negotiating with the outplacement firm, Leo heard of an opening at Farleigh Dickinson University to be director of the George Rothman Institute of Entrepreneurial Studies.

"I had my eye on this ever since I left banking. I had heard about it from the university's president. When I learned officially that the institute's director was leaving, I called the university, received a job description, and sent in a resume along with a cover letter summarizing why I felt I was well suited for the job. I was told that a search committee had been established, and then I got a letter saying that I was among 75 very qualified candidates for the job. Then another letter told me that they had screened the resumes, and that I was one of six selected to meet with the committee."

Leo met with the committee and soon afterwards learned that he was one of two finalists. "They invited me back to make a presentation. I worked on it for four days. Then after the outplacement firm's offer, I heard that the Fairleigh Dickinson job was mine."

Similar to his banking days, Leo serves as the institute's key representative in the business community. Now, however, he's an advocate of entrepreneurship rather than banking services. Leo is also the institute's representative in the academic community. He finds that getting things done here differs greatly from business. "At the bank, we would meet, discuss an issue, and reach a decision. In a university, one needs to be patient because decision making is more collegial and takes much longer."

During the 2001–2002 academic year, Leo was named interim dean of the university business school. Returning to the Rothman Institute afterward, he launched a drive to raise funds for an "incubator" to nurture students and adult nonstudents who want to start their own businesses.

After ten years as director, Leo retired. By then, he had introduced a number of curriculum innovations. One change requires that all undergraduate and graduate business school students be required to take a course in entrepreneurship, recognition of the growing interest on campus in small-company management.

Retirement, however, did not mean an end to business, academic, and community involvement. He serves on the institute's Family Business Forum, a corporate board, and an advisory board of a small family-owned business.

Looking back on his academic career, Leo, who had wanted a career in academia after graduating from college, felt like he had returned home.

---

## POINTS TO REMEMBER

- **Giving back to the community or society** in which one has enjoyed success is one of the primary reasons that members of the 50-plus set work as volunteers.
- **There is no shortage of opportunities** to serve as a volunteer.
- **There's a volunteer job to fulfill every interest.**
- **Professional and management skills are always in demand.**
- **Many mangers and professionals prefer hands-on volunteer work**—not administrative work.
- **You can learn new skills** as a volunteer.
- **Corporate America is packaging volunteer programs** for early retirees.

# Hobbies: The Pleasure Is All Yours

*"Don't ever give up; don't ever give up."*

—Comments by Jim Valvano, basketball coach at North Carolina State University, prior to his death in 1993

To some, a hobby becomes a way of life. A hobby can be just as captivating as any career. Sometimes a hobbyist decides to convert it from being a delightful pastime into a retirement career. However, dangers lurk, as Patricia Thomas discusses later in this chapter.

Name the field and there are hobbyists. To some, hobbies are a lifetime pursuit, while others acquire the interest as retirees, whether it's handicrafts, cooking, collecting, or traveling.

A hobby may involve attending public events or becoming a participant. Attendees favor movies, sports, and amusement parks; doers prefer a nearly unlimited array of active hobbies—amateur theatricals, playing sports, home improvement/repair, and gardening.

Some hobbies are costly, requiring special equipment and training. Books, craft hobbies, and travel rank high in expenditures by the 50-plus set, while other hobbies cost nothing but the effort of imagination. Hobbies can be done individually, in a group, or both. Many are very time consuming; others take only a few minutes a day.

Some hobbies fit best into the lifestyle of 30- to 40-year-olds. The hobbies of interest to the greatest number of retirees can be pursued over a lifetime. You're more likely to find most in the 50-plus set walking rather than running marathons and gardening

## FAVORITE SPORTS

In order of frequent participation:
- Exercise walking
- Fishing (fresh and salt water)
- Exercising with equipment
- Swimming
- Golf
- Camping
- Bike riding
- Bowling
- Aerobic exercising
- Billiards/pool

Source: SGMA International.

instead of bungee jumping. Even so, it seems that nearly everyone knows someone who's defying the odds—a 77-year-old who plays tennis five times a week or an 82-year-old downhill skier. Witness also the success of the Senior Olympics sponsored for those aged 50 and over. Whether they are competitive or just doing it for fun, chances are many of these athletes learned and perfected their sports skills long before retirement.

About 10,000 athletes participated in the 2005 National Senior Games. NSGM (*www.nsgm.com*), a trade group representing sporting goods manufacturers, reports that 250,000 in the 50-plus set currently participate in state senior games or the Senior Olympics.

## Getting Started

Getting involved in a hobby is as simple as visiting a local library or bookstore, or attending an adult education workshop given by community colleges, high schools, or hobby organizations. As a first step, obtain the course listings from community college and high school extension programs. Hobbyists have their own "birds of a feather" groups, and they, too, sponsor workshops to attract and train new enthusiasts.

Hobby supply and craft supply shops, as well as other retail outlets catering to the clothing, equipment, and literature needs of all kinds of enthusiasts, usually post notices of related classes, meetings, and outings. If you're lucky, you might enjoy a productive chat with a knowledgeable clerk—also likely to be an enthusiast—in such a store or nowadays via the Internet.

How-to books and magazines abound in nearly every field, appealing to both novices and advanced hobbyists. To test this theory, visit a neighborhood bookstore. Browsers will find that hobby-related books make up roughly one-third to one-half of the nonfiction books. Selecting a new hobby depends to some extent on the hobbyist's income, aptitude, and personality. Some hobbies, due to more costly equipment and training, naturally attract fewer people. But don't let expenses become a deterrent. If the goal is to make pottery, instruction and access to wheels and kilns are available on a shared basis through community and extension schools and hobby-related clubs. This same cooperative spirit aids flying enthusiasts who individually can't afford the cost of buying and maintaining a plane.

How about finding new ways to expand the scope of a current hobby? Bird watchers do more than track birds. They lead hikes, attend workshops, and join environmental groups. A hobby can broaden in scope, as Iris S., a retired New York City high school English teacher, discovered. Iris grows African violets in her apartment and is an officer in a group that meets regularly to discuss and show their plants. For those wanting to take their hobby to the next step, she points out, there is a worldwide society devoted to African violets, which publishes a quarterly magazine and conducts regional, national, and international meetings.

Also, don't fall victim to the notion that one needs to be an expert to enjoy a hobby. Listen to Dr. Joyce Brothers's assessment of someone lugging that burden: "You believe you have to do everything at an 'A' level. If you can't, you feel you aren't accomplishing anything at all. You may give up."

Right on, Joyce. I'm a lifetime piano player. I wouldn't dare call myself a pianist. I no longer read music, but I can play most tunes by picking out the melody. My approach is homemade. I play the melody with my right hand, and the same chords for all songs with the left hand. At times, the sound

## SUGGESTED READING

- *Years of Your Life,* by Mary Helen and Shuford Smith (McGraw-Hill, 2000).
- *How to Enjoy Your Retirement Activities from A to Z,* by Barbara Day and Patricia Wagner (Wanderway & Burnham, 2002).
- *How to Start a Home-Based Crafts Business,* 4th edition, by Kenn Oberrecht (Globe Pequot Press, 2004).

## WOMEN AS HOBBYISTS

The Craft & Hobby Association (CHA, *www.hobby.org*), until recently the Hobby Industry Association, has a vested interest in hobbies, estimated to be a $29 billion industry. CHA members produce and sell craft supplies, such as art supplies, needlecrafts, and floral crafts. In its most recent industry analysis, the association noted that 97 percent of adult women (ages 55 to 64) participated in a craft activity in their lifetime, and 88 percent of them continue to do crafts as they age. Cross-stitching, crocheting, décor painting, scrapbook/memory crafts, and floral arranging are the most popular crafts among women. The only thing that stops them is poor health, especially bad eyesight.

can be somewhat discordant. My wife is tolerant of my playing; my children have different views. The end result is I enjoy playing, and it's a great way to let out tension and relax.

## Not a Substitute for Work

Some hobbyists personify perfection in their dual roles as professionals at work and hobbyists at home, with equal devotion to both throughout their lives. Others balance what they often consider lackluster or uninteresting careers with more spectacular extracurricular lives. Whereas a 9-to-5 job provides income, a hobby is the real focal point of their lives. Retirement offers an opportunity to put their priorities in order and act on them at will. But members of either group value their hobbies as a creative outlet that differs radically from day-to-day workplace challenges. Still others show more interest in hobbies in retirement than they showed during their workday lives. Even among the upper echelons of corporate managers, there are differences.

Top executives typically do not have hobbies, observed Jeffrey Sonnenfeld of Yale University in his book *The Hero's Farewell*, a study on the retirement habits of CEOs of major corporations. "Their greatest gratification was generally in the job they left and not in deferred recreation or outside organizations." The executives interviewed by Sonnenfeld frequently asked, not at all rhetorically, "How much tennis can you play before you look for something bigger to do?"

A hobby has its limitations even for the most enthusiastic fans. As much as Russ Larson, the recently retired publisher of the monthly magazine *Garden Railways,* enjoys writing about model railroad hobbyists, he does not advocate "spending 40 hours a week on a hobby after retiring. I suspect that for most people a mix of more serious pursuits along with hobbies and games would be the most satisfying."

The late Jules Willing, a human resources executive with Revlon, candidly wrote about the problems of trying to substitute a hobby for a lost job in his book *The Reality of Retirement:*

"When work no longer provides activity, interests and hobbies are substituted. Early in retirement, there is a carry-over of attitudes—you tend to approach your hobbies as you did your work: intensively. The hobby gets the highest priority, the most time, the greatest energy, the extensive investment. . . . In retirement, hobbies are not pursued at all in a leisurely way, but more as a matter of job replacement than of pleasure, the anxious need to fill an unendurable void."

Willing was quick to point out that successful managers normally find hobbies "unsatisfying as major preoccupations. Hobbies do not generate the kind of psychic satisfaction your work did. They may entertain or amuse and occupy but they rarely make the adrenaline flow the way winning a budget battle did. With a hobby you generally have nothing to risk."

Hobbies are often viewed as a leisure-time pursuit, something layered between more important functions—somewhere between sleeping and working. That's a trait from a time when occupational tunnel vision was the order of the day. The first priority was to the workplace, a habit that might be difficult to break.

---

## CRAFTY BUSINESS GUIDES

Barbara Brabec, a former publisher of *Barbara Brabec's Self-Employment Survival Letter*, gave up newsletter publishing to concentrate on writing business self-help books for craft people who want to be self-employed and also work at home. Her titles (found at *www.barbarabrabec.com*) include *Creative Cash—How to Profit from Your Special Artistry, Creativity, Hand Skills and Related Know-how; Handmade for Profit—Hundreds of Secrets to Success in Selling Arts & Crafts; The Crafts Business Answer Book and Resource Guide; Homemade Money: Bringing in the Bucks; How to Improve Your Google Ranking with the Right Keywords in the Right Places;* and *Starting a Home-Based Scrapbook Business.*

Only you can decide to what extent one or more hobbies can replace the demands and satisfaction of the workplace, and how much time in retirement needs to be filled. At the least, a hobby can be one part of a total portfolio of activities.

## Got the Travel Bug?

Many members of the 50-plus set find that travel is only one part of a much larger leisure-time pattern that goes beyond cruises, overseas travel odysseys, and other once-in-a-lifetime travel events. In some instances, retirees combine walking and hiking or explore different areas by car and camper. Opportunities also exist to travel and study on an Elderhostel trip in the United States or overseas, or to build homes for Habitat for Humanity in a third world nation. In sum, a hobby is whatever you decide you want to make of it.

Travel to many in the age 50-plus set is more than an annual vacation. Travel often relates to a hobby, with involvement and planning that starts long before leaving home. They read about their destination, attend lectures, and brief themselves about the places that they will soon visit. Or, as Robert Louis Stevenson wrote nearly 130 years ago: "For my part, I travel not to go anywhere, but to go. I travel for travel's sake. The great affair is to move."

For the hobbyist, there's no shortage of travel opportunities. Affinity groups offer an opportunity for people with like interests to travel together. These trips bring together folks who enjoy and want to know more about art, music, religion, crafts, cooking, sports, hiking, golfing, and fishing among countless others. They can be as exotic as an overseas trip to Italy to study Renaissance art or as basic as an overnight visit to a regional flower show. Name the subject, and rest assured at least one affinity group sponsors a U.S. or overseas trip to complement a special interest audience. That said, it's no wonder that the 50-plus set represents a multi-billion-dollar travel market.

Unlike the occasional traveler, hobbyist travelers have a set agenda. They are not just taking a vacation. As hobbyists, their trips are fashioned to be learning experiences. Later on in this chapter read about Perry Colwell's visit to Italian auto factories. His trip was consistent with a lifetime interest in cars and motorcycles. Perry's comments are followed by Sandy and Joe Thompson's travel adventures as National Park Service rangers.

## PHASING INTO RETIREMENT VIA PAINTING
### Pamela George
### *Moves from Classroom to Studio*

Pamela George learned a lesson about retirement from her mother, Ruby, who until her retirement at age 62 was an assistant to the president of Centenary College of Louisiana. Ruby left the college when a new president was appointed. "She could have down-shifted and taken another job at Centenary. To this day, she has rued her retirement and says that she's been bored to tears ever since," says Pam.

Unlike her mother who retired abruptly and without a plan other than to take care of an ill husband,

**Although Pam embarked on a different career path, she never lost her passion for painting.**

Pam, now in her late 50s, has already started to unfold her new career as an artist. In 2005, Pam, a tenured professor of education at North Carolina Central University in Durham, completed the terms of her phased retirement.

"I've been painting since I was five. But being from a working-class family, painting was not considered a profession but a hobby. One had to earn a living. In many ways, painting was my first calling. Even as a hobby, it was central to my life." Although Pam embarked on a different career path, she never lost her passion for painting.

Graduating from Louisiana State University in 1969, Pam got a master's degree in special education the following year at the University of North Carolina at Chapel Hill. Afterward, she spent two years in Samoa with the Peace Corps, where she met David Austin, who became her husband. She traveled with him overseas for another two years before returning to the United States, which was followed by a four-year stint as a middle school teacher. By 1979, she had received a doctorate from UNC.

Since 1978, Pam has spent her entire academic career at Central as an educational psychology teacher, researcher, and supervisor. For four years in the late 1990s, she chaired and taught four courses a semester in the Department of Leadership, Policy, and Professional Studies, a job with a 60-hour workweek. "It kind of burned me out and got me interested in taking early retirement."

With a daughter in college, Pam entered a new phase of her professional life. "I'm now in the midst of a three-year phased retirement program. I paint three full days a week, spend another day doing research for my painting, another day with my mentor who is also my art teacher, and work 20 hours a week at Central."

Phased retirement was first offered though the University of North Carolina statewide system about five years ago to encourage faculty retirement. The arrangement enables Pam to receive the equivalent of a full salary. The package consists of her pension, which is roughly 50 percent of her faculty pay, along with one-half of her faculty salary. Sales of her paintings produce another $6,000 a year. Pam's primary goal over the next few years is to replace the loss of academic income with increased revenues from her paintings.

With painting taking on increased importance to her financially, Pam can no longer think like a hobbyist. "In the past, I gave away paintings as gifts to local groups that could use them to raise funds, or I used them to illustrate the books that I've written.

In beefing up her studio operation, P'Gale Studios, to function more efficiently and to be financially sound, Pam wrote a business plan with the help of Dub Gulley, the director of Durham Technical Community College's Small Business Center. "Dub made me think of painting as a business, not as a hobby. I now know what it costs to paint and have a gallery show. To sell a $1,000 painting entails spending several hundred dollars on oils, canvas, and framing. I know that I can make up to $100 an hour teaching or doing consulting, while painting comes to only $25 an hour. One of my immediate goals is to complete several paintings a month—enough that I can have a one-woman show."

As part of her retirement due diligence, Pam accumulated data on different ways to operate a profitable studio. "When I attended educational conferences in other cities, I spoke to artists on how they run their studios. I came away with the impression that few artists make a living from their work." As part of this exercise, Pam continually searches for ways to lessen her dependence on art shows because galleries charge a 40 percent to 60 percent sales commission.

While creating her new lifestyle, Pam, along with a recently retired Central colleague, prepared this formula for retirement, which she calls her "Retirement E's":

■ **Education,** including the need for a mentor, a painting teacher, and advisors like Dub Gulley

> With painting taking on increased importance to her financially, Pam can no longer think like a hobbyist.

**"After such a profound year of extraordinary involvement and service, I am uncertain about the meaning and the seclusion in the life of an artist."**

- **Enterprise,** that is, operating her studio as a profitable business
- **Earnings** from retirement, painting, and academic research
- **Exercise** to stay physically fit
- **Enlightenment** from involvement in her community and expression of spirituality

Pam and David, a health research specialist at the Research Triangle Institute, spent a momentous post-Christmas period in 2004. Pam had a one-year Fulbright assignment in Sri Lanka and the Maldives (David took a leave from RTI). One task was to train university faculty members in research methodologies. "We were there during the tsunami and had the chance to see firsthand the courage of people in the face of enormous devastation. We helped to raise money for schools, which had been badly damaged."

Returning to Durham, Pam began what she calls her "new life" as a part-time educational consultant and full-time artist. "After such a profound year of extraordinary involvement and service, I am uncertain about the meaning and the seclusion in the life of an artist. I was also credentialed by the U.S. State Department as a Senior Fulbright Specialist making me a kind of fancy international consultant."

## TREATS HIS HOBBY LIKE A JOB
### Zen Palkoski
#### *Biomedical Designer Becomes a Wood Carver*

At age 10, Zen Palkoski vacationed with his parents in Quebec. He was fascinated by a man carving a small figure out of wood. The fascination was nearly forgotten for 50 years. Other than carving a few pieces such as a British grenadier soldier and a key rack for the kitchen wall, Zen didn't take up carving again until he retired.

As a Seton Hall University student, Zen's goal was medicine. But his dream was quashed when he did not get into medical school. Drafted into the Army for two years, he spent 18 months in Germany, and, following his discharge, he was hired by Hoffmann-La Roche (now Roche Holdings) to work in a preclinical cardiovascular lab designing biomedical equipment. Over the next 37 years in the same lab, he both observed and participated in the evolution of medical equipment from somewhat crude equipment by today's standards to complex computerized and electronic gear.

Zen's watershed year was 1994. "I had no personal retirement plan. I was expecting to retire in another five years, when I would be 65. But I got a good buyout package, because the company wanted to cut costs."

After a short stint helping a friend start a picture frame business, Zen was at liberty to find new outlets. "He got me to go to carving club meetings, which met one evening a week in a high school shop. It was called the 'Whittle Club.' We drank coffee and ate Dunkin' Donuts, exchanged ideas, gained confidence watching others do their carvings, and we picked up some new skills. I started to carve, mostly Santas and shore birds." Zen found that many of the hand skills that he had previously used to tie dry fishing flies and to design intricate medical equipment were similar to those required in carving.

Zen and his wife, Jane, decided to move from Ramsey, New Jersey. Their decision was forced by a jump in real estate taxes to more than $8,000 a year and the need to live on a fixed income that was based on a pension equal to one-half of his final Hoffmann-La Roche salary. Only 60, Zen was not yet eligible to receive Social Security. Another factor of the move was Zen's interest in the outdoors. A longtime canoeist and fisherman, he wanted to move somewhere more amenable to his interests while he was still young enough to carry a canoe and wade into streams.

The transition from New Jersey to North Carolina was not easy. "I felt detached. No job, no friends. I

**"I was advised to treat my wood carving as a job. I built a workbench in one-half of our two-car garage."**

even missed the harassment at work. When I worked, I complained like most people. When I retired I missed the work and the way my day had been scheduled. I realized that those things had been part of my life for 37 years.

"Then a friend taught me a lesson. I was advised to treat my wood carving as a job. I built a workbench in one-half of our two-car garage. I go to work at 8 AM; about 9:30 I take a brief coffee break and then return to work. I do this until lunch when I usually quit for the day. I've made it something like a job with my morning schedule. And I work this way about 20 hours a week."

Carving requires more than skilled use of an array of tools. Research is important. If Zen is carving an owl to sit on top of a wooden fence post, he reads about owls to ensure that its proportions and features are accurate.

Zen is fortunate that he incurs few raw material costs. Cedar, his termite-resistant choice for outdoor pieces, and bass wood, for indoor carvings, are readily available. When storms rip through North Carolina, his backyard and neighborhood are filled with downed trees, an ample source for future birds, gnomes, and other carvings.

The Palkoskis have decorated their home and yard with dozens of carved figures. Even though he sells an occasional piece, Zen prefers to give his carvings as gifts to family members, friends, and garden groups. He's not in it for the money. As he puts it, "I can make more money as a part-time clerk in a store." Even so, the income from sales offsets the costs of entering the annual Chatham County House tour and buying new tools.

Several summers ago, Jane saw a notice in a homeowners' newsletter. The advertiser was looking for someone to housesit a suburban Paris home during the summer. Zen stayed in North Carolina the first summer but accompanied Jane the following year to the same Paris house. While in Paris, Zen became interested in Rodin's sculptures and was inspired to begin sculpting in clay. Returning home, he took several sculpting courses at UNC in Chapel Hill to improve his skill.

Wood carvings, however, remain Zen's primary interest. He's carving more abstract pieces that are larger and more creative than his earlier works. As an outdoorsman, he has applied his observations in his carvings. "I noticed how beavers cut down trees. I became bolder, and, like the beaver, I work with larger chunks of wood when I do my carving. I've also been creating some small bronze figures. It's labor intensive but very gratifying perhaps because of all the effort to produce a piece. One thing is certain: what began as my retirement hobby in 1994 is now my passion."

## SHARES PIANO PLAYING WITH OTHERS
### James Freund
#### *Finds New Outlets After Legal Career*

"I took piano lessons as a kid, but I didn't like classical music. I wanted to sound like Horowitz but I couldn't. My epiphany came at 13 at a girl-boy party. One of my friends could play 'Near You,' and I wanted to play like him. I stopped taking lessons and taught myself how to play popular music with a practice keyboard and sheet music."

James Freund put his musical interests aside for 50 years. Come his early retirement, he revived them and made them the focus of his retirement lifestyle.

Jim graduated from Princeton. Having a Navy ROTC scholarship meant that Jim had a contractual obligation for three years of active duty. As a junior officer, one assignment was as a defense attorney on minor courts martial. He won a sufficient number of cases to kindle a career as a lawyer.

Graduating from Harvard Law School, he worked at one firm for three years. In 1966, he joined a new law firm, Skadden, Arps, Slate, Meagher & Flom. It would evolve from a smallish mid-1960s firm to a legal

## "Unlike some other lawyers who retired, I was able to repot myself."

giant. Mergers and acquisitions was one of the firm's specialties, and over the years Jim was a key participant.

"When I turned 50, I was excited about my work. Our business was running high. I had just met the woman who was to become my second wife. By 60, the work was not as exciting. I was no longer getting a kick out of it. I was burning out."

The following year, Jim gave the firm a year's notice of his plan to retire at 62, eight years shy of the normal retirement age. Some of his partners couldn't believe that he was leaving. Being a comparatively young firm, retirement to date had not been a major Skadden concern. "I never considered how I would keep busy. I left law as a success.

"I would give up a large source of income. I was assured by my financial advisor that I could do it; I wouldn't have to change my standard of living."

His wife, who owns a New York City real estate firm and is a number of years younger than Jim, was concerned whether Jim could stay busy while she pursued her career.

A year after leaving Skadden, Jim wrote six articles on retirement-related issues for the American Bar Association's *Business Law Today*. In many ways, they summarize his personal views on retirement, including such factors as a lawyer's ego.

"Unlike some other lawyers who retired, I was able to repot myself." As a starter, Jim brushed up his piano-playing skills. To be sure, they weren't totally dormant since his teenage awakening. He played the piano at Skadden parties as well as for his own amusement.

Retirement is one thing. Finding a meaningful replacement is another matter. Writing in *Kiplinger's Retirement Letter*, Jim said for "maximum fulfillment I believe you need to become immersed in at least one activity with the following characteristics: It should be something you can do primarily by yourself without the need of a supporting cast. That's because you'll have a lot more time to yourself once you retire. It involves a skill that will require some effort on your part in order to become proficient—one that you will continually seek to improve. And it produces something you can view with pride and show off to others."

Jim has made the piano a key part of his current lifestyle. The living room in his New York town house is filled with musical instruments. Besides a grand piano, there are several bass violins, a drum set, and other instruments that Jim or his two grown sons have played.

He's taken piano playing to the next level. Once a week, Jim plays the "oldies" with a jazz flair at two Upper Westside senior centers. Songs of World War I, for example, serve as the basis of a senior center sing-along. This session and others, such as "Autumn in New York," have been produced at Jim's expense into CDs, which he gives to friends or as leave-behinds at the centers.

Some retirees, as noted in Chapter 4, are consummate volunteers or leaders of nonprofit agencies. Jim takes a different route by structuring and financing volunteer services on his own without the umbrella of a structured nonprofit group.

Since retiring, Jim has also accelerated his interest in photography. Hardly the typical albums of vacation and family photos, his photos center on New York City. The results have been a series of exhibitions and several photographic books on New York, including *Central Park: A Photographic Excursion* (Fordham University Press, 2001) and *2004 Slices of the Big Apple: A Photographic Tour of the Streets of New York* (Fordham University Press, 2004).

His photos range from those shot with a digital camera to one picture in each book that was taken with a disposable camera. It's consistent with his view that there's more to good photos than expensive equipment. As he noted in *Kiplinger's Retirement Letter,* "Every year, I supply disposable cameras to groups of students from an inner-city high school. I lead them on an instructional tour of Central Park. Their shots are enlarged, and I award a prize to the winner."

The fact that he is no longer a practicing lawyer does not mean that Jim has forgotten what it's like to be one. These memories and past workplace experiences represent the core of a collection of 22 fictional short stories about lawyers, which he hopes to have published.

When Jim was about to retire, he met with several Princeton classmates, and they discussed the concept of retirement. He found that some were fretful of their life outside the workplace. "I don't miss the law and I've never been concerned about ways to fill the time."

## RISKS IN CONVERTING A HOBBY INTO A BUSINESS

### Patricia Thomas

*Keeps the Hobby as a Hobby*

A hobby can be a fulfilling pastime, but if you take the next step and convert it into a business, the hobby is now work. Such is the saga that Patricia Thomas relates.

Pat, unlike so many folks in this part of the South, was born, educated, and worked in North Carolina. She has an undergraduate degree in English and political science from East Carolina University.

At college, she got hooked on making her own clothes. "It was a way to have nice things to wear." Even with this interest, fashion design was never a career goal. Instead, she interned with the Institute of Government, which was followed by a job with state government, a specialty in human resources, and a series of state and local human resources jobs. Along the way, she got a master's degree in public administration.

Eleven years later, Pat switched jobs. She was appointed Director of Human Resources for Chapel Hill and was responsible for the personnel practices of about 400 employees with diverse skills in police, fire, library, and public works. Sewing once again took a back seat to her career.

In her late 30s, she helped to start Management & Personnel Services (MAPS), where a small number of state government–trained and experienced HR managers would serve as consultants. The goal was to provide consulting services to state and local government. The firm was structured so the partners could do consulting on vacations or leave time. Little did she realize that 20 years later MAPS would enable her to reenter the workplace.

In 2002, after 33 years as a HR manager, it was time to make the break. "When I retired, I thought I would travel, relax, sew, and never go near human resource work again. I liked the idea of not having to get up at 6:30, and drive about one hour to work." It was her aim to go into the sewing business as Dragonfly Fiber Arts.

Her jackets and vests mix expensive and colorful fabrics, which she priced accordingly. Pat puts it this way: "I love to play with fabric and color, and I enjoy the process of creating wearable art.

"I didn't want to start mass producing clothes, duplicating any item, or meeting deadlines." She thought it would be a "fun" business to have, but Dragonfly Fiber Arts soon lost its allure. It was now work and no longer a hobby.

After six months, Pat took on her first MAPS human resource consulting assignment. To simplify its internal operations and eliminate a layer of administration, MAPS had affiliated with the NC League of Municipalities. The league finds MAPS assignments, and it also handles contract billing and other administrative chores. What started out as an occasional assignment now consumes 75 percent of Pat's workweek.

Her assignments are primarily in smaller cities, towns, and counties in North Carolina. Travel, however, is extensive, considering the state is more than 500 miles wide. "When I'm home, my schedule changes. I still get up early. Then Mike (her husband) and I take a long walk. I rarely get to work before 10, and I work straight through to dinner. For each day I'm with clients, I need another day in the office to do reports."

**"I love to play with fabric and color, and I enjoy the process of creating wearable art."**

Pat expects to continue consulting for at least another five years. "My major challenge is to stay up-to-date on changes in HR laws and regulations." Her life now represents what she says is a strong balance between HR consulting, a part-time to full-time work schedule, and a chance to sew for pleasure.

Even with her priorities, sewing is hardly relegated to the back burner. "It took me a year to get back to the joy of sewing. Now, I sew strictly for fun." Because her designs are not for sale, and she makes about one item a week, her closets are soon filled with last year's Dragonfly designs. "I have periodic closet sales where I sell the clothes in my own closet. The money from it pays for new fabrics."

## DIVERSE LIFESTYLE: CARS, TRAVEL, AND VOLUNTEERISM

### Perry Colwell

*Former Corporate Executive Creates Vibrant Lifestyle*

As Perry Colwell anticipated the end of his 45-year AT&T career, he had two goals: to finish his career in a positive and productive way, and then to decompress from a demanding corporate job in which he had worked 60 to 70 hours a week.

Over the next decade, Perry subsequently found a substitute for the workplace by spending more time with two old "friends," namely, cars and motorcycles, and discovering two new ones, volunteerism and travel. As such, he's been able to combine cars and motorcycles with frequent American and overseas vacations.

Perry began his working life as a Navy seaman and a college dropout. Without a college education, he worked his way up the career ladder in the telephone industry—lineman, then lower and midlevel telephone company manager, and then corporate and staff executive. Just prior to retirement, Perry was AT&T's acting chief financial officer. "Starting about a year before my retirement, I retained a consultant. She helped me to plan my last year at work so that I would focus on the things that were important to AT&T and the people there. The goal was to help me feel good about the way I had completed my career."

Rather than remain in central New Jersey following his retirement in early 1992, Perry wanted to leave the area. He and his wife, Betty, selected Chapel Hill, a university town with good health care, and recreational and social activities. Influencing the move was Juanita Kreps, an AT&T board member, who at the time was a Duke economics professor and previously President Carter's secretary of commerce. She helped Perry and Betty become established in the community.

Perry's goal was to keep busy in the months following their move to Chapel Hill. "I always wanted to build my own car. I bought a Caterhan Seven kit, and it took Betty and me about ten months to build it." When he finally drove it, Perry found that the interior was somewhat small for his six-foot-plus frame. He sold the car a few years later, but building it gave him time to adjust to his new lifestyle and to find challenging replacements for his former 12-hour corporate workday.

Juanita Kreps provided two key introductions to organizations that would become the focal point of Perry's initial community involvement. The first was the University of North Carolina's Ackland Art Museum, where Perry's AT&T skills were applicable to the museum's financial-planning process. As a result, Perry was named to Ackland's national advisory board. Kreps, a board member of the National Executive Service Corps in New York (now the Executive Service Corps Affiliate Network), introduced Perry to that organization's local affiliate, the Executive Service Corps of the Greater Triangle.

In the nonprofit world, skilled corporate executives are a valuable commodity, especially when they're willing to apply their business talents in a different environment. For Perry, volunteerism would be a new experience. His previous nonprofit partici-

**Cars and motorcycles also provide a platform for many of his vacations.**

pation had been limited to being a board member of a New Jersey group that built reasonably priced retirement homes.

Perry is no token board member or one who rests on his past corporate laurels. He's a hands-on worker who, so far in retirement, has served as both a board member and chairman of not only the Executive Service Corps but also Planned Parenthood, the Center for Child and Family Health, and Museum of Life and Sciences. Perry was asked to join the Planned Parenthood board when it received a $1 million bequest. As with the Ackland Art Museum, he was recommended to Planned Parenthood based on his financial management skills. "My AT&T financial experience has been useful. As a manager, I know how to work with diverse types of people."

By design and somewhat similarly to his old AT&T schedule, Perry puts in a full workday with the nonprofits. "I've tried not to change my work habits now that I'm retired. I organize myself as if I'm still going to work. Before going to bed, I put together a checklist of things I need to do the next day. I still get up early. I'm at the spa at 6:15, and I work out for 45 minutes to one hour."

Perry's longtime interest in cars and motorcycles started at age 17 when he bought his first bike. Fast forward 30 to 40 years. Perry, now a senior AT&T executive, would commute by motorcycle to the company's headquarters. This longtime hobby became one of the cornerstones of his retirement lifestyle. To this day, he continues to do much of the basic maintenance.

Cars and motorcycles also provide a platform for many of his vacations. Chip (his son by a previous marriage) and I both like motorcycles. Perry owns and rides four bikes—two modern and two vintage models. "For the past summers, we've gone on bike tours in Europe. Our relationship was not always this way, but we've become friends as a result of these trips and our common interest in bikes."

Besides Perry and Betty's frequent Smithsonian trips to Europe, the Far East, or India, they have done a number of Antique Motorcycle Club of America road runs in California, Washington, the Smoky Mountains, Colorado, and New Hampshire. Cars and motorcycles have influenced other vacation destinations. On a recent trip, they went on a car devotee's dream vacation—a ten-day Smithsonian Study Tour of northern Italy visiting Fiat, Lancia, Ferrari, Lamborghini, and Alfa Romeo design studios, factories, and auto museums.

## TO THE PARKS AND BEYOND
### Sandy and Joe Thompson
### *Travel Integrated into Their Lifestyle*

Most summers, Sandy and Joe Thompson play hooky by leaving Tucson, Arizona, to work as paid rangers with the National Park Service. While they enjoy the opportunity to live outdoors and escape Arizona's summer heat, it's just as important for them to make additional money to supplement their retirement income. And equally important, it has proven to be a cost-effective way for them to travel.

The Thompsons retired young—54 for Sandy; Joe, two years younger. Living in Bethesda, Maryland, they started a voice mail and paging-service company in the early 1980s. "We had about 15 employees. We sold the company in 1993 when we got tired of running it and saw that it was becoming more difficult for a smaller company to compete. We got out when it was to our advantage to do so," Sandy says.

"When we sold Compuvoice, we had no master retirement plan, nor did we plan to move or work again." Instead, they bought an RV. For three years, they roamed the western United States, Canada, and Mexico. By 1999, they decided to sever their eastern ties. They sold their house and the RV and became permanent Tucson residents.

Though they officially consider themselves retirees, the Thompsons had little desire to be sedentary. Long-

**Though they officially consider themselves retirees, the Thompsons had little desire to be sedentary.**

time outdoor enthusiasts and hikers, they had volunteered for several summers with the National Park Service. Some ranger friends encouraged them to apply to become uniformed seasonal rangers. They were accepted and assigned to Glacier National Park in Montana. "There are definite pluses and minuses to being a ranger versus a volunteer. A volunteer can come and go more freely than a ranger. A ranger gets paid, puts in a minimum 40-hour workweek, and gets a job evaluation," says Joe. "We're not the oldest couple. There are seasonal rangers who have been doing it for 35 and 40 years."

Joe and Sandy each had a different Park Service task. "I issued backcountry permits," Joe says. "I helped operate a ranger station and acted as a resource counselor for visitors going into Glacier's backcountry." Sandy's job included collecting fees, answering questions at the gate, and patrolling the campgrounds. They earned between $15,000 and $20,000 for a season lasting up to five months. The income, though not large, has helped to offset the slump in the value of their investment portfolio.

The Thompsons hoped that their outdoor adventures would take on an additional dimension. They applied to the National Science Foundation for a five-to-six-month assignment in Antarctica, where they would do administrative and odd jobs. "Age was not a factor; we've had friends our age who've done it," says Sandy. "What's more, the pay is good." Unfortunately, they did not receive the NSF assignment. In 2003, they completed their last Glacier summer gig. It was a difficult summer due to widespread forest fires in the park and the surrounding area. They were evacuated for a week. "It was a good summer to decide to leave," says Joe, "because we didn't have fond memories of a wonderful summer as we had in past years."

The following year, the Thompsons worked on their home and were involved in some community projects. A new travel adventure was about to begin. They were asked by a former Glacier Park supervisor to work as Park Service volunteers at Kalaupapa, Moloka'i, Hawaii. "Kalaupapa is an isolated medical facility used for the treatment of leprosy (Hansen's disease). It is the most remote of all the National Parks, and access is strictly controlled. It's one of the most remote places by virtue of its geographic isolation from the main part of the island."

Kalaupapa is the home for 38 patients, all of whom are adults in their mid-60s or older and have lived there most of their lives. When the last patient is gone, Kalaupapa will become a park open to the public.

As volunteers, the Thompsons were given an oceanside apartment and a small stipend to offset the cost of flying and food. Their work related to an archival facility being built by the Park Service. Sandy cataloged materials for the research library; Joe worked on a World War II collection of Civil Air Patrol radio equipment. "We felt privileged to be part of this community," says Joe. "Very few outsiders are allowed to visit while the patients are still in residence. We had a chance to learn about a disease that once meant a death sentence, and to associate with some of the kindest and most inspiring people we have ever known."

---

## POINTS TO REMEMBER

- **Hobbies can be demanding,** absorbing large blocks of time.
- **Some people need several hobbies.**
- **Some retirees convert their hobby** into a new career.
- **Don't be disappointed** if you never build the same enthusiasm for a hobby as you did for your job.
- **If you don't already have one, it might take a couple of false starts** before you find a suitable hobby.
- **There's no shortage of opportunities** to explore a new hobby.
- **Schools conduct courses to help** hobbyists learn and perfect their skills.

# Staying Put, with Business as Usual

*"Absence of occupation is not rest,*
*A mind quite vacant is a mind distressed."*
—William Cowper, 18th century English poet

In advising owners and managers of smaller companies how they can stay put, management consultant William Buxton Jr. likes to cite an example in his immediate family. "My father, William Buxton (now deceased)—or 'Mr. B.,' as he was called—was president and major stockholder in the Peoples Trust & Savings Bank, founded by my grandfather in Indianola, Iowa. Mr. B. planned to step down as president and let my brother run the bank. But unfortunately my brother died, and Mr. B., then 75, was once again president. Soon afterward he sold the bank to Iowa National Bank in Waterloo."

Instead of stripping Mr. B. of his lifelong career, the new owners gave him a small office in the bank. While no longer an officer or on the payroll, he went to the bank two to three hours a day. As the bank's volunteer goodwill ambassador, one of his unofficial duties was compiling a newsletter called *Words of Wit and Wisdom,* which the bank mailed to customers throughout the region. "The bank was more than my father's career; it was also his hobby," Bill says.

By and large, Mr. B. is the kind of person you'll find profiled in this chapter: men and women who can't imagine being turned out to pasture and for whom work is their abiding passion. These are the people who can't fathom retiring in any traditional sense. For them, hobbies and other recreation—volunteer work, going back to school, and spending more

**These are the people who can't fathom retiring in any traditional sense.**

time with family—are pale alternatives to the invigoration of the workplace. The motivation is the same for the chairman of a multi-billion-dollar company, the owner of a hardware store, the partner in a law firm, or the corporate manager—to stay involved, responsible, and challenged.

In his book *The Hero's Farewell,* author Jeffrey Sonnenfeld describes one group of CEOs who exemplify this attitude: "Monarchs do not retire, but wear their crown until the end. . . . These monarchs led their enterprises for lengthy reigns that ranged from 20 to 60 years. They were often in office until the last day they breathed." Sonnenfeld portrays Justin Dart, who built United-Rexall Drugs into a national drug chain and proclaimed at 72 that "I want my death and my retirement to be simultaneous." Three years later, Dart got his wish. He died after merging United-Rexall with Kraft.

And what about Maurice Greenberg? Now 80, he presided over American International Group, a large international insurance company, for over 35 years. In early 2003, Greenberg and the board designated but hadn't yet publicly announced the name of his successor. Greenberg, the *New York Times* noted, has "no immediate plans to leave, and he provided no further insights into his timing." But times change even for corporate chiefs. Greenberg was forced to resign in March 2005 after the disclosure of financial irregularities at AIG. Even so, a number of old-timers still run corporate giants. In his mid-80s, Sumner Redstone heads Viacom, a media company, which controls CBS and Paramount Pictures. Redstone has no plans to step down. Nor does Warren Buffett, chairman of Berkshire Hathaway, a holding company with assets in excess of $100 billion. Buffett, in his mid-70s and personally worth more than $40 billion, continues as Berkshire's active CEO.

Then again, not everyone hangs on by choice. Some do it out of financial necessity. They can't or don't want to maintain their current standard of living from pensions, savings, and investments alone. Perhaps a large part of their retirement nest egg is tied up in a business that they haven't yet been able to sell.

For others, continuing to work has additional benefits, including being able to take advantage of tax deductions on entertainment and travel or enjoying the fellowship that comes with being an active member of the business or professional community.

For many workhorses, staying on in the workplace is simply a matter of "not whether you win or lose but how long you play the game."

To Chris Crenshaw, who operates a financial services firm of the same name in Durham, North Carolina, the word *retirement* has a connotation of finality. It's definitely not part of his vocabulary. "Before you put your feet on the floor when you get up in the morning, you need something to look forward to doing that day." Chris finds his answer in work and, along with his wife, Elena, who's in her mid-40s, in raising their two children. Though he was previously married, Chris became a father for the first time in his mid-50s. Now in his late 60s, Chris lives the lifestyle of men 20 years younger. He attends school events, travels to soccer tournaments, and occupies the driver's seat of his business.

Chris plans to stay active in his business for many years even though he's considering merging or affiliating with another firm. In any scenario, he will keep a strong equity position in the new enterprise. As part

**"Before you put your feet on the floor when you get up in the morning, you need something to look forward to doing that day."**

---

**SUGGESTED READING**

- *50 Plus!: Critical Career Decisions for the Rest of Your Life*, by Robert Dilenschneider (Citadel Press, 2002). A public relations expert challenges readers to consider career and related decisions.
- *Reengineeering the Corporation*, by Michael Hammer and James Champy (HarperBusiness, 2004). This revised and updated bestseller will help you look at the same old problems differently.

of his game plan, he expects to add a few younger people to do research and to work with clients. "This will leave me more time to bring in business, and be the firm's rainmaker."

## The Risks They Run

One of the privileges enjoyed by a Warren Buffett—or just about anybody who is self-employed—is the greater likelihood of staying put, adapting their role at work to their needs and continuing to work if they want to. Why retire? Chances are they have more control over their fate than most corporate employees do. But even they may encounter inhibiting forces.

Even if they continue on by choice, some old-timers may encounter resistance to their decision by a board of directors that maintains the company needs new blood and new direction. Other times, there's an heir apparent who's champing at the bit. Despite the longevity of a Sumner Redstone or a Warren Buffett, there is a trend toward younger CEOs. The majority of the CEOs of 500 companies listed by Standard & Poor's are in their 50s, according to executive search firm Spencer Stuart *(www. spencerstuart.com).*

Although their lives, souls, and egos may be wrapped up in the business, many old-timers remain in family-owned businesses and professional services at a cost to the firm. More often than not, the operation is reduced in scope, size, and quality of service as the owner gets older and less aggressive.

Retirement-age professionals who want to stay on in midsize to larger firms have little choice but to produce. They're allowed to remain with the firm just as long as they are rainmakers and bring in new business. The logic goes that the day-to-day professional work can be done by younger partners for less money. But in smaller enterprises or one- or two-person professional firms, there may be no one looking out for the best interest of the business—say, if it fails to update and install the latest in computer or manufacturing equipment, or if it continues to operate with outdated methods.

Many professions recognize the danger of getting into a rut and have instituted educational programs to improve quality performance among all members, not just the 50-plus set. The accounting profession, for example, requires that certified public accountants enroll in continuing education each year to maintain their professional credentials. But, in effect, the requirement particularly affects some older professionals who might have a tendency to let ongoing education take a back seat.

Ideally, the sole proprietorship or professional firm can take steps to assure continuity and to provide an opportunity for the owner to work past "normal" retirement age by bringing in a younger associate to share responsibilities. The owner agrees to take home less money in return for working few hours each week. This sounds good, but more often than not it doesn't work. Egos get in the way. After years of running the business, the owner still wants to be boss even though he's working less. Too many times the associate ends up leaving because the owner was not totally committed to changing his work habits or to sharing the profits or ownership.

Some "die with your boots on" advocates face this possibility and take a more realistic approach. By design rather than attrition, they reduce the size of their operation and run a truncated law or accounting practice, or operate a small and usually not too dynamic retail or service business.

## One Man's Story

Harold T. maintains nearly total control of a closely held, $40 million industrial testing company that he started more than 30 years ago. Harold prefers to remain anonymous because it would hardly be in his best interest to tip off competitors about his corporate strategy. "Not a month goes by when I don't get a call from someone who might like to buy the company. We've even had some serious talks with two companies. Sure, I would get some money and stock, but they would want me to remain with the company after the takeover. I'd end up working harder than ever for the new owners so I could collect more money if my company increases sales and doubles profits. It would mean changing the friendly yet effective way we run the company. As you see, I'm not too interested in retiring and selling out." Harold feels that time is on his side. His father, a Nebraska farmer, retired when he was 75.

But Harold is also a realist, and he's concerned about the company and its future. His two sons are college age. He estimates that even if they were to become interested, it would take five to ten years before they would be ready to enter the company. By then Harold will be in his late 60s. He's hedging his bets. He's setting up an employee stock-ownership plan that permits his 50 full-time employees to buy some of his holdings. "At least this way, the ownership will be shared by our people."

## It's Harder for the Corporate Workhorse

Corporate or government managers, and partners in professional-services businesses normally don't have the options that are available to the self-employed or owners of smaller businesses. Employment contracts may force them to leave. Or they may be forced out by downsizing or lured out by early-retirement packages. They can be pushed out by diminished rewards, unwelcome transfers, or work rules that make any sort of flexible or creative approach to retirement impossible. It might be nothing you could call age discrimination per se, but the message is still clear.

That's unfortunate when you consider that, given the option, folks in the 50-plus set prefer to work, an observation initially noted in the 1990s by the Commonwealth Fund *(www.cmwf.org),* a nonprofit group that studies social issues. It found that more than half of workers between ages 50 and 64 would extend their careers if their employers provided training for a different job, continued pension contributions past age 65, or offered a position with less pay but fewer hours and responsibilities as a transition to full retirement.

Each successive survey by outplacement firms and groups like AARP *(www.aarp.org)* confirms the earlier findings of the Commonwealth Fund. There are some hitches. To illustrate, employee tenure, reports AARP, is on the decline. Over a 20-year period, AARP noted a decline in the median employment tenure among men ages 55 to 64. In 1983, it was 15.3 years; and it fell to 9.8 years in 2004.

Most 65-plus men who continue to work are either at the "top or the bottom of the occupational ladder," said author Betty Friedan. It's mandatory for some men to hang on just to pay the bills, she noted in her book *The Fountains of Age.*

The possibility of staying in the corporate workforce would be enhanced if both employer and employee accepted such practices as flexible work schedules, telecommuting, job sharing, and phased retirement. But the pros and cons of flexible staffing and scheduling notwithstanding, these corporate programs usually don't extend to most midlevel to higher-level managers and professionals. At best, we hear about a 62-year-old executive who wants to continue working

---

### RULES FOR SCALING DOWN YOUR BUSINESS

- Start off with a business plan.
- Maintain a core of dedicated customers.
- Make sure you're running your business on at least a break-even basis. It doesn't make sense to sap your financial resources with a dying enterprise.
- If you can, move your business to your home or at least to a less-expensive office space.
- Invest in good office equipment. Chances are there's no staff to do routine office work.
- Don't downscale business at the risk of being bored.

---

**Olga plans to stay put and has no intention of retiring anytime soon. But she is making sure that others will be able to take over for her once she's out of the picture.**

but would like to avoid commuting three hours a day to and from work.

Employees are in the driver's seat when they are highly skilled, and the employer has difficulty in finding suitable replacements. In nursing, for example, where there's a critical shortage of skilled nurses, hospitals have introduced flexible work rules in order to retain or recruit retirement-age nurses.

## SHE'S NOW A MUSICAL INSTITUTION
### Olga Bloom
#### *Musician and Impresario*

Chamber music performed on a barge on the East River in New York City just opposite Wall Street? Despite the unlikely setting, Olga Bloom had a dream that she made come true.

But as rewarding as a Bargemusic concert is, part of the joy in attending the year-round, four weekly performances (Thursday, Friday, and Saturday evenings and Sunday matinees) is watching Olga in action. Olga, who started the concert series in 1977, is Bargemusic's lifeblood. As president, she is actively involved in management, taking on fundraising and public relations duties. But she also attends to the details. She sells and collects tickets, positions folding chairs in the auditorium, serves refreshments, and personally greets the 130 or so people who attend a typical performance. Olga plans to stay put and has no intention of retiring anytime soon. But she is making sure that others will be able to take over for her once she's out of the picture.

"It takes as much energy doing things in retirement as it does to work. Going dancing or playing golf takes energy. If you like your work, why retire?" Her own schedule gives testimony to her words. She works six days a week, from 8 in the morning to 4 in the afternoon.

"I still don't have a job description. When I clean floors, I'm the floor cleaner; when I'm raising funds, I'm a fundraiser. Other than music, I have few interests. My life is identified with the barge."

Even with her hectic schedule, Olga is still a performing musician. About once a month in a concert not open to the public, she invites three other musicians to join her on the barge in an evening of chamber music.

Olga never expected to get rich from her music or from Bargemusic. She admits to living rather simply on less than $40,000 a year, her income from Bargemusic. She lives by herself in a small house that she owns in Brooklyn—an improvement over the late 1970s, when she lived on the barge. If she ever retires, she will collect her Social Security, as well as her pension payments and those of her deceased husband.

Born in Boston, Olga attended Boston University to study music. "I left when my mother got sick. This was deep in the Depression years. I played in WPA (the Works Projects Administration, a federal agency supporting the arts during the 1930s) concerts and in chamber music groups—first the viola and then the violin."

She moved to New York in 1943. "I decided it was time to stop being a student and to work as a musician. I met my first husband, a violinist in an army band. He had more noble purposes and did not want to spend the war years as a musician. He switched into the Air Corps and was killed in action in the South Pacific."

For the next 30 years, Olga played wherever she could, from symphony and ballet orchestras to chamber music. During this time, she recalls, "my philosophy about music was developing."

One of her observations was that music as a profession was being restricted to the wealthy who could afford to buy costly instruments. She knew this firsthand. Her second husband, Toby, a violinist in Arturo Toscanini's National Broadcasting Company Sym-

**"When musicians finish their studies, they need a place to perform. There are more good musicians than we can absorb. The barge is my answer."**

phony Orchestra, mortgaged most of his possessions to buy more-expensive violins.

Olga and Toby were living on Barnum Island, off the south shore of Long Island. They gave chamber music recitals at their home for friends, and at these informal concerts Olga began to explore the relationship between music, water, and the environment. Toby encouraged her to pursue the idea that would eventually become Bargemusic.

After Toby's death, Olga read in a newspaper ad that a barge was for sale. That seemed like an answer to everything—a concert hall on water. The first two barges that she bought had acoustical problems from heavy planking that absorbed sound. On the third try, she found a 102-foot, 80-year-old steel barge lined with cherry wood. It made the difference. A year later, in 1977, it was refurbished and towed to its current mooring in Brooklyn. The location, a few hundred feet south of the Brooklyn Bridge and directly across the East River from Wall Street, proved ideal. Getting a mooring in Brooklyn was no easy task. But Olga by then had a number of influential supporters and the ability to attract "friends in high office who could look after us."

Her intention in the late 1970s was to present concerts by students from New York's leading conservatories. That changed when violinist Ik-Hwan Bae was named as Bargemusic's artistic director. He convinced Olga that they should not rely exclusively on students for the level of performance that sophisticated New York audiences demand. Nowadays the pool of nearly 100 musicians she utilizes is made up of all professionals. With four concerts every week, Bargemusic has a schedule that is matched by few other musical venues. The program is consistent with Olga's original concept that Bargemusic concerts should, above all, further a young musician's career. "When musicians finish their studies, they need a place to perform. There are more good musicians than we can absorb. The barge is my answer."

In the late 1980s, Olga began to think about ways to operate Bargemusic more efficiently. She appointed a board of overseers consisting of professional musicians, a board of directors drawn from community leaders, and a business manager to administer the organization, all calculated to leave Olga with more time for fundraising. The scheme partially fell apart when a number of board members resigned as their plans to institute managerial systems came into conflict with Olga's impresario style. After the rift, friends and patrons, who consider Bargemusic synonymous with Olga Bloom, contributed $30,000 at a dinner and concert on the barge to help pay off debt and meet expenses.

Olga's dreams extend beyond her Brooklyn Bargemusic concerts. She would like to see other cities with waterside locations develop similar chamber music concerts on the water.

## ONCE A JOURNALIST, ALWAYS A JOURNALIST
### Pete Johnston
### *University Professor*

No sooner had Donald "Pete" Johnston retired from the faculty of the Columbia University Graduate School of Journalism than he walked across campus and joined the faculty of another Columbia school, the Graduate School of International and Public Affairs. Teaching is Pete's forte and his love, and he doesn't see giving it up just because he's turned 80. Pete's approach to college teaching has stayed constant over the years. Despite the way that computer technology has changed the processing of data, it hasn't much changed how a journalist reports and writes. "I spend a lot of time with students, criticizing their work and helping them reach decisions relative to their careers. I have always let a job expand beyond its normal dimensions," says Pete.

**"Ever since I've been a teacher, I have felt I'm contributing something very useful in motivating my students."**

As an adjunct faculty member, Pete officially works half-time, but keeping to official working hours has never been his strong suit. Pete enjoys helping students improve their basic communications skills, something he does in his "off" hours in one-on-one sessions. "Ever since I've been a teacher, I have felt I'm contributing something very useful in motivating my students."

For a change of pace, he serves as the volunteer editor of the Columbia Journalism School's alumni newspaper.

Born in Buffalo, Pete served in the air force during World War II. He graduated in 1949 from Cornell University and the following year from Columbia's journalism school. He worked as a reporter with the United Press International bureau in Buffalo for several years and then was transferred to the foreign desk in New York where he covered the United Nations. The *New York Times* then hired him for its Sunday "Week in Review" section to report on national and international events and on trends in social issues.

"I always wanted to be a journalist. Little has changed. When I worked for UPI and the *Times,* I commuted from Westchester. The other commuters, who made more money than I did, sounded disgruntled with their work and their pay. They couldn't wait until the weekends. I never felt that way toward work."

While at the *Times,* Pete taught journalism part-time at one of the colleges in the New York City university system. The experience encouraged him to apply to Columbia Journalism School as a full-time faculty member.

Pete found his true challenge as a teacher and mentor. "I like people, I like the Columbia environment, and I particularly like working with younger people—they make you feel younger." Students enjoyed his enthusiasm. He gave more time to the job than was required. His comments on student writings were both critical and helpful. None of that changed over the years.

During the mid-1980s, Pete, then an associate professor, was promoted to associate dean for academic affairs as well as director of admissions. When a new dean was named, Pete was replaced as an administrator. He returned to teaching. His effectiveness as an instructor aside, Pete had an academic problem: He had neglected scholarly research, a critical factor in receiving tenure. Years earlier he had been denied tenure, but his faculty position wasn't jeopardized because he was also serving as associate dean, a position protected by university regulations. When he reached age 65 and lacked tenure, it appeared his teaching career was at checkmate. This time he would have to leave the journalism school, with lifetime health care benefits and a pension based on 15 years of service.

At that point, Pete knew one thing. He did not want to stop working, unlike his older brother who worked as a sportswriter for 40 years, retired to Florida, and has not written a word since. "He is content to play tennis, walk, read, ride his bike, and watch TV. I'm not ready for that yet."

Fortunately, Pete's teaching credentials did not go unnoticed. As an associate dean, he knew other Columbia administrators, including those in the Graduate School of International and Public Affairs. They asked him to join the faculty as an adjunct professor, teaching basic journalism courses and working part-time. For the past 15 years, he's been director of the school's International Media and Communications Program.

In that capacity, Pete has run United Nations–sponsored training workshops for journalists from developing countries and served as the editor-in-chief of a four-volume *Encyclopedia of International Media and Communications*. The project, says Pete, took five years to complete and "contains 219 articles written by media specialists from across the globe. The main focus is on the status of the media in every country."

As long as Pete works no more than half-time, he can earn income and continue to collect his pension.

Pete's experience with an apparently seamless switch from one faculty to another on the same cam-

**Students enjoyed his enthusiasm. He gave more time to the job than was required.**

pus has carryover value for many managers and executives exiting the corporate workplace. Rather than retire, perhaps they, too, can find another department within the same organization that can use their skills.

Pete's five children are all grown. His wife, Jane, a former high school English teacher, is a published writer of murder mysteries. Jane brings in a small pension, Social Security benefits, and some book royalties.

Pete thought that at 70 he and Jane would leave New York and move to their summer home on Cape Cod. Jane spent about six months a year there; Pete lived there during the summer months. But any consideration of Cape Cod as a full-time home has been dropped. They found it too quiet and lonely in the off-season. They sold the house after spending 33 summers on Cape Cod. This way they have more time to travel.

Consistent with a desired New York City lifestyle, the Johnstons bought an apartment within walking distance of the Columbia campus. "We like the energy and action. We plan to stay here indefinitely."

## WORK IS THEIR FAMILY TRADITION
### Sally Rhine Feather and Bill Hendrickson
#### *She's a Clinical Psychologist, He's a Businessman*

Meet Sally Rhine Feather and Bill Hendrickson. They were college classmates, went their separate ways after graduation, married other people, raised children, pursued different careers, faced family traumas, and in the mid-1980s, they met again and were married the following year. More than 15 years later when most of their contemporaries are retiring, Sally and Bill are active workplace participants. They pursue separate careers yet participate together on one rather demanding project, the Rhine Research Center.

**Sally.** Looking back, it seems that Sally's future was somewhat predictable. As a youngster, she was interested in her father's research in parapsychology, which is commonly referred to as extrasensory perception. Photographs in magazine articles from Sally's youth show her playing games to test ESP.

Sally's father, J.B. Rhine, a Duke University psychology professor along with his wife, Louisa, another psychologist, made ESP the focus of their academic and research careers. After 38 years on the Duke faculty, J.B. Rhine founded the Rhine Research Center in the mid-1960s when he neared retirement.

"After I graduated from the College of Wooster in 1951, I got a job as a technical writer in Washington with the Library of Congress doing abstracts on Department of Defense materials. Perhaps, in the back of my mind I was interested in my father's work at Duke, but I was not too goal directed at the time."

Like many women college graduates of that era, career took second place to marriage. Sally married, and she worked to put her husband through medical school. The couple returned to Duke for his residency.

In 1962, Sally enrolled at Duke in a research and experimental psychology doctoral program. "It took me five years, and I got my degree the same year I was divorced. My aim was to work full-time at the Rhine Research Center."

Sally found that a research job did not fit the needs of a single mother. "I needed a 9-to-5 job, a steady income, and benefits. I was hired to run an adolescent clinic in Charlotte, but I stayed only two years because a job opened up in Durham." She worked until the early 1980s with several mental health clinics until she felt it made financial sense to become an independent clinical psychologist. Sally continued her practice until 1987, when she married Bill and moved to his home in Ridgewood, New Jersey. "The hardest part of the move was getting patients. I took assignments from the courts and had a part-time practice."

Six years later, Sally and Bill moved again—back to Durham. As soon as they settled in, she set up a private-practice office in Durham and one in her home in Hillsborough, a few miles north of Chapel Hill. She

**"Even though it might be wonderful to have more time to relax, retirement is for sissies."**

established new ground rules for work by limiting her load to 20 hours a week. "First, it is hard to regain a full-time workload when you've been away, and secondly, I was in my early 60s and I didn't want to work that hard. It's nice to choose and do what you want within the framework of your career path but still be able to devote more time to volunteer work, gardening, family, and other things."

But Sally's relationship to the Rhine Research Center moved front and center. Her father and mother died at ages 84 and 91, respectively. Both had worked nearly to the end of their lives. Their deaths had left a leadership hole at the center that was filled for nearly 20 years by a series of directors.

In January 2002, Sally, who had been a center board member since the mid-1960s, was named full-time director. In that capacity, she averaged 30 hours a week of work. It was unpaid due to a budget crunch. Sally's goal is to get the center on a sound financial basis, expand its academic research, get it more involved in consumer-related ESP programs, and attract more grants and contributions. New responsibilities have meant a flip-flop in Sally's work schedule. As she expanded her work with the center, she cut back her private practice from 20 to 4 hours a week. Retirement is not part of Sally's (or Bill's) vocabulary "Even though it might be wonderful to have more time to relax, retirement is for sissies." She plays tennis a few times a week but finds that even a sport that one enjoys has its limitations in one's retirement plans. "How many times a week can you do it?" she asks.

In 2005, Sally's professional life took on a new dimension. As the coauthor of a nonacademic book, *The Gift: ESP, The Extraordinary Experiences of Ordinary Press* (St. Martin's Press, 2005), she was engaged in book signings, radio interviews, and other promotional events.

One part of the Feather-Hendrickson's lifestyle, however, might change. Living in a home on a multi-acre rural site poses physical limitations. As a lifestyle alternative, the couple is considering the possibility of moving into a retirement community. "That still does not mean that I have to play bridge; I can still work. Like my parents, I expect to be involved professionally and in the community wherever I live," says Sally.

**Bill.** The son of a Presbyterian minister, Bill was born and lived in Ohio and, like Sally, graduated from the College of Wooster. "I thought I would teach history or I would go into radio broadcasting." Like many other classmates, he went into the army and was assigned to counterintelligence for two years in Europe. Three months after his discharge, Bill was married.

Over the next 34 years, Bill became an employee benefits specialist for several insurance companies, ending his career in New York with Marsh & McLennan as a sales and marketing vice president.

When he left Marsh in 1985, retirement was not part of Bill's plan. His pension income was limited due to having changed jobs in an era before portable pensions. As an alternative to early retirement, Bill formed Hendrickson & Company to sell employee benefit insurance to small and midsize firms and to members of trade associations. He launched the company about the time that he married Sally.

Six years later, Bill faced another hurdle when he relocated to North Carolina. "At first, I commuted to New York about every two weeks, then every three or four weeks, and by 1999, every six weeks. Now, it's more like every two to three months."

Bill's lessening involvement reflects the increased involvement of his eldest son Doug. In the mid-1990s, Doug, who was an executive with Chemical Bank in New York (now JP Morgan Chase), came to work with Bill with the idea that he would like to join, buy, and take over the business. "Doug's decision made sense to me because it would provide for an orderly succession consistent with my own plans." Following the takeover, Bill became a Hendrickson & Co. consultant.

Make no mistake, though. Fewer business trips to New York does not mean that Bill is retiring. Hardly. He does much of his work from North Carolina via telephone, fax, and computer. He spends about 40 percent of his time on insurance matters. Until mid-2003, he owned an interest in a local land development company, Red Hill Farms, which he subsequently sold. For several years, he served as the Rhine Research Center's unpaid treasurer.

Like Sally, Bill became an author in 2004 with *You Can Survive the Corporate Culture* (Publish America, 2004). "I discovered that books rarely sell by themselves, and authors need to keep priming the sales pump." As a result, Bill, the insurance marketer, is actively promoting his book.

Differing from Sally, Bill has no role model when it comes to retirement. His father died in his mid-60s. "My idea on retirement is to continue to work and enjoy the psychic benefits of my income and fees. I'm also following the advice of one of Sally's uncles: 'Don't ever retire.'"

## NOW CARRIES A PART-TIME UNIVERSITY WORKLOAD

### John Shelton Reed

*Officially Retired, but Still an Academic*

John Shelton Reed spent his entire professional career as a member of the University of North Carolina faculty. In retirement, John's lifestyle is in many ways still colored with a strong academic hue as he continues to teach at different universities in the United States and overseas.

By 2000, John, then in his late 50s, felt he was ready to retire. His plate was full as a tenured professor and director of the Howard Odum Institute for Research in Social Science, a position he had held for 12 years. Previously, John had been one of the founders and then director of UNC's Center for the Study of the American South. Besides the usual academic papers and books, John has written and edited a number of consumer books, including *1,000 Things Everyone Should Know About the South* (Doubleday, 1996t), which he cowrote with his wife; *My Tears Spoiled My Aim and Other Reflections on Southern Culture* (Harvest Books, 1993); and *Whistling Dixie: Dispatches from the South* (Harcourt Brace Jovanovich, 1992). And John proudly claims that he's the only sociologist to be included in Southern author and humorist Roy Blount Jr.'s *Book of Southern Humor.*

"I left UNC after 31 years. I enjoyed teaching, but due to my administrative duties with the center, I was spending about half my time in committee meetings and writing reports. In many ways, I had a great job. There was little supervision and one-half my time I could do what I wanted. Now I do it all the time."

John admits that he spent his first retirement year in leisurely fashion. "I had little trouble adjusting to my new lifestyle. Unlike some other people that Dale (his wife) and I know, my life and identity had not been tied up completely in my job. We spent the spring semester at Stanford University about 30 miles from our 'number one' daughter. In our drive to and from California, we visited our 'number two' daughter in Houston." While at Stanford, John worked on a number of articles and a few book chapters. After returning home and continuing his research, John admits that he spent more time in the UNC library than he had spent in the previous ten years.

The tempo picked up the following year. "We only spent two months in Chapel Hill. I taught four weeks in January at Centre College in Kentucky, and then from February through June, I taught an American studies course at the University of London. That was a great deal. I didn't get paid. I got free airfare for Dale and me, plus a free apartment near the university." During the fall semester, John taught a graduate course at East Tennessee State University, about 20 miles from where he was raised. It gave him a chance to visit regularly with his parents.

Growing up in Kingsport, Tennessee, John, the son of a small-town surgeon, was not planning on an

> "In many ways, I had a great job. There was little supervision and one-half my time I could do what I wanted. Now I do it all the time."

academic career. He went to the Massachusetts Institute of Technology to study mathematics, drifted into statistics, and drifted once more into statistics and how it relates to sociology. This led to a doctorate in sociology from Columbia University and a thesis on the sociology of the South. It was only logical in 1969 to return south and join UNC's sociology department.

The Reeds live modestly. Dale, a piano teacher, retired when John did. Their source of income is John's UNC pension, slightly more than half of his faculty salary. John also retired with lifetime family medical benefits. The Reeds will be eligible for Social Security in several years. In the years before he retired, John also taught summer school, which increased the size of his pension.

In retirement, John discovered a new interest unrelated to academia. A vacation in Mexico triggered what John calls his first serious hobby, collecting Mexican silver pieces. So that they can spend more time in Mexico, the Reeds are trying to learn Spanish. In early 2003, they spent a month in Guatemala taking a Spanish-immersion course.

John also revisited England and Oxford University in 2004 where he had a yearlong fellowship earlier in his career. "I was a visiting fellow at All Souls College for eight weeks working on a project that relates to my 1996 book *The Cultural Politics of Victorian Anglo-Catholicism.*" John's schedule became somewhat burdensome in 2004 from teaching in both England and the United States. As a result, the Reeds that year were only home six weeks.

"I'm now teaching at various colleges and universities every other semester, sometimes just for the chance to spend time in nice places, sometimes for the pay, and occasionally for both reasons. The money is not really needed, but it pays for various luxuries.

The Reeds are also looking ahead at different lifestyle arrangements. "In ten or so years, we might move to Carol Woods, a retirement community in Chapel Hill and the home of many retired UNC faculty members. We're not ready or old enough yet, but someday we might want to give up housekeeping and live with some of our friends."

*"Retirement is not a very useful word; it means withdrawal. I expect to do what I'm doing as long as I can."*

---

## ADVISES OTHERS ON CAREERS AND RETIREMENT
### William Stanley
#### *Outplacement and Coaching Consultant*

William Stanley practices what he preaches. A career-coaching consultant, Bill, now in his early 70s, advises men and women who are 10 to 20 years younger than him on the strategy that they should follow if they've been pink-slipped or given the option of early retirement. Bill's decision was easy—continue to work.

Providing this type of assistance is not new to Bill. Since graduating from Princeton and completing his military obligations as a naval officer, he has focused on human resource issues.

Bill spent 20 years at Connecticut General Life Insurance Company (now merged into Cigna) and 13 years with an outplacement firm. Since 1995, he has worked as a self-employed outplacement and coaching consultant.

*"Retirement* is not a very useful word; it means withdrawal. I expect to do what I'm doing as long as I can. I find that my clients (which include a large communications industry equipment supplier and a metro New York hospital) don't care how old I am. They like my experiences and want to learn more about how to deal with the last one-third of their lives. I try to give them the feeling that what I'm telling them is me. It's the way I live. In this way, age has its advantages.

"My job is to get at each person's personality and show them how to fulfill their needs. When I coach some people, I get a blank stare and rolling eyeballs.

"I try to stay in touch with some of the people I coach. Some have developed consulting businesses. Others have used their energies in hobbies or as vol-

**His independent consultancy posed another challenge— keeping his network going.**

unteers. Others just give up and escape into the life-style of a gated community."

Because of Bill's expertise, he has twice been invited to speak to his Princeton classmates at their reunions. At their 35th reunion, he asked them to describe their plans for the last third of their lives. By then, the class was balanced between those who had already retired and those who were still working. Their primary questions, other than those related to health, were: Why retire when there's so much left to do? How do you find structure in retirement? How do you learn a new routine? How do you stay busy yet not feel stressed or rushed?

After more than 30 years of working a structured business day, Bill discovered that becoming an independent consultant in 1995 and working from an at-home office in Ridgewood, New Jersey, called for some fine-tuning. No longer was his 9-to-5 day scheduled with meetings to attend, reports to prepare, and "make work" assignments to handle. His independent consultancy posed another challenge—keeping his network going. "That has become more difficult as people who I knew in the corporate world have retired. My Princeton classmates, who are now mostly retired, can no longer refer people to me."

Bill works three days a week. Despite his reduced workweek, revenues from coaching are surprisingly strong—boosted somewhat by an unsettled job market where people in their 50s are asking themselves, "What's next?" Besides consulting fees, Bill's income consists of Social Security benefits, income from a few 401(k)s, and a Cigna pension from which he's been receiving payments since he was 55.

Interestingly, when Bill was a Cigna human resources manager, he recommended that the company lower the pension age for retirees to 55, recognizing that by that age, employees may have already worked for 30 years and be able to retire yet not be able to collect their pension.

Bill's wife, Viola, is in her late 50s and teaches fifth grade in a neighboring community. She has every intention of working another nine years until she's eligible to retire on a full pension. When Bill is between coaching gigs, he has other responsibilities to keep him busy. He calls himself a "house husband," an assignment with many roles: cooking, a longtime hobby; maintaining their home; and taking care of his mother-in-law, who lives in another house in Ridgewood, and his mother, who lives in Wallingford, Connecticut. Besides all that, there's constant maintenance to do at their 150-acre rural weekend and summer retreat in upstate New York.

## TELLING THE STORY ON FILM
### Garner Simmons
### *A Hollywood Filmmaker*

When it comes to retirement, Garner Simmons had a mentor—his father, Louis. When Louis was 50, he was the national sales manager of a company that went out of business.

Rather than have a pity party for himself, he put together a series of financial and marketing deals whereby he would own the products that his previous employer once produced.

Louis, according to his son, believed that one took chances in life by betting on one's self. His formula must have been successful because he ran the company for another 25 years. His father imbued Garner with a spirit of independence that has influenced his work as well as his attitude toward the so-called retirement years. Garner's life to date has been based on taking risks, something he inherited from his father. And having spent a lifetime without a regular company paycheck, he rarely considers the issues facing most corporate employees.

"I never wanted to have a 9-to-5 job. As a kid, I always wanted to do something interesting." This is something that he's done for 30 years as an independent TV/film writer and producer.

**With this background, it's no wonder that Garner, now in his early 60s, has no plans to retire.**

With this background, it's no wonder that Garner, now in his early 60s, has no plans to retire. Why should he? Garner is an independent television and feature film writer, who has been practicing his trade ever since he received a doctorate degree in 1975 from Northwestern University's School of Communications. His thesis, which was later published as a book, was on Sam Peckinpah, a noted Hollywood filmmaker who died in 1984.

Garner is a Chicago native. He was an English and fine arts major at Colgate University. "I wanted to be a painter. My timing wasn't too good." It was 1965, and the Vietnam War was becoming a national issue. Instead of going to graduate school and further art training, he returned to Chicago, and, to avoid the draft, he enlisted in the Illinois National Guard. Three years later, he was mobilized following two 1968 events—the assignation of Martin Luther King and the Democratic National Convention. "At the same time, I worked at various jobs from tending bar to hacking a cab to teaching school before going to Northwestern for graduate work."

While in graduate school, 20th Century Fox optioned a screenplay he wrote, which prompted Garner and his wife, Sheila, to move to the Los Angeles area, their home ever since. The rest, as they say, is history. Garner, unlike so many of his contemporaries who worked in corporate America, has been a free agent for his entire career. "I live by my wits. I've never been a corporate employee. I'm used to the irregular work of a freelance independent writer and producer. I take jobs writing for TV to bring in revenues. It also gives me the funds to write and produce other things on 'spec.'"

In many ways, his approach to the workplace can continue indefinitely. He's not tied in with an employer's retirement program, mergers and acquisitions, or other vicissitudes of the workplace that he says affects many of his contemporaries.

Sheila, who is several years younger, is a school administrator. Their three sons are grown, and interestingly all three are involved in some way in the film field.

Since 1981, Garner through his company, Equuleus Productions (*Equuleus* means little horse, and one of the smallest constellations in the heavens), has written, rewritten, or produced over 200 television episodes, movies of the week, and miniseries. His credits include *Poltergeist: the Legacy, Spencer for Hire, Falcon Crest, Yellow Rose,* and *Buck James* along with such feature films as *The Last Samurai* and *The Easter Rebellion,* which is based on the 1916 Irish uprising.

At 62, "I find it hard to image being retired and not working. Unlike friends my age or even younger, I don't worry about being cut loose since I work for myself." His independence carries through his daily workplace routine. "I prefer to work at home. In a typical day, I run three miles in the morning, then write for four to six hours, play some golf, and write some more when I return. To survive in my type of work, you need to know how to live in an up-and-down environment."

## THERE'S LIFE AFTER IBM
### Larry Bumgardner
#### Corporate to Small-Company Software Designer

For several years prior to Larry Bumgardner's retirement, IBM was offering early-retirement buyouts. Larry was undecided whether he should stay or leave. The dilemmas he faced—deciding if and when he should accept a buyout package and, if not, what to do next—are being faced by countless other managers in the 50-plus set. Larry now admits that he should have accepted an earlier buyout package, but he remained at IBM because he hadn't yet determined the next step in his personal game plan. The factors that were involved in his decision making are complex and typical for anyone weighing a buyout offer.

> **"Taking the IBM package was one thing, but finding something I really wanted to do was something else."**

After considering a number of postretirement jobs and actually teaching school, Larry returned to what he knows best, computer software development, and this time working for a small company.

Change for change's sake wasn't in the cards for Larry. Contrary to one of IBM's many nicknames—"I've Been Moved"—Larry's career and lifestyle had been rather consistent. "Same company, same location, same house, and the same wife. As you can see, I didn't follow the 'grass is always greener' concept."

As a youngster, Larry thought about being a teacher or minister but found that he was better suited for and more interested in science. He received undergraduate and graduate engineering degrees from North Carolina State University and Duke University, joined IBM, and a few months later was activated as a U.S. Army Signal Corps officer. Other than two years of military service, Larry's entire life had been spent in North Carolina with IBM. Larry was officially classified as an IBM group leader in charge of designing software for retail-related computer systems. Ironically, as IBM downsized, his division achieved record sales.

Larry found it difficult to realistically consider any form of early retirement. He felt he was much too young, and retirement contradicted his philosophy that work is critical to survival—not in the sense of financial survival but in usefulness. "I didn't believe in being idle. Taking the IBM package was one thing, but finding something I really wanted to do was something else." Initially, Larry felt that he couldn't leave until he decided on a new pursuit.

Prior to retirement, he was optimistic about life after IBM. "I felt that when I left IBM, there would be a number of options." Larry had plenty of contacts through his work with retail computer systems. He believed he "could join another software company or become an independent contractor and earn the difference between my IBM pension payout and my living expenses."

Larry also considered becoming an entrepreneur. He tried to purchase an auto machine shop from owners who wanted to retire. Hardly a newcomer to this field, he first learned how to repair cars from his machinist father. But the business had some serious environmental problems that would be too costly to remedy.

As a trained scientist, Larry considered teaching. "I only wanted to work in urban public schools where I could teach science to city and disadvantaged kids. Teaching in a private or church school didn't interest me. It wasn't where I was needed."

Practicing good works was nothing new to Larry. Besides his wife and their three children, his family includes several children from troubled families. He also donates 20 percent of his gross income to charity.

In his mid-50s, Larry retired officially in 1997 from IBM. Since then, he has had three different jobs. Consistent with his preretirement plan, he became a teacher. Rather than seeking a safer haven in an independent school, he worked for several months at a Durham middle school teaching science and math, but his idealism was shaken by school conditions. Soon after he left teaching, IBM asked him to return as a contract worker, a relationship that lasted slightly less than a year.

In early 1998, he joined QVS Software, a small company in Raleigh that produces point-of-purchase software systems, an area that he knows well from his IBM days. He describes it as the "best job I've ever had." As an IBM retiree, Larry is also a "double dipper," collecting both his IBM pension and a QVS salary.

Larry's children are self-supporting. His wife, Nancy, does not work. Like her husband, she is also a community activist involved in leadership positions with several nonprofit groups. "Even if I made less money, we knew that we could live on less," says Larry.

> **"When we set up the new firm, we developed a blueprint suitable to my lifestyle interests and to some others in the firm."**

## WORKING FEWER DAYS WITH LAW FIRM
### William Kennon
*Legal Work Shaped to His Lifestyle*

William Kennon dissolved his law firm in 2003. "What's next?" he asked. He and several of his former partners set up a new firm, Kennon, Craver, Belo & McKee.

Bill, then in his early 60s, told the other principals in the firm that he wanted to reduce the hours that he would work to the equivalent of three days a week. He was willing to take less monthly income and a commensurate part of the profits.

His approach runs contrary to many professional services firms where partners want to continue to receive a large piece of the pie but don't want to put in the hours to deserve it.

"When we set up the new firm, we developed a blueprint suitable to my lifestyle interests and to some others in the firm." It was never a goal of the firm to expect partners and associates to bill clients up to 80 hours a week.

Bill was born in Durham, went to Duke, and majored in political science. If he had it to do all over again, he would have majored in English, which he finds to be even better training for a legal career.

As expected by his family, he went to law school at the University of North Carolina. "I'm a fourth-generation lawyer. My great grandfather and grandfather practiced in the Midwest. My father had a one-person firm in Durham. I joined him." Bill said with a grin that "I worked myself to the top. A year later I was made a partner. We don't have to worry that there will be a fifth generation of lawyers in the family." His two grown sons already have different careers.

"I practiced with my father for ten years until he got ill when he was 66. He died a year later. He was a tax lawyer. So am I. Over the years, we provided certain types of legal services to one of the older law firms in Durham. I already had a relationship with the firm, so I joined them and soon became a partner."

Over the next 25 years, the firm grew to 25 lawyers. When Kennon Craver was set up, the staff consisted of mostly business and trust law specialists. The other lawyers in the old firm, who were primarily litigators, started another firm.

"Frankly, when we formed Kennon Craver, I wanted to take more time off. At the old firm, I was also managing partner, which meant administrative and management responsibilities." It's one duty that others now handle at Kennon Craver.

Bill and his wife, Martha, own a vacation home in Morehead City, about 175 miles northeast of Durham. It's here that Bill wants to spend more time to fish, hunt, and play golf. He also has some real estate investments in the area as well as a few local clients.

One of his challenges is addressing his inner feelings on retirement. "Do I really want to retire or continue working a few days a week in return for a fair part of the firm's proceeds? I don't want to have the younger people in the firm feel that they are working to support me." In practical terms, it means that he's rarely at the office on Fridays or on a number of Mondays. Clients can see me Tuesday through Thursday in Durham.

Tax law, he notes, is highly complex. There's lots of reading, continuing education, and mastering of complex tax and estate laws. Bill feels he can do this even if he works fewer hours. Fortunately he receives backup from his partners.

Also in his favor is the nature of the firm's legal specialties. "Our practice is not urgent. It lends itself to normal business hours. We're not doing merger and acquisition or litigation law."

Even so, he intends to continue practicing law. And consistent with his interest in both fishing and trust law, Bill's license plate appropriately reads: PROBAIT.

## POINTS TO REMEMBER

- **Many in the 50-plus set intend to continue working.**
- **Additional income is only one of many reasons** for working.
- **You can work without being a workhorse.**
- **There are ways to continue** to work on your terms.
- **Flexible work patterns** are one answer.
- **You may want to pass along your business.**
- **You may want to stay involved** but take on a different role.

# Starting Over

*"Most people in the age of Integrity (over 65) will continue to work in one way or another . . . because they will have to be prepared to support themselves for greatly elongated lives."*
—Gail Sheehy in *New Passages*

## Chapter 7

You're 50- or 60-something and you've just been pink-slipped. What's the next step? Do you look for another job (the subject of Chapter 8), buy an existing business, start your own, purchase a franchise, begin a new career, or become a consultant?

Chances are the 50-plus set won't find a friendly welcome mat at most Fortune 500 companies. Many employers, while respecting your credentials, assume that you've been overpaid, that your work skills have plateaued, or that you're no longer as aggressive as a 42-year-old.

Now's the time to downplay the traditional job market and consider some form of self-employment or career change, an idea that the fictional Rabbi David Small contemplated in *The Day the Rabbi Resigned*. "Because I'm 53, it occurred to me that in a few years I'd be too old to be considered for a teaching job. Maybe I'm too old now, but I'd like to give it a shot."

The rabbi was not alone. Slightly less than 10 percent of all nonfarm workers ages 55 to 64 are self-employed, reports the Bureau of Labor Statistics *(www.bls.gov)*. The rate nearly doubles when workers are over age 65. Perhaps one reason for this spurt is that owning a business has become a prime way to remain employed. That does not mean that all older entrepreneurs are putting in a 60-hour workweek. Some operate seasonal businesses; others are consultants who work two or three days a week. The move toward self-employment seems endemic. By 2020, AARP predicts that 18 million people over age 50 will be self-employed. Compare this with about 6 million in this age bracket who presently work for themselves.

## Want to Own Your Own Business?

You've probably daydreamed about owning your own business. But before taking the plunge, be hard-nosed. Starting a business calls for enormous amounts of energy and endurance, a tough hurdle for anyone but more so for new business owners who are 50-plus and especially so for those past 60. Above all, it means risking capital—a small amount for an at-home consultancy but much more for buying or starting other types of businesses. Surely, your lawyer or accountant will point out the pitfalls of jeopardizing retirement-related resources on any new business venture.

As an entrepreneur, George Krassner personally knows the risks shared by most owners of start-up businesses. "They fall in love with an idea yet fail to do adequate research. They underestimate the cost of being in even the most modest type of business and at the same time overestimate their market potential." Krassner finds that retirees go into business for many reasons: "They're bored with retirement, or they have an 'A' type personality that needs to be stimulated."

Is it a risk worth taking for the 50-plus set or, in fact, for would-be entrepreneurs of any age? It probably depends on whether you're an optimist or a pessimist. The Small Business Administration *(www.sba .gov)* estimates that about one-half of start-ups terminate within the first four years of inception.

At age 54, 60, or 65, it makes little sense to gamble a life's savings on a new business. Of course, there are exceptions—for example, a former executive with money to spare as the result of a favorable corporate buyout or the seller of one business who is in a strong cash position to invest in another. There are success stories, however, such as retired high-income Chrysler CEO Lee Iacocca, who started ventures including a food and wine company. Don't think that Iaccoca lost his flair for the corporate limelight after retirement. In 2005, he even appeared again as the advertising spokesperson for a series of Chrysler TV ads. Then there's Marvin Traub, a former chairman of Bloomingdale's, who formed his own marketing and merchandising consultancy.

If you get the itch to be an entrepreneur, be aware of the pitfalls. There are a number of investment vehicles that fetch a better return than most new businesses. The 3 to 5 years it will likely take to establish the business may seem like an eternity. Other than early or wealthy retirees, most other retirees no longer have the luxury of 20 to 30 years to recoup any money that they could ultimately lose in a failed business venture.

Business turnaround expert William Buxton does not court retirement-age people as prospects to purchase businesses up for sale. "Other than those people with extra money to spend or who know a specific business 'cold,' I advise people in their late 50s to 60s to avoid risking it all in buying or starting a business."

Aside from the financial risk, there are some serious considerations:

- **How prepared are you for the rigors of self-employment** after spending 25 to 30 years working in corporate America?
- **Do you really know the business** that you hope to start or buy?
- **Who is going to teach you the ABCs** of being a business owner?
- **Are you both mentally and physically prepared** to be a business owner?
- **Are you prepared to work longer hours** than you did in your previous job?

---

## MUSTS FOR NEW BUSINESSES

- **Doing your homework is critical** before going into business.
- **A preliminary, one-year, realistic business plan** is mandatory.
- **Avoid blue-sky proposals;** they accomplish nothing. Remember, the planning is not an exercise in fiction writing. The object is to set realistic and achievable goals.
- **Prepare a tentative operating budget.**
- **Decide whether there's a need for additional financing.**
- **Know if there is sufficient income** to support both the business and personal needs during the start-up period.
- **Decide whether the business needs any other full-time or part-time employees.**

---

# Is a Franchise a Better Choice?

Is franchising a good option for potential entrepreneurs? Many new-business experts feel that franchising represents a strong start-up opportunity for the 50-plus set who have risk capital to invest resulting from severance or golden-parachute payouts. The risks are sharply lower than those of starting a business from scratch.

Franchise industry growth figures are impressive. Depending on who does the counting, there are approximately 769,000 U.S. franchise-owned businesses with an estimated $1.5 trillion in annual industry sales. A new franchise unit opens somewhere in the United States about every eight minutes. Most retail or service chains are franchises. The roster, according to the International Franchise Association (*www.franchise.org*), includes food retailers (McDonald's, Burger King, and Dunkin' Donuts), tax service companies (H&R Block and Jackson Hewitt), and executive search firms (Management Recruiters International).

Franchising is not for everyone. Watch out for possible culture shock, especially when shifting from a corporate lifestyle to a mom-and-pop business environment. Gone are the 9-to-5 workdays. Hands-on work begins with the boss and is the order of the day in most franchises, as well as in any other start-up business. It can be especially shocking to a former white-collar administrator turned fast-food franchisee. Interestingly, the transition may be easier for some older and more seasoned professionals who are less interested in frills and titles, have their feet firmly planted on the ground, and are more willing to do what's necessary to get the job done.

A franchise, at best, represents an entrepreneurial compromise. The buyer obtains what, hopefully, is a proven business formula and a strong marketing image along with training and an array of ongoing support services. In return, the franchisor sets the ground rules regarding prices, use of the company's logo, quality control, product marketing, advertising, and purchasing.

Buying a franchise is not forever, says John Hayes, a consultant to would-be franchisees. "It is not like a family-run business passed along from generation to generation but rather a business that might be sold after eight years, hopefully at a profit. This might become your retirement nest egg, or you could use the money to buy another franchise." Other franchise owners leverage their investments. They parlay a single franchise unit into a regional chain or create miniature franchise conglomerates.

Nearly 20 percent of franchise operators own more than one unit, says market researcher Frandata (*www.frandata.com*)—sometimes with the same franchisor, other times in different businesses to increase diversification and lower risk if one franchise concept goes sour. Frandata reports that more than one-half of all franchises are controlled by multiunit operators.

The International Franchise Association says that McDonald's has the largest number of outlets followed in order by Yum! Brands (KFC, Taco Bell), 7-Eleven, Cendant (Howard Johnson, Century 21), Subway, H&R Block, Jani-King (cleaning services), Dunkin' Donuts, and Curves.

**A franchise, at best, represents an entrepreneurial compromise.**

Some franchise operators actively seek former corporate managers as franchisees. ProForma *(www .proforma.com)*, a distributor of printed items, including promotional printing and advertising specialties, seeks owners with previous sales experience. In recent years, about 25 percent of ProForma franchise owners were age 50-plus. Some franchise operators look for franchisees with related industry know-how. The Golden Corral chain prefers to recruit experienced restaurant industry personnel. "When they aren't food people and they still want to invest in our franchise, we get them to partner with a food guy," says Golden Corral's Stephen Fortlouis. Depending on size, a 282-seat Golden Corral might gross upward of $2.8 million a year while sales at a 468-seat unit has the potential to gross more than $4 million.

Learning how to run most franchise businesses is not that difficult. The good franchisors have developed easy-to-learn operating formulas, and they are experienced in training recruits. UPS Stores (previously Mail Boxes Etc.) trains franchisees at its in-house "university" in San Diego. Other franchisers offer ongoing educational programs via the Internet. The education and training in the practical day-to-day operations can start in advance of buying a franchise. One approach is to work for a franchisee part-time in the evenings or on weekends. Here's a chance to learn whether that type of franchise or the field itself holds any interest.

Start-up costs vary. It is safer but more expensive to be part of a proven, successful franchise company than to join a newly established franchise operation. Some franchises, due to their success, are naturally costlier. Storefront fast-food and retail operations are generally more expensive to acquire than most behind-the-scenes business-to-business and customer-service franchises. Expect to invest approximately $510,000 to $1 million in a McDonald's franchise. To get going with a Subway sandwich shop, the investment is between $86,000 and $252,000, with 50 percent of the cost payable in cash. Curves, which grew in 11 years to about 9,500 fitness and weight loss centers catering exclusively to women, requires a $42,000 to $53,000 cash investment.

More often than not, the franchise fee represents just a part of the start-up costs. If it is a retail operation, there may be the cost of building or renting the store. Bona fide franchisors provide checklists that show the average cost for training, store design, inventory and equipment, leasehold improvements, working capital, and fees for advertising, legal help, accounting, licenses, and insurance.

Franchisees constantly gripe that they are required to buy products and services from authorized suppliers. They contend that these practices increase overhead costs while franchisors maintain that their rosters of approved suppliers help to assure better quality control.

You can also get into business by buying an existing franchise outlet. About 15 to 20 percent of franchises are resold annually. Some potential owners prefer buying an accepted winner, and they don't mind paying a premium for it. Distressed or marginal operations are even less costly to buy. One suggested buyout formula: The buyer should expect to pay three to four times net earnings plus the depreciated value of assets, the current franchise fee, and the liabilities as of the closing.

## A Franchisee Speaks Out

At age 49, Tom (who prefers to remain anonymous) faced a situation familiar to many men and women his age. He lost his job as a marketing executive at a subsidiary of a Fortune 100 company when the company was sold. At the time, Tom was earning more than $125,000 a year plus an excellent benefits package. As part of his severance package, Tom's former employer gave him severance pay equivalent to one year's salary and referred him to the local office of one of the nation's larger outplacement firms.

Tom was married, and his wife worked. One son had already graduated from college, another was

**About 15 percent to 20 percent of franchises are resold annually. Some potential owners prefer buying an accepted winner, and they don't mind paying a premium for it.**

**"At 49 to 50 years of age, I was very concerned about the prospect of failure. I felt that franchises offered me the most insurance against failure."**

completing college and a daughter was a high school junior. Tom needed to decide whether to take another job or start or buy a business.

"When I went to outplacement, I was looking for a job, but I was also seriously considering the alternatives. My outplacement counselor advised me to use a business broker. I spent some time with a broker who told me about the companies he had for sale. I also met with my accountant and asked questions about ways to finance a small business. Both the broker and accountant introduced me to a couple of bankers who were small business finance specialists.

"I looked at some franchises on my own. Why franchising versus another type of business? At 49 to 50 years of age, I was very concerned about the prospect of failure. I felt that franchises offered me the most insurance against failure. I didn't have any special business management skills, and I felt that a tried-and-true franchised formula would be better than 'hunting and pecking' on my own. I also looked at nonfranchised businesses—a sports clothing and equipment store, a couple of liquor stores, and even a store that cashed checks. Each one had its own risks. I dismissed all food-related businesses because I had no food experience, and the cost of entry was too high. I dismissed liquor and check cashing due to their long hours and personal risk—they get robbed.

"I became interested in a franchise in the 'pack and ship' field. It was a business that I thought I could understand, and I had become somewhat familiar with these stores and their business model in my last job. I went to the company's Web site and read its literature. I read franchise magazines, read the 'business for sale' ads in my newspaper, and talked to everyone that I could. The price of buying a start-up store was a bit steep compared with buying an existing store, an option that the franchisor never told me about. So I visited and talked with a couple of owners of existing stores.

"I finally decided to buy an existing store from an owner who was retiring. It had a central location with a residential and commercial mix of business in a town about 15 minutes' drive from my home." Instead of financing his purchase through the seller over six years, Tom worked with his local bank, which offered a better rate of interest.

"I think I made a smart decision" said Tom. "When I went for training at the franchisor's corporate offices, I met guys who were building new stores and were frustrated with zoning issues and construction and had no customers. One guy was supposed to have his store up and running by August, but its completion was delayed for three or four months. That was something I didn't have to worry about."

Tom took over his franchised store in June 2002. After six months, he reached the point where he could pay himself a nominal salary even though he had to take other steps to meet his personal obligations. He refinanced the first mortgage on his home at a favorable rate, borrowed on his credit card, and opened a line of credit from his bank. "In a nutshell, I'm leveraged beyond belief, but I'm betting this will all work out."

By buying an existing store, Tom already had a base of existing customers; the secret was to keep them as customers and obtain new ones. On his first anniversary, he reported that the franchise had done about 20 percent to 25 percent better in his first year of ownership than the previous owner had done in his last. Offsetting the sales rise was an investment in equipment, advertising, and supplies plus a lot of mistakes on Tom's part. Hopefully, he says, "I'm getting better at it, but there isn't much margin for error.

"I still worry about revenues, net income and cash flow, and bad weather that adversely affects the number of customers served each day. The enjoyable part is helping customers and watching their packages leave the store on a truck." Tom sold the franchise less than two years after buying it. The franchisor was squeezing profits from the existing business formula. Tom was often working six full days a week, and the take-home pay was rather modest. He sold the fran-

> **By buying an existing store, Tom already had a base of existing customers; the secret was to keep them as customers and obtain new ones.**

**Determine whether there is some form of local or area market exclusivity or whether the franchisor has the right to open additional outlets in a nearby area.**

chise at a profit and actually recouped his investment. Tom now works as a senior speechwriter for a large national organization. The one catch: His current take-home pay is considerably less than what it was several years ago as a corporate marketer.

## Protecting Yourself

Due diligence should be the order of the day before making any commitment. This is the time to study the marketplace. By attending regional shows where franchisors exhibit, you have a chance to increase awareness of the range of different franchise businesses. Start to read how-to business books on franchising that are available in most bookstores and public libraries.

Prior to purchase, the franchisor is obligated by law to send all prospective buyers either the Uniform Franchise Offering Circular (UFOC) or an extensive disclosure document that discusses such basic issues as the history of the franchising company, any bankruptcy records, fees, and royalties. For fear of potential liability, most franchisors will avoid being specific about an anticipated return on investment from a franchise.

The UFOC guidelines, which went into effect in 1996, provide information on the franchise operations in understandable English rather than "legalese." The guidelines require franchisors to reveal the names, addresses, and telephone numbers of franchise owners, including all franchisees who have sold out or gone bankrupt. Franchisors must also reveal any litigation in which they have been involved. No longer can they list only the names of successful franchise operators.

This said, potential franchisees should do their homework and do it thoroughly. Personally check out the franchisor. Determine whether there is some form of local or area market exclusivity or whether the franchisor has the right to open additional outlets in a nearby area. Most important, visit other franchisees licensed by the same company and talk to the owners.

---

| **KNOW THE ANSWERS BEFORE BUYING A FRANCHISE** |
| --- |

■ **What type of experience is required** in the franchised business?

■ **How many hours and what level of personal commitment are needed** to run the business?

■ **Who is the franchisor?** What is its track record? What is the business experience of the officers and directors of the company?

■ **How are other franchisees doing?**

■ **What are the start-up and licensing costs?** How do they compare with similar franchisees from other franchisors?

■ **Are franchisees required to buy supplies and business services** from the franchisor?

■ **What is the turnover rate** among other franchisees?

■ **What are the terms and conditions** under which the franchise relationship can be terminated or renewed?

■ **Is the franchisor in sound financial health?**

Source: International Franchise Association.

# Consultants Abound

Question: What is a consultant? Answer: Any unemployed person 50 miles from home wearing a suit and carrying a briefcase.

There is no shortage of consultants. It doesn't take any particular skill to call yourself a consultant— just print some business cards and letterhead. Except in a few specialty areas, consultants do not need a state license or professional accreditation.

The reasons for starting a consultancy vary. Sometimes the incentive is purely defensive. Downsized managers and early retirees become consultants as a shelter against further job loss. The start-up and carrying costs are minimal because the consultancy is usually launched at home.

It's easy to become a consultant. For $10, a print shop will produce 500 business cards. The secret even for a part-time consultancy is to obtain new clients, retain existing ones, do the work, and handle the paperwork. Past corporate employment is not necessarily the best training for the retiree turned consultant. In corporate America, one works in teams. Decisions are made that way. Corporate managers can rely on support services and backup staffs. Not so for most one-person consultancies where the owner/operator

**The start-up and carrying costs are minimal because the consultancy is usually launched at home.**

does everything. Consultants are independent contractors. In the consultant-client relationship, the client does not pay fringe benefits or payroll taxes. In return, the consultant receives tax advantages and business exemptions. For example, consultants (and any business owner or self-employed person) may shelter up to 25 percent of their compensation or $40,000, whichever is less, in the most popular types of Keogh retirement plans.

Another fully tax-deductible alternative is the simplified employee pension (SEP or SEP-IRA), which in many ways is even easier to set up and maintain than a Keogh. As of January 2005, one is permitted to contribute as much as 25 percent of net self-employment earnings, or $42,000, whichever is less.

In 1998, a new form of IRA, the Roth IRA, became available. It seems that the Roth IRA was designed with baby boomers in mind. Although contributions to a Roth IRA are not deductible, the new plan has several advantages that should interest boomers. Taxes are paid up front so the savings are in after-tax funds. Investors in a regular IRA or Keogh plan usually can't withdraw any contributions until they reach age 59½ without paying a penalty. When owned for at least five years, Roth investors can withdraw their contributions before that age without paying penalties or taxes. Thus the Roth IRA offers early retirees a potential source of funds for investing in business ventures.

Some ex-managers in the 50-plus set blossom as consultants, with incomes eclipsing their highest corporate achievements. Other consultants are only marginally successful. In fairness to them, strong financial performance may never have been their primary business goal. To many early retirees, a consultancy represents a way to stay active, maintain business or professional skills, and, most important, bridge the earnings gap between their former salaries and their retirement benefits and investment income.

Consulting, though a practical entrée into business for retirees, is not for everyone, says outplacement consultant John Challenger of Challenger, Gray & Christmas *(www.challengergray.com)*. The upside is that, depending on how much the individuals want to work or earn, they control the decision whether to work part-time or full-time. But there is some risk. While the investment might be small for starting a consultancy, the business can easily dwindle unless there's an infusion of new business. "It's not know-how that gets the new business," Challenger says, "but the willingness to spend 70 percent of one's time selling."

■ **The consultant's lifeblood is new business.** The consultant's first rule of survival is to obtain business. Signing the first client is usually not the problem. Many times, it is a former employer. Client number one emerges, but few consultants can exist on assignments from a single client. Herein lies the challenge: find additional clients.

■ **Avoid doing battle with the "big guys."** Consultants come in all shapes and sizes. The large national and international firms can afford to be generalists, offering clients what seem like an unlimited range of services. Smaller consultancies need to pursue a different strategy because they can rarely compete across the board with the larger firms. The successful one-person consultancy wisely becomes a niche specialist and, more often than not, a subniche specialist, obtaining new business by convincing clients of its unique expertise.

■ **The consultant must be self-sufficient.** Many consultants go into business directly from a sheltered corporate environment. Staff assistants previously handled simple tasks like ordering stationery, maintaining office equipment, and billing customers. A consultancy and, in fact, nearly all start-up businesses operate differently. Nothing gets done unless the consultant does the word processing, printing, photocopying, faxing, and telephoning.

■ **There's a need to know more about the consulting business.** Take nothing for granted. Know the basics of running a consultancy. It means paying attention to such details as billing and collecting fees. Learn

**To many early retirees, a consultancy represents a way to stay active, maintain business or professional skills, and, most important, bridge the earnings gap between their former salaries and their retirement benefits and investment income.**

the consultancy fundamentals well in advance of opening day. One good way is to talk with other consultants or read some "how-to" books written by consultants for other consultants.

■ **It pays to be frugal.** Control expenses. Remember, it might take up to 90 pays to get paid by some clients, and cash flow can be a problem. Don't overspend on equipment and supplies. An alternative is to lease office equipment and furniture for a few months with an option to buy. Managers in corporate America are trained to "think big." This caveat often works in reverse for start-ups. If mailing only five letters a day, why rent an automated postal meter when postage stamps will do?

## Life in a Home Office

Whether it is an engineer or technician starting a high-tech company in the garage or a marketer launching a consultancy in the den, there are immediate advantages of a home office. Even so, not everyone is suited temperamentally to work at home.

But the home office has become an acceptable venue for many 50-plus-set consultants, as well as for start-up entrepreneurs of all ages. There are some obvious advantages, such as eliminating office rent, avoiding a commute, and enjoying the ambiance that comes with a more informal business lifestyle.

The home office has some slight tax advantages, primarily a deduction of that portion of the home that is totally dedicated to an office.

The availability of low-cost computers and communications equipment means that even the most remote home office is only microseconds away from customers and important business hubs. A home office can be set up for less than $5,000. The basic equipment should consist of a desktop or laptop computer, a printer, a self-standing fax/copier and scanner,

Internet service, and voice mail. The cost of furniture and decoration is a discretionary expense.

Before redesigning an attic or spare bedroom into a home office, be aware of some of the realities and myths of this workplace.

- **Find out whether the community, condominium, or landlord permits a business to operate in the home.** Zoning regulations, for example, may prohibit posting a business sign, causing increased traffic, or parking in front of a home. Most manufacturing processes are banned in residential areas

- **Working at home is more than trading in wing tips for sneakers.** Business is still the order of the day despite the informality of attire.

- **Try to resist the temptation of a 24-hour workday.** With an office across the hall from your bedroom or in the basement, it's often hard to separate business from personal life. Modern technology can help on that front, too. After-hour telephone calls can be intercepted by voice mail, and a fax machine can operate unattended.

- **There's no reason to be a recluse.** It's lonely working at home. The exception is the much-traveled consultant who only returns to the office to read mail, make telephone calls, and prepare reports. To offset work-at-home loneliness, make a point of meeting regularly with business friends and associates. Also, keep up with trade and business groups, and attend their meetings. This serves another purpose, too; networking can lead to new business prospects.

- **Don't be defensive about a home office.** A consultant is supposedly an expert. Consultants are normally retained for their expertise, not for the size of their office or its décor.

- **Avoid routine household chores during working hours.** Start by separating business from home life. It is as fundamental as refusing to answer the family telephone during business hours. The same guidelines apply to trees that need pruning and closets that plead for cleaning.

# Changing Careers

The media thrive on publicizing dramatic career changes, but those are the exception in the 50-plus set. Few people in their 50s or older are prepared to face the academic demands, the dual rigors of learning a new trade and obtaining professional accreditation, or the cost in time and money in order to change careers.

Take Dale Graff. He had just turned 50. "I was working 65 hours a week, and my wife, Paula, and I weren't getting a chance to play golf and enjoy life." A nuclear engineer with an MBA, Dale worked for Argonne National Laboratory on reactor safety, then for Bell Labs as a project manager, followed by ten years with Fujitsu and another two years with Lucent. Dale has a desire to more fully develop another aspect of himself—a certain psychic ability that he strongly experienced in a couple of instances. On September 9, 2001, Dale had a psychic sensation. He acted accordingly the following day when he sold his stock holdings. He had had a similar sensation 11 years earlier when Iraq was about to invade Kuwait, and he sold stock then as well. "I always liked things that were strange and wacky; the difference is that I now live it."

Dale is building his psychic awareness in the hope that it might lead to a new career. He attends workshops at the Rhine Research Center, a nonprofit parapsychology institute in Durham, North Carolina, as well as other psychic-related meetings. "I've done more than 100 free readings over the past few months on the telephone. I've done them for people of all ages. I hope I'll get to the point where I might charge a fee to help people understand their psychic experiences. But I'm not ready for that yet."

Dale's goal is to live on earnings from his investments and stock trades, although this idea has been made more difficult by the market slide. Even though his 2001 stock sales shielded him from the market downturn, he didn't have sufficient money to retire in the style he wanted.

Meanwhile Dale looked for a job to help recapture some of his lost funds. He found a consulting job with a telecommunications company. "I work mainly from home, and enjoy it. It's a nice transition back to the working world. At 52, I see this job helping to supplement our investments over the next several years.

"I continue to do psychic readings over the telephone and at psychic fairs. I've done over 200 readings without any advertising—just word of mouth. I also continue to get very clear warnings on the stocks I own. My MBA and financial background make it hard to disengage my logical mind and sell the stock I've researched so hard."

# Teaching as a Career Change

How many times do we say or hear a friend say, "I'd like to teach when I retire"? Colleges and universities are inundated with employment applications from would-be instructors in the 50-plus

---

## SUGGESTED READING

### Consulting
- *How to Success as an Independent Consultant,* 4th edition, by Herbert Holtz and David Zahn (Wiley, 2004).
- *Getting Started in Consulting,* 2nd edition, by Alan Weiss (Wiley, 2003).

### Franchising
- *Franchising: Pathway to Wealth,* by Stephen Spinelli, Sue Burley, and Robert Rosenberg (Financial Times Prentice-Hall, 2003).
- *Franchising from the Inside Out,* by Ed Teixlira (Xlibris, 2005).

### Owning Your Own Business
- *Starting on a Shoestring,* by Arnold Goldstein (Adams Media, 2002).

- *The Entrepreneur and Small Business Problem Solver,* by William Cohen (Wiley, 2006).
- *Starting Your Own Business,* by Rieva Lesonsky (Entrepreneur Press, 2004)
- *The Complete E-Commerce Book: Design, Build and Maintain a Successful Web-Based Business,* by Janice Reynolds (CMP Books, 2004).

### Working at Home
- *Best Home Businesses for People 50+,* by Paul and Sarah Edwards (Tarcher/Putnam, 2004).
- *The Work at Home Sourcebook,* 9th edition, by Lynie Arden (Live Oak Press, 2005)
- *101 Best Home-Based Businesses for Women,* 3rd edition, by Priscilla Huff (Three Rivers Press, 2002).

**Forty-seven states plus the District of Columbia have implemented alternative teacher-certification programs to quicken the transition.**

set. They, like the corporate world, have few openings as they reduce the size of their faculties. Employment opportunities differ in elementary schools and high schools. Perhaps they might be interested in a chemist as a science teacher or an editor to teach English composition. Practical as it sounds, the concept never really flourished, even with the acknowledgement of a chronic teacher shortage.

A few years ago, educational leaders reasoned that the entry of midlife to later-life career changers into education could offset that shortage of classroom teachers. A number of colleges developed teacher-training programs to attract to the classroom early military and corporate retirees, particularly those with engineering and scientific skills.

More than lip service is needed to encourage early retirees and boomers in their early-to-mid-50s to become teachers. The IBM-sponsored Transition to Teaching program is open to about 100 IBM employees with science, math, and related workplace experience. Prior to making the changeover from the workplace to the classroom, these employees will take academic courses to meet state certification, and they'll be given up to three months' paid leave to do student teaching in a classroom.

As teacher trainees, they'll be reimbursed a maximum of $15,000 to cover classroom and related academic expenses.

The National Center for Education Information (NCEI, *www.ncei.com*) reports that 47 states plus the District of Columbia have implemented alternative teacher-certification programs to quicken the transition. Compare this with the 8 states that offered these programs 20 years ago. To date, more than 250,000 teachers have been licensed this way, says Emily Feistritzer, NCEI's president. California, New Jersey, and Texas lead the way with aggressive alternate certification programs. Approximately 18 percent of the new hires in California enter teaching via alternative routes; nearly one-half in Texas and about 24 percent in New Jersey. Almost 35,000 individuals are entering teaching nationwide through alternative teacher-certification routes each year, NCEI notes. Each state has a department of education and a Web site that lists specific information on public school accreditation. Dr. Feistritzer, who has surveyed what has taken place in alternative teacher certification since 1983, points out that "alternative teacher-certification routes provide opportunities for people from various educational backgrounds and walks of life to become teachers. They open doors to teaching for persons from non-traditional backgrounds, including people transitioning from other careers or from the military, liberal arts graduates, and early retirees."

Teaching opportunities are more readily available for the 50-plus set in independent schools where state licensing and accreditation are not required, and prior work and professional credentials are often accepted in lieu of teaching experience. What's more, the independent schools, unlike most public schools, can set salaries for entry-level teachers based on past work experience. For more information, contact the National Association of Independent Schools *(www.nais-schools.org)*.

> **For nearly 20 years, he worked evenings and weekends on first one, then two newsletters dealing with imaging technology.**

## HE GOT A GOOD HEAD START
### Mitch Badler
*Corporate Public Relations Executive
Turned Newsletter Publisher*

Long before the reality of downsizing dawned on most managers, Mitchell Badler was playing "what if" games. What would happen if he lost his job as a corporate public relations executive with Eastern Airlines or, later, with Amax, a mining and energy conglomerate? Mitch's newsletter-publishing sideline was his cushion. For nearly 20 years, he worked evenings and weekends on first one, then two newsletters dealing with imaging technology. How Mitch handled his dual career could serve as a model for people age 50-plus that are anticipating the possibility of downsizing and plotting their next move. Little did Mitch realize that he was creating the base for a retirement career.

"It began for several reasons," said Mitch. "To see if I could make money, to keep my hand in editorial work since my PR responsibilities were becoming increasingly more managerial, to have a possible fallback because I instinctively distrusted the corporate world, and for something to do if and when I ultimately 'retired' from the corporate world. Looking back, it worked on all four counts."

Mitch started to hedge as far back as 1969 when he launched the *Microfilm Newsletter* as a part-time activity. He learned about the microfilming industry earlier in his career as the editor of several photography trade magazines.

At the time, Mitch was working as a public relations writer for Eastern Airlines.

Even though his career had proceeded steadily uphill, Mitch had good reason to distrust corporate employment. Prior to Eastern Airlines, he had worked four years for Citibank editing the bank's publications. "When I was at Citibank in the mid- to late 1960s, I got caught in a power struggle between two executives competing to be CEO." His boss straddled the fence during this succession fight. Realizing that the new head of public relations would reorganize the department, Mitch left before it all happened. He joined Eastern Airlines and stayed with the company until it relocated to Miami.

Mitch then was hired by Amax and a few years later was named its director of public relations. In the 1980s, Amax suffered a reversal in fortunes and lost $2 billion in three years. Heads rolled, but Mitch kept his job. In 1991, he left Amax after it was acquired by another mining company. He retained a lawyer and negotiated a favorable severance package in the form of a one-time payout along with lifetime health care benefits.

Other executives might have looked for another corporate job but not Mitch. "I decided that enough was enough. No more corporate jobs; I didn't need that anymore." Neither did Mitch need to retire. He held some valuable trump cards.

Throughout his corporate career, *Microfilm News-letter* "went its merry way" as a sideline endeavor. In the early days, it was strictly part-time for Mitch and an assistant, another moonlighter, who handled circulation. After a few years, Mitch hired a full-time office administrator while he continued to write and edit the newsletter.

As a part-time editor and publisher for more than 20 years, Mitch's life was hectic. "My routine until I left Amax was to work on the newsletter at least one full day each weekend and most evenings." His one-newsletter company grew. He introduced a biannual industry directory. He started, and then dropped, two other newsletters, and in the late 1980s, he spun off *Imaging Technology Report,* previously a supplement in *Microfilm Newsletter,* as a separate monthly. The newsletters were Mitch's long-term security blanket, a way to control his destiny. It was employment that he totally controlled.

Newsletter publishing rarely conflicted with his corporate life. He spent vacations at microfilm industry trade shows. There were few problems with either Eastern Airlines or Amax because the subject of the newsletters did not conflict with his line of work at either company.

When he left Eastern Airlines, Mitch briefly considered becoming a full-time editor and publisher, but the income from newsletter publishing at that time wasn't sufficient to support his family. It did, however, produce enough supplementary money to send his children through college and graduate school.

With the corporate workplace behind him after he left Amax, Mitch now had the time to work as editor and publisher five days a week. His staff consisted of a full-time office manager, a part-time circulation manager, and freelance editorial correspondents. Compared with his former schedule, Mitch notes, "It was like being on a part-time holiday. I actually had

> **"My employer never owned me on a full-time basis. Above all, publishing (the newsletter) did not depend on the whims of other people."**

time to watch TV at night. I'd get to work about 10 in the morning and home about 6." He supplemented his newsletter income by tapping his investment portfolio so his lifestyle didn't change after leaving Amax.

Looking back at his dual corporate and publishing career, Mitch knows that the relationship, though complex, gave him career options. "My employer never owned me on a full-time basis. Above all, publishing (the newsletter) did not depend on the whims of other people."

As he got older, publishing newsletters furnished still another benefit. "I never considered retirement. I'm not a golfer. I wanted to keep my hands in something useful."

In 2000, Mitch began to back down a bit from work. "I decided that I no longer wanted the responsibility for day-to-day circulation drives, advertising sales, and maintenance of subscriber lists."

Two years later, Mitch sold *Micrographics & Hybrid Newsletter* to Micrographics Marketing, Ltd., in England. "To date, the sale has worked out very well. Besides paying me the sale price, the company retained me as the North American editor. They merged it with their U.K. publication, and created an international English-language publication that took on the nickname of my old newsletter, 'The Green Sheet.'" I contribute a monthly recap of what's happening in the U.S., and cover two big trade shows a year. I'm only doing editorial work, spending about one-third to one-half the time I did before, and getting what I feel is a fair fee."

---

## DOES BUSINESS IN THE DESERT
### Al Croft
#### *Public Relations Executive Turned Industry Consultant*

For decades, Al Croft read *Arizona Highways* and dreamed of someday living in the Southwest. The dream began to become reality when Al and his wife, Irene, bought a second home in Sedona, Arizona, about 110 miles north of Phoenix. Though they initially rented it. Al mused that someday it would be their full-time residence and the site of his home office. He put the next phase of his plan into effect, somewhat unexpectedly, the next year.

At 61, he left his job as a senior executive in the Chicago offices of one of the nation's larger public relations firms following what Al describes as a "difference of opinion" with some of the firm's managers. A 25-year veteran of the public relations agency business, Al had already decided to use his agency management skills to start his own consultancy, one that focused on ways to better operate and manage public relations firms.

The day after he left his job, Al invested his severance package in office equipment and direct-mailing costs to launch his consultancy. His objectives, then and now, were to offer a range of management services to public relations firms of all sizes, work at his own pace, and, above all, live and work in Sedona. Being familiar with PR agency management and marketing practices, he felt confident that there was a ready market for his niche specialty.

The Crofts waited four years, long enough for their daughter to graduate from college, before they moved to Sedona. By then, Al's consultancy was well established. Sedona became their permanent residence and the headquarters of A.C. Croft & Associates.

Sedona, a community of approximately 15,000 people, is a tourist haven, drawing more than four million visitors annually. The mountain landscape is the prime attraction. A number of other small consulting firms in other fields call Sedona home for reasons similar to the Crofts. Most of these consultants find that they can carry on their work as easily in Arizona as in a metropolitan center.

The area is hardly isolated in the computer age. Computers and telecommunications have eliminated geographic isolation, and overnight delivery services

**The nature of Al's work has changed dramatically from his days as a PR agency executive.**

are omnipresent. "On a trip to Flagstaff, 50 miles away, I counted nine United Parcel Service trucks making early-morning business deliveries along the route," says Al. His clients, scattered throughout the United States and Canada, can be readily serviced through personal visits, e-mail, fax, and telephone. In reality, Al finds that e-mail has almost supplanted the telephone for much of his direct contact.

No formidable snags occurred in moving from Chicago to rural Arizona, and Al has found many pluses. "Clients like to take a few days off from their offices and meet with me in a leisurely fashion in Sedona. Some come from as far as Washington, D.C.

The nature of Al's work has changed dramatically from his days as a PR agency executive. "I don't do public relations for companies. I counsel the principals of public relations firms, represent a buyer or seller in an acquisition, conduct in-house account-management seminars, and produce a monthly newsletter. Everything I do is geared to help agencies market their services and manage their operations more effectively."

Marketing is critical to building his client base. Toward that end, Al actively promotes his business with a newsletter on management strategies for PR firms. Al also sponsors the Sedona Roundtable, an annual three-day management workshop for the principals of public relations agencies. His 1996 book, *Managing a Public Relations Firm for Growth and Profit* (Haworth Press) was updated with a second edition in 2006.

Being a niche specialist has certain advantages. He can bill clients up to $350 an hour. And, of course, because he is working at home, his overhead is minimal. Irene, who has a sales and marketing background, handles the administration of the Sedona Roundtable.

Even with his good cash flow, Al had to make some adjustments when he became self-employed. "After 35 years of regular paychecks and 18 years as an independent consultant, I'm still not used to not knowing exactly what my income is going to be for the next month, or from year to year."

By corporate standards, Al might appear to be semi-retired. "I work as hard as I want to, traveling outside the area two to three times a month. I make almost as much money as I did in the agency business, but I also play tennis a few times a week. The most important thing is that it keeps my brain active. I couldn't imagine being retired, and I'm not the volunteer type. Why retire, when I like what I'm doing and I'm making money at it? I'm not ready to turn my brain off."

While Sedona has a reputation as a retirees' haven, Al points out that he's not alone in pursuing an active lifestyle. "One of my tennis partners is an 83-year-old plumber. After two hours of doubles, he goes back to work."

---

## A NATURAL SEGUE

### Susan Weinberger

*Makes Transition from Administrator to Consultant*

To Susan Weinberger, retiring was hardly a traumatic experience. She changed the locale of her office and continued to work full-time as a mentoring specialist. But this time, instead of working as an administrator with the Norwalk, Connecticut, school system, Susan would head her own firm, the Mentor Consulting Group. As an independent consultant developing partnerships to support school mentoring programs, Susan could spread her enthusiasm and experience.

Susan's firm has received contracts from Allstate, the office of Juvenile Justice and Delinquency in the U.S. Justice Department, and the Ministry of Education in Bermuda, among others. One program brings together graduate students at Arizona State University in Tempe and school children on Indian reservations; another involves linking the Canon City, Colorado, district attorney's office with teenagers who are on probation.

Susan travels at least three days a week to train, consult, and speak at conferences. A trip might include

**As an independent consultant developing partnerships to support school mentoring programs, Susan could spread her enthusiasm and experience.**

spending a day training educators on mentoring techniques in the Houston (Texas) Independent School District or two weeks doing a media tour in support of the mentoring programs sponsored by Big Brothers/ Big Sisters of Canada.

As an experienced classroom teacher, Susan still enjoys working one-on-one with children. Every Friday she mentors a student for one hour at the Silvermine Elementary School. He was in the second grade when Susan started with him two years ago. When she's away on a business trip, she faxes him things that he can consider. This work helps keep Susan on the cutting edge of mentoring by practicing what she preaches.

Raised in Brookline, Massachusetts, Susan majored in modern languages at Carnegie-Mellon University; met and married Norman, then a premed student; taught high school Spanish while Norman went to medical school; and moved to Norwalk when he completed pediatric training and went into private practice.

Thirteen years and two children later, Susan returned to the classroom as a Spanish teacher. She became coordinator of bilingual and English as a Second Language programs in the Norwalk school system. "In 1983, I got interested in a new concept in school mentoring and the formation of partnerships to support it. The idea was to get local businesses to let employees spend one hour a week mentoring kids in the Norwalk schools."

Over the next 15 years, Susan, who by now had received a master's degree in elementary and bilingual education from Manhattanville College and a doctorate in educational administration from the University of Bridgeport, had built a local network of businesses who provided mentors for Norwalk school children. She was ready for the next step after receiving national recognition. In 1995, she renegotiated her Norwalk contract, which enabled her to spend 25 percent of her time on projects not associated with Norwalk.

Three years later, Susan was ready to leave the Norwalk system and retire with a pension based on 23 years of service. Her objective as a consultant was to share her mentoring knowledge and know-how with other schools, companies, and governmental agencies. "When I asked my husband whether I could go into business, he said, 'Seize the opportunity.'"

Connecticut's governor, John Roland, requested that Susan devote one-quarter of her time to the state's mentoring partnership program. The assignment helped to launch her business.

Consulting has paid off in many ways. In Susan's first year as a full-time consultant, she earned more money than she did as a school administrator. As a mentoring proponent, Susan's schedule is often frenetic with trips to Singapore to address the first Youth Conference on Mentoring; or to discuss mentoring with teachers assigned to Defense Department schools in Spain, Germany, Italy, and the United Kingdom; or to set up mentoring programs on native American reservations in six western and north central states.

Susan's advocacy on behalf of mentoring is infectious. Her son, whom she describes as an entrepreneur, and her daughter, a graphics designer, are also mentors.

> **In Susan's first year as a full-time consultant, she earned more money than she did as a school administrator.**

## WORKS SOLO IN FAMILY LAW
### Daniel Hill
#### *Professor Gives Up Tenured Post for Law School*

At 47, Daniel Hill had no plans to retire. A tenured professor in health administration at the University of Alabama's Birmingham campus, Dan could have easily waited another 10 years. By then, he would have accumulated a total of 27 years of college teaching in Alabama and previously at Pennsylvania State University.

Yet Dan, who is married and has twin daughters, did not want to become a victim of what he calls academic malaise, a condition experienced by many professors who get in a rut years before they retire but linger on solely to increase the size of their pensions. "I felt that I had gone as far I could go as a teacher and researcher. I wanted to be more productive."

**"I don't like to look back at things. I wanted a fresh start in a different field."**

Dan decided to make his career change while age was still in his favor.

A sabbatical is the usual approach taken by academics who need to recharge their energies. This approach didn't meet Dan's need to do something different and do it now. He decided on law school—a new idea to him and not the fulfillment of a lifelong dream. "Looking back, I had negative feelings about being a lawyer when I was a youngster."

Up to then, Dan's academic career had been on course. After graduating from Ohio University, where his father was a professor, Dan got his doctorate from Purdue University in 1971. The topic of his dissertation was "An Economic Analysis of Health Insurance with Special Reference to Blue Cross." The thesis formed the groundwork for his academic career at Penn State and the University of Alabama at Birmingham, and for his appointment to state, national, and international health administration study groups.

Before deciding to switch careers, Dan talked with his wife, Ellen, who he says was nervous yet supportive; his sister, Charlotte, a former social worker who had already made a midlife career change into law; a number of lawyers; and his daughters. The twins were primarily concerned over whether the family would have sufficient money to pay for their college educations.

Dan decided against going to Alabama's law school, located about 50 miles from his home. "It would have been a much simpler decision and less costly, but I wasn't sure where I wanted to practice. I turned down a few scholarships and went to the University of North Carolina Law School, which had more of a national reputation than Alabama. Looking ahead, Chapel Hill was the type of place where Ellen and I wanted to live." The Hills sold their house in Birmingham. They used the proceeds to pay for the move and to help pay for law school. Ellen, who had already finished two-thirds of the requirements for an MBA degree, was hired by UNC Law School's career placement office. Three years later, Dan graduated with honors at age 50 as the oldest member of his class.

Dan was now looking for a job. Finding one would have been simpler if he had opted to fuse his knowledge of health care and law into a hybrid career. He could have followed a logical career path into health administrative law with a law firm or health care facility. He decided against that route. "I could have gone back to Birmingham and joined the largest law firm in the state, but it would have involved health law, which I felt was just another type of corporate law. Anyway, I don't like to look back at things. I wanted a fresh start in a different field."

As a teacher, Dan had enjoyed dealing with students, and that experience provided a natural bridge into family law, a specialty that calls for people skills. This interest led him to a small Durham law firm, Hayes Hoffler & Associates, where he was "of counsel." Six years later, he became a solo practitioner although he kept his offices in the Hayes Hoffler suite. His specialty within family law has evolved into what he describes as collaborative family law and mediation.

In his mid-60s, Dan, unlike many of his former faculty colleagues who are preparing for retirement, has no target date for retirement. Being self-employed, he can practice as long as he wants. Dan already receives a pension from the University of Alabama and is covered by its medical plan.

"Because I was connected to the medical center at Alabama, I was paid more than professors on the main campus in Tuscaloosa. I didn't go to law school to make more money but to do something different and to avoid getting into a rut."

**In his mid-60s, Dan, unlike many of his former faculty colleagues who are preparing for retirement, has no target date for retirement.**

## A NEW TWIST ON FINANCIAL SERVICES
### Robert Southerland
#### *Retirement Not on His Agenda*

Bob Southerland's career over 40 years has seesawed between being an employed bank executive and managing his own financial services company. It's a field

**With self-employment still a primary goal, Bob made a modified career change within the financial services field.**

he knows intimately and one that is the thrust of his postretirement career.

As they say here in North Carolina, Bob is "a Tarheel born and a Tarheel bred." Born in Rocky Mount, he deferred going to the University of North Carolina in Chapel Hill for several years. "I didn't think at the time that I was ready for college. I took a job with Wachovia Bank in Raleigh as an accounting clerk at $231 a month. Faye and I got married; I was 19."

Three years later, Bob was ready to go to college. Unlike most of his classmates, he was married and, by then, a father. Instead of living in Chapel Hill, he commuted 35 miles each way from Raleigh to Chapel Hill, receiving a degree in industrial relations in three years.

It was the mid-1960s. The Vietnam War was on the top burner. Bob was safe in terms of the draft. "I was too young for Korea and too old for Vietnam." Bob returned to Wachovia. The first three years he handled mortgage loans, followed by another seven years in commercial loans.

It was time for Bob to make an earlier career goal a reality and become president of his own bank, which was easier said than done. It meant developing a business plan, raising capital, and recruiting a board of directors. At 34, Bob started the Carolina Federal Savings & Loan Association. Eight years later, his S&L with $70 million in assets was sold.

With self-employment still a primary goal, Bob made a modified career change within the financial services field. He went into real estate investments as the founder and president of Realty Capital Investments. By 1990, it was necessary for him to switch careers once again as a result of changes in the Tax Reform Act of 1986, legislation that Bob felt was restricting the growth of firms like his.

Bob started the Southeastern Financial Group, a specialist in retirement and estate planning. It was a way to continue to be an independent operator. Seven years later, Wachovia, his employer 22 years earlier, asked him to return to the bank as a senior vice president heading retirement estate and estate plan programs in its Raleigh office.

It seems that Bob's career runs in seven- to ten-year cycles. In 2004, Bob retired from Wachovia. Since rejoining Wachovia, he had found corporate employment not as stimulating the second time around. His exit package included a small pension along with retirement health coverage. Fortunately, he was not required to sign a noncompete clause. Thus, Bob's career options were open in areas akin to his Wachovia work.

"I had no plans for full-time retirement, then and now." Like so many people who have operated their own businesses, Bob's skills were applicable to working on his own in financial services. He started Risk Management and Benefit Services, once again piggybacking on his experience in estate planning and related areas, such as life, long-term care, and disability insurance.

The advantages of a computerized home office fits in with his plan to work three days a week. "I estimate that I work between 15 and 20 hours. I'd like to increase this since I'd want to work closer to full-time since I'm not ready to retire, and I like to work as long as I can. It's a formula that keeps me busy, involved, making money, and using my business skills. More tennis and golf are not the answer."

> **Like so many people who have operated their own businesses, Bob's skills were applicable to working on his own in financial services.**

## LEAVES THE BIG CITY FOR SMALL TOWN
### Gregory Marotz
#### *Gives Up Wall Street for B&B Inn*

Greg Marotz knows how to switch gears. He's been a minor league professional baseball pitcher, a sales executive with several small manufacturing companies, and an institutional funds sales manager for a large investment banking firm.

Yet he gave up that career in his mid-50s and moved from a New York City apartment to Hamilton, New York, a town 200 miles to the north and the home of Colgate University. Where some contemporaries might have taken early retirement, Greg was

**Where some contemporaries might have taken early retirement, Greg was embarking on a career with a different twist and new demands.**

embarking on a career with a different twist and new demands. Greg is originally from the Chicago suburbs. As a teenager, he excelled in baseball. His college goal was a business career, not professional baseball. Baseball, however, was a serious interest, sufficient enough that he signed a contract while at Colgate with the Pittsburgh Pirates.

The contract meant that he lost his standing as an amateur athlete. He was no longer eligible to play college baseball. His professional career took place during the late spring and summer months. While a Colgate student, he played for the Salem (Virginia) Rebels and the Gastonia (North Carolina) Pirates. Come September, he returned to college. It was hardly a big money maker. "I got a signing bonus of $8,000 plus another $9,000, which covered two years of college expenses."

He got married three days after graduation. "I married Christy Wolff in 1967; we've been sweethearts since the first grade. Three or four days after we were married, I went on a road trip with the Raleigh team. It was our honeymoon."

Greg's major league dream soon came to an end. He returned to Chicago and worked in sales-related jobs over the next ten years with three small manufacturers of industrial products. Although he had completed about 60 percent of the class work as an evening student at the University of Chicago business school, he dropped out. "I had three responsibilities: family, career, and business school. Business school became a casualty."

He left the third of the family-owned businesses he had worked for and took a job with Merrill Lynch. It ran what was considered at the time to be the finest training program for stockbrokers. A year later, a college classmate lured him to Lehman Brothers

Greg spent the next 17 years with three different Lehman offices, starting in the Chicago office, then a position in Boston, which culminated in a transfer to the New York headquarters as a senior vice president and sales director for several institutional funds.

In 1994, Greg and Christy bought an early 19th century farmhouse in Hamilton on three acres abutting Colgate's golf course. Adjacent to the two-bedroom farmhouse is a 1950s-era three-bedroom house they intended to use as a guesthouse where their five daughters and visiting friends could stay. Little did they realize that this vacation home and annex would become their full-time home as well as the site of a business venture.

"In 1996, I joined Intervest Holdings, which was involved in electronic securities trading. I left two years later. I was trying to get financial support to start a consulting company. The deal was derailed due to a merger of one of my supporters."

With four of their daughters college graduates and no longer living at home, the Marotzs left New York City and moved to Hamilton. They had no hesitation about leaving their Battery Park apartment for rural Hamilton.

Greg was retained as a consultant with Vantine Imaging, a Hamilton-based company and a leading niche producer of composite photos for college fraternities and sororities, and member organizations. He left Vantine after five years as executive vice president.

Interestingly, Greg was working once again in a familiar corporate environment. "In many ways, Vantine was a flashback to my work at Northern Screw (one of his Chicago employers) where there was similar father-to-son baton passing taking place. Both companies were 'big' in customer services and both interested in growing the business."

The farm that started out as a vacation retreat and then a year-round residence was about to change again. A neighbor, who ran a B&B, called in a panic. She had overbooked reservations. She asked whether the Marotzs would take one of her extra guests. "We said yes, got the customer's payment, and decided that we liked putting the money in the bank." Thus the Guest House at Weathervane Farm was born.

Neither Christy nor Greg had inn experience. "We never took a course in how to run a B&B. We

**The B&B pays many overhead expenses— debt service, real estate taxes, and insurance— for the entire property.**

travel a lot by car. We like to stay at good places. We had observed how they ran."

Though they have only three guest rooms, Greg admits it's hard work. "You're constantly on duty attending to a guest's needs. Christy cleans the rooms and does the breakfast baking. I make the other breakfast dishes and maintain the property."

The inn has never been a big moneymaker. That's not a vital factor. Greg has a comfortable investment income from his years at Lehman Brothers. The B&B pays many overhead expenses—debt service, real estate taxes, and insurance—for the entire property.

Business comes by word of mouth, primarily from Colgate visitors. In January 2005, the inn added a Web site *(www.weathervane.com).* Until then, Greg or Christy would spend at least ten minutes on the telephone describing the inn and its services. The Web site helps presell the inn. Now, people see the rooms on the Web. They select the room and know the cost."

Greg is already considering the next move. Still too young to retire, he's considering whether to add rooms to the present inn or open another one. As for reserving a room, Greg says that rooms are already booked for graduation weekends through 2009."

## OPENS ACCOUNTING FIRM IN HER MID-50S
### Carolyn Dalby
#### *Why Call It Quits?*

In their mid-50s when so many Americans are considering retiring or, in some instances, actually retiring, Carolyn Dalby was moving in another direction. She became her own boss.

Born toward the end of World War II in Brookfield, a western suburb of Chicago, Carolyn's career goal, like so many women of her generation, was to teach school. After a few years at Drake University in Des Moines, Iowa, she left college and married Tom. She became a stay-at-home mother and did not work while Tom's banking career took the Dalbys and their two children on a round of corporate relocations to Park Forest, Illinois (a Chicago suburb), Tulsa, Oklahoma, and Little Rock, Arkansas.

Her future career started to incubate as a University of Tulsa student. "I was getting a science degree, but I was also taking philosophy, history, and other non–career path courses. A friend of ours was chair of the accounting department, and he said when I got done broadening my horizons, I should come and learn how to do something practical.

"I started accounting while finishing the undergraduate degree. My goal was to get a degree. I loved botany and the closest I could get to that was biology. There is not much one can do with a BS in biology except fill test tubes. To get an interesting job in science means additional degrees, and I was not that motivated. The idea of accounting just clicked.

"After dealing with sciences, becoming an accountant was easy. I got flextime jobs as a part-time bookkeeper doing financial work. It allowed me to be an active mom, still travel, and play golf. My ambition wasn't too strong. One day I woke up. It was time to start rowing my own boat."

Carolyn's workplace commitment continued to change when she and Tom moved in 1990 to Durham. The following year she was certified as a public accountant. As a CPA, she worked for several smaller accounting firms.

Her last staff position was made to order. It is a normal practice for staffers to sign noncompete clauses, which state that the firm's clients are not portable. Leave the firm, and clients remain with the firm. Not so with Carolyn. Her boss had no such ruling, a situation that encouraged Carolyn to strike out on her own in 1999.

Compared with her friends who worked for large companies, she found going into business less of a gamble. Friends her age or younger were losing their jobs when their companies downsized or were acquired.

"Some friends couldn't believe I would go out on my own. I had up to then never worked for myself, but I learned what to do and what not to do by working for others." Tom, who worked for an investment firm, cheered her decision.

It was initially a one-person office. When it became financially feasible, she hired an administrative assistant. Thanks to computers, Carolyn, like so many entrepreneurs and professionals, can operate effectively in her small office setup.

Though officially in business about six years, she views her firm like a college sophomore rather than like a senior. Others her age have been working since their 20s. Thirty or 40 years later, they're either retired or looking for new opportunities. Not so for Carolyn, who's only been self-employed for a handful of years.

"I'm now developing a time line for the next five to six years. By then, I might cut back. Up to then it's going to be business as usual. Each client has a different challenge. Each faces different and changing issues."

In looking back on her past lifestyle, Carolyn finds that it's a far cry from her earlier days in school when a typical report card said that she could do better. "I now have a stake in the ground. Anyway, as an exaggerated late bloomer, I am planning to peak the day before I die."

---

## POINTS TO REMEMBER

- **The business-as-usual concept no longer applies** to the job market.
- **Be mentally, physically, and financially ready** to start a business.
- **Franchising has its advantages** as well as its pitfalls.
- **Thorough homework is important** for entrepreneurial hopefuls.
- **Running a successful consultancy requires a different set of work skills,** especially the ability to get out and hustle the work.
- **Operating from a home office calls for different work habits.**
- **Opportunities exist** by changing careers.

# Escaping from Retirement

*"Work is a basic experience of life. It is too important and too valuable to be forfeited to the young."*
—Robert S. Menchins in *New Opportunities for Older Americans*

**F**or some of us, retirement can't come soon enough, but when it does, often it isn't what we expected. Consider my friend, who retired at age 61 and moved to a rented apartment in Florida. He went to the swimming pool and was greeted by one of his new neighbors: "Welcome to God's waiting room." That capped his impression of his new life. Disillusioned, he returned to New York the following day and asked for and got his old job back. He escaped from retirement.

Early retirees and others who thought their working days were over are changing their tune. They are finding ways to go back to work, either as their sole pursuit or as one part of their retirement portfolio.

This is hardly a surprise to Dr. Letitia T. Chamberlain, who, until recently, directed New York University's Center for Career, Education, and Life Planning. She finds that it normally takes people at least two to three years to settle down into a retirement lifestyle. Retirees want to stay productive and, above all, be active. Some in the 50-plus set want to return to the workplace to fill an income shortfall between realistic cost-of-living expenses and their retirement income. But many others miss the challenge of the workplace and its camaraderie, or they want to maintain their technical and professional skills. As Dr. Chamberlain observes, there are many people who are not satisfied working as volunteers or hobbyists.

Employment is what they knew and what they like. Paid work is their antidote to a "retirement lifestyle."

Robert Mallernee, a managing director of U.S. Trust Company, sees retirement issues from the vantage point of representing folks with seven-figure portfolios. Oftentimes, he says, they wish that they were still working. Having had high-level corporate or professional positions, they cannot, because of their egos, take a lesser type of job.

From the American Bar Association, I learned of one lawyer who wants to avoid the pitfalls faced by the people such as those that Bob Mallernee describes. The lawyer in question (who shall remain nameless) still practices with the midsized firm that he founded, a specialist in business and commercial real estate law. He no longer works full-time, but he continues to manage several large corporate accounts. Of retirement age, he's married to a former member of the state legislature who is about the same age. They plan to live in the Virgin Islands, and he's determined to remain professionally active. In preparation, he's taking the Virgin Islands bar exam so he's licensed to practice law on a limited basis once they relocate.

## The Sidelines Weren't for Him

Dr. Lawrence Walker was a downright miserable spectator. When Larry retired in 1991 as superintendent of schools in a rural North Carolina county, he learned some real-life lessons about early retirement. Following retirement, he managed a statewide political campaign for a friend. His friend lost the election, and Larry was out of work.

Fortunately, Larry's expenses were pretty well controlled. He and his wife, Mary, a nurse, owned their home in Yanceyville, a town of 2,000 and the county seat of Caswell County. Too young to collect Social Security benefits, Larry had a pension, health care benefits, and savings. A few years before retiring, he bought a convenience store as an investment. He worked there a few hours each day, had others manage it, and subsequently sold it. But Larry's retirement would soon turn into a litany of disappointments.

"I got tired of tending my garden. Working in the store full-time was not for me. My golf is miserable, so it made me feel even more miserable. My hobbies—collecting antique fountain pens and old American coins—are not the type of activities that keep you too busy. Neighbors and friends hearing that I retired thought I left due to illness. Their concerns made me concerned. I'm an optimist but I got down.

"I missed the camaraderie of school work. I found that I was starting to lose education and government contacts. It doesn't take too long to be out of the loop, and once you are out of it, it's hard to get back in.

"I also did some consulting, but it's not the same as a full-time job. I needed a more solid base of operation."

Larry attended a meeting of retired school superintendents and returned home depressed. Mary said, "You don't belong in that group yet."

Less than two years after retiring and as a result of networking among fellow educators and government officials, Larry was activated as executive director of the Central Carolina Consortium, one of seven regional groups established in the state to link schools at all levels with industry and business. To take the job, he had to temporarily forgo a pension based on 33 years of service as a North Carolina educator. The state forbids "double dipping" for state employees who take another state job.

When the consortium assignment ended in the late 1990s, Larry was named executive director of the Carolina Regional Education Service Alliance, which serves 290,000 students in 16 school systems and one institution for hearing-impaired children. He spends about 50 percent of his time with the alliance and the balance with his educational consultancy, Technical Services Associates. And, most important, the double-dipping restriction no longer applies, so he receives a state pension and health care coverage.

> **"I found that I was starting to lose education and government contacts. It doesn't take too long to be out of the loop, and once you are out of it, it's hard to get back in."**

---

### RULES FOR GOING BACK

- Don't think like a "pampered corporate baby."
- Applicants still need to convince a company that it should hire a 62-year-old.
- Don't expect to get a prestigious title.
- Be prepared to do hands-on work, even in a manager's job.
- Be prepared to accept less money than in past jobs.
- Above all, be flexible.

---

## Everyone Can't Be a CEO

Paul Rizzo retired from IBM in 1987. Two years earlier, he had been considered a prime candidate to become CEO. Passed over, he left to become dean of the business school at the University of North Carolina, from which he had graduated and had been a football star. In mid-1992, Rizzo retired from UNC. Within four months, he was summoned back to a troubled IBM on a full-time basis to help run the company as a "counselor and advisor" to then chairman John Akers. When Akers was ousted, Rizzo was promoted to vice chairman by the then new CEO, Louis Gerstener; Rizzo retired from IBM a second time at the end of 1994. And even then he didn't retire. Now, he's the board chairman and a partner in Franklin Street Partners, a North Carolina investment firm, as well as a member of several corporate boards.

Unfortunately, the mobility that permits an older, high-profile CEO to slide into another corporate job or become a director of one or several corporate boards does not readily apply to the typical 50-plus-set manager. And odds are stacked against most managers getting another high-paying job in corporate America.

There are some notable exceptions. As midlevel management jobs are abolished, it is ironic that people with hands-on technical, financial, and sales experience are in far greater demand than their immediate supervisors. To confuse matters even more, it is easier to place a 54-year-old downsized executive who has worked for four different companies over 27 years than someone who has worked for a single employer during the same period. Compared with a decade ago, says executive recruiter Randall Bye, employers now seek managers who have worked for several companies and have proved that they have the flexibility to adapt to different types of corporate cultures.

## A New Way of Doing Things

The situation may appear bleak, but it does not mean there is a total absence of job opportunities. The rules have changed and early retirees need to adapt to a new workplace environment. The job-search winners are those applicants who recognize a need for new tactics and have updated their game plan.

Outplacement consultant Temple Porter of the Raleigh Consulting Group *(www.tricoach.com)* advises clients to disregard old road maps in favor of nontraditional and alternative routes to the job market. "Clients need to show their 'unique leverage' in terms of reputation, special knowledge, and professional skills. Save your talent and energy for the important stuff; don't sweat the rest."

Avoid shooting yourself in the foot when trying to get a new job, says John Challenger of the outplacement firm Challenger, Gray & Christmas *(www.challengergray.com)*. He finds that job prospects for the 50-plus set rise when they follow a few simple rules:

- **Sell them on your expertise.**
- **Look and act young.**
- **Avoid looking dowdy at interviews.**
- **Address yourself to the employer's needs, not your own.**
- **Above all, do not announce personal timetables,** such as a desire to work for only four more years before retiring.

Job searches are changing, and the Internet is one reason. The 55-plus set, according to a Census Bureau *(www.census.gov)* report, looks for jobs on the Internet and searches job listings on career sites like Careerbuilder.com, Monster.com, and Brilliantpeople .com.

What's the alternative when an employer doesn't offer outplacement services? For some, it's Forty Plus *(www.40plus-dc.org)*, which operates in 20 cities and the District of Columbia. Forty Plus is not an employment agency but provides the road maps to new careers for managers and professionals age 40 and over. And don't be misled by the organization's name. A large proportion of the members are in their 50s and 60s. Membership in the Washington, D.C., chapter is limited to folks who earn at least $40,000 a year in either a management or professional job.

# Alternatives to Business as Usual

### Placing Retirees in New Jobs

The National Executive Service Corps, as noted in Chapter 4, has been reorganized. It is now the Executive Service Corps Affiliate Network *(www.escus.org)*,

---

### A RESUME TELLS A STORY

The resume for the 50-plus set is practically an art form.

- **The resume is a selling document.** Tell the reader what makes you unique. Simply put, what assets do you bring to the party?
- **Above all, give readers a fast career overview.** Stress what happened over the past 20 years. The rest is ancient history, and chances are the earlier jobs were stepping stones anyway.
- **A similar rule applies to education.** List the college degrees and, when possible, omit the graduation year.

---

though the metropolitan New York operation continues to be called NESC.

While its prime mission is management assistance to nonprofits, it also deals with retirees who have had a taste of retirement and want no more of it. Retirees seek jobs for different reasons. A need for additional income notwithstanding, one retiree noted that "after my retirement, I thought all of my knowledge would be locked up like concrete in the brain, never to be used again."

Like so many organizations dealing with retired executives and professionals who want to return to work, the agency has a backlog of several thousand resumes. Its focus is on filling nonprofit management positions. Paul Barrett, a senior vice president in the New York office and a former marketing executive, places the 50-plus set in nonprofit management jobs. They earn 25 percent to 50 percent less than comparable jobs in the corporate sector. In return, what most nonprofits receive is a seasoned manager at an affordable price.

In preparing candidates for nonprofit job interviews, Paul encourages them to think like nonprofit executives rather than corporate executives. He helps them to prepare resumes that show how their corporate financial, marketing, or computer experiences are transferable to a nonprofit agency. He finds that applicants, who have served on nonprofit boards or have been volunteers, often have an advantage because of their exposure to nonprofit operating procedures.

Jackie Reinhard lost her job as executive director of information technology for the College Board when it reorganized. At 53, she had no interest in retiring. "I went to search firms looking for a technology job, but I found very few openings, and the competition was fierce. While I wanted to make the transition into a director's position with a nonprofit, I didn't know how to go about it."

Paul encouraged Jackie to become a volunteer before she asked for a paid job. She hoped this exposure would lead to a job. The opportunity presented

---

### CLUE TO A WINNING INTERVIW

- **Act your age but don't overdo it.** Start by leaving the grandchildren's pictures and similar mementos at home.
- **Watch the narrative.** Avoid talking about the 1980s or even earlier business trends. These events might predate the interviewer's own date of birth.
- **This is not the time to tell "war stories"** about the old days.
- **Talk in present and future tense.** Emphasize recent achievements and goals.
- **Above all, be yourself.** The interviewer is well aware that you didn't graduate from college in 1990.

---

itself faster than she expected. Recognizing that Janet's skills were indeed transferable, Paul recommended her to the New York chapter of the Lateral Sclerosis Association, which works to benefit patients with ALS, also known as Lou Gehrig's disease. She was hired as executive director responsible for the New York chapter's day-to-day operations.

### The Part-Time Alternative

Make sure you know the differences between part-time and temporary work. The part-timer is a company employee, while the temporary worker may be an employee of a temporary agency. Part-timers, depending on the number of hours worked, may receive fringe benefits and may be eligible for paid vacations.

Some employees, particularly those who are nearing retirement age and whose skills are in demand, are switching from full-time to part-time employment as part of a phased retirement plan.

AARP (*www.aarp.org*) notes that "68 percent of workers ages 50 to 70 plan to work in retirement, and 57 percent expect to work in their 70s, 80s, or as long as they are able."

Not everyone is motivated or financially able to set up a business, buy a franchise, or start a consultancy.

Some boomers will negotiate with their employers to stay on the job in some capacity. This is a comparatively easy task when the worker has a skill in demand. For others, it's a return to the job market.

Accordingly, AARP launched its Workforce Initiative in early 2005 with 15 charter corporate members, including MetLife, Pitney Bowes, Borders, Walgreens, and Home Depot. "The tough part in fully evaluating the reasons people continue to work is that many are reluctant to indicate that they are working for the money," says Emily Allen, director of AARP's Workforce Initiative.

CVS, though not a part of AARP's program, hires and rehires retirees, with 16 percent of its workforce over age 55.

The Conference Board *(www.conference-board.org)*, a nonprofit research group, noted in *Managing the Mature Workforce* that "the maturing workforce is often seen as an issue to be dealt with instead of a great opportunity to be leveraged. Working in retirement, once considered an oxymoron, is the new reality." It also found that the retirement of mature workers represents a potential brain drain.

Escaping from retirement is also a reality as the result of technological advances. Tasks that until recently were restricted to the office can be done in a home office. The International Telework Association and Council *(www.workfromanywhere.org)* estimates that there are 24 million employed teleworkers.

## No Need to Be a Kelly Girl

Do you remember the "temps"? They were folks who came to your office to answer the phones, do copying, or perform some other necessary but often low-level chore when a regular staff member was ill or on vacation. The temp field has expanded and in many ways changed directions. Now there are executive temporaries who are politely referred to as interim managers. Kelly Services, employer of the temps that used to be known as Kelly Girls, has a professional and technical division.

**Because it's such a good opportunity for the employer to get to know the worker's skills, there's a growing trend toward converting temporary to full-time positions.**

Even with the growth in temporary employment services, temps account for less than 2 percent of the total workforce. About 2.6 million people work as temporary and contract workers, and they earn more than $12 an hour, the American Staffing Association (*www.staffingtoday.net*) points out. Workers with technical and other in-demand skills earn considerably more. Several years ago, the median average pay was $20 an hour for professional and technical contract workers. The U.S. Labor Department's Bureau of Labor Statistics (*www.bls.gov*) reports that 12 percent of workers ages 55 to 64 work as independent contractors, on-call workers, temporary agency workers, or for contract firms.

The temporary service field has benefited from downsizing, early retirement, and the trend to get retirement-age employees off the corporate books. As staffs are thinned, the corporate appetite for skilled managers and professionals hardly diminishes, resulting in interim-management firms that place managers and professionals in temporary jobs.

Still, finding an interim-management job is a long shot. The best candidate for a temporary job is the highly skilled professional or technician in a niche field that's in demand. The chances of getting a job as an interim executive are slim at any age. The ratio of applicants to job openings on file for people of all ages at the more than 100 firms that specialize in placing management and professional personnel is staggering, sometimes as high as 1,000 to 1. Dahl-Morrow International (*www.dahl-morrowintl.com*), a suburban Washington, D.C. specialist in the information systems and communications fields, has little difficulty attracting candidates to add to its database of more than 20,000 names. At Dahl-Morrow and most other interim-management firms, temporary assignments range from three months to one year.

Even with the low odds of success, retirees should not overlook the interim-management market, says Andy Steinem, one of the firm's principals. At Dahl-Morrow, about one-half of the interim-management

---

## SUGGESTED READING

- *Too Young to Retire—101 Ways to Start the Rest of Your Life*, by Marika and Howard Stone (Plume Book, 2004).
- *Occupational Handbook* from the U.S. Department of Labor (distributed by VGM Career Opportunities). Published in alternate years. Provides vital information on dozens of professional and management careers that you might never have considered.
- *Over-40 Job Search Guide*, by Gail Geary (Jist Works, 2005).
- *Switching Careers*, by Robert Otterbourg (Kiplinger Books, 2001).
- *What Color Is Your Parachute?* by Richard Bolles (Ten Speed Press, 2005). Since 1970, a perennial guide for job seekers of all ages.

---

assignments turn into full-time jobs. Because it's such a good opportunity for the employer to get to know the worker's skills, there's a growing trend toward converting temporary to full-time positions.

---

## SELLS NEW YORK CITY CONDOS AND CO-OPS
### Dorothy Arnsten
#### *School Psychologist Turned Real Estate Broker*

"Larry [her husband] and I do not like to hang out. I don't like going to lunch with the girls and I don't like shopping. We have lots of interests, but other than work, no other single activity can fill up a day," says Dorothy Arnsten.

When Dorothy retired several years ago as a psychologist with the New York City public school system, she took a retirement route normally not associated with someone with a doctorate degree and over 25 years of classroom and counseling experience. Like many retired psychologists, she could have concentrated on her private practice and enjoyed the income

**It didn't take much to convince her that in-depth research on behalf of clients helps to clinch a sale.**

from an ample pension. Dorothy, however, was looking for a different stimulant consistent with her attitude toward retirement.

Dorothy started to plan a career switch several years before she left the school system. Her husband, an accountant, also owns and manages some property. "Larry would give me papers to look at. He asked me to read and then sign them. I discovered that I was the general manager. When I asked about the title, Larry said, 'I work for you, sweetheart.'" This whetted her appetite to learn more about real estate.

She subsequently met Ileen Schoenfeld at a party and learned that Ileen, another former teacher, was selling New York City co-op and condo apartments. "The work interested me. Selling real estate would add something different in my life. I took a real estate course and was licensed by New York state." Real estate added a third dimension to an already busy lifestyle as a full-time school psychologist with a part-time private psychology practice.

Dorothy's big break came when Ileen had to go to Florida to visit her ailing mother. She asked Dorothy to be her proxy. In her absence, Dorothy sold two apartments. Ileen and Dorothy became partners. "It's a great relationship since I can work my own schedule, and we can spell each other on weekends and vacations."

While many retirees would be satisfied with a single postretirement job, earlier on in her postretirement career, Dorothy worked as both a full-time real estate broker and as a part-time psychologist. She limited her psychology practice to a few patients, all in short-term relationships. This, too, has changed. Dorothy no longer has a psychology practice. Her focus is totally on real estate sales.

As a broker, Dorothy brings strong research and computer skills to the workplace. She was introduced to computers in the early 1980s when she took several courses in conjunction with her doctorate studies. Computers provide a key research and marketing tool for real estate brokers. It didn't take much to convince her that in-depth research on behalf of clients helps to clinch a sale. From a home or office computer, Dorothy feeds information on clients' needs into the computer to generate lists of apartments or town houses that fit the clients' specifications. Her computerized listings are read by potential buyers in places as diverse as New York, Hong Kong, and London.

## ONE YEAR OF RELAXATION WAS ENOUGH
### Barbara Hallan
### *Returns Part-Time to a Nursing Job*

From the get-go, retirement didn't turn out exactly the way Barbara Hallan had anticipated. "When I retired, I thought I would have a great life with time for a cup of coffee and the crossword puzzle. I could do all the things I had put off when I worked—gardening, putting photos in albums, spending more time with my grandchildren, and going to Duke's fitness center." Her plans went slightly awry when she was assigned to a fitness program that met early in the morning, requiring her to rise early. Though fitness was important to Barbara, having a chance to relax and not having to adhere to a schedule was even more important. She dropped the fitness center.

And after only a year of retirement, Barbara Hallan was ready to return to work.

Barbara was a Depression baby. Her family lived in Newport News, Virginia, where her father worked in a shipbuilding yard and for the C&O Railroad. She recalls that money was short, and though she liked to draw, the family never had money for art lessons—a fact of her childhood that she still hopes to overcome.

After graduating from high school, Barbara attended a three-year nursing school program at a local hospital. After two years of work as a nurse, she attended an 18-month nurse anesthetist course at Washington University in St. Louis. As a nurse anesthetist, her salary would be two to three times more than that of the average floor nurse. Soon after completing that

**"I felt very fortunate to have a profession that I could return to after all that time and still love it."**

training and obtaining a job as a nurse anesthetist, Barbara married, moved to North Carolina, and worked as an anesthetist for three years.

But after bearing three children in 6 years, a nursing career became secondary in Barbara's life for the next 20 years. She returned to nursing in 1982, following the trauma of a divorce. "I took a 12-week, nursing-update program. I was too out-of-date to go back to work as a nurse anesthetist. I would have had to go through retraining since things had changed so much."

In her early 50s, Barbara became a floor nurse at the Duke Medical Center in Durham. "It was the first time I had done this type of nursing since finishing nursing school. I felt very fortunate to have a profession that I could return to after all that time and still love it." She moved to an assignment on the neurology floor, followed by one in the recovery room.

A family medical crisis forced Barbara to leave work in the recovery room and switch to another nursing specialty, the outpatient heart catheterization laboratory. Her mother had developed Alzheimer's, and Barbara's daughter, who had been living at home and helping with her grandmother, married and moved out. With no one available to care for her mother at night, Barbara could no longer alternate between day and night shifts. The heart catheterization lab met Barbara's need for a 9-to-5 job.

Barbara's decision to retire in 1995 was precipitated when Duke offered a package that would boost her 12 years of employment to more than 17 years for purposes of calculating retirement benefits. "Except for this reason, I would not have left, but I decided it was a good idea, because I didn't know what my life would be like over the next 5 years. Would I stay well? I had my mother to take care of.

"I had to retire to take advantage of Duke's plan. Because I wasn't expecting to leave at that time, I did little planning when I retired. When I left, it was with a mixture of joy, relief, and sadness, all at the same time."

One year later, Barbara relished returning to work in the catheterization lab. She had missed the discipline of nursing and medicine. While Barbara was at work, an attendant cared for her mother. The balance of the time, Barbara attended to her mother until her death in 1998. As a retiree, Barbara is limited in the number of hours she can work without affecting her Duke pension. With this arrangement, she could only work the equivalent of two-and-a-half days a week, or no more than 999 hours a year.

But working as a part-timer offered Barbara some needed tangible and personal benefits. Her pay was at the top of the salary range, and she said it was "good pocket money" to supplement her pension, Social Security, and savings.

"I feel more fortunate than many of my friends. Some of them have to do menial work when they want to work because they don't have a skill. My plan was to do nursing as long as my mind and body would hold out. When I leave, I want to go with a good record, so I won't work beyond that point. Then maybe I'll finally take art lessons. This was something I liked to do as a youngster."

Barbara retired for the second time from Duke Hospital in late December 2004, a month after turning 75. Interestingly, her tenure lasted a few years longer than some of the hospital's cardiologists who retired at 70.

**"My plan was to do nursing as long as my mind and body would hold out."**

## LIVING HER DREAM—AGAIN

### Jackie Wooten

*Retired, Then Returned to Work as a Classroom Teacher*

Jackie Wooten is a consistent person. Ever since she was a youngster, she wanted to be a teacher. And that's what she's done her entire adult life. No sooner had Jackie retired than she was ready to return to the classroom. Retirement was not to her liking.

"In the past, I was asked why I didn't become a principal, since I'm so well organized. But I have no desire. I get my energy from teaching; it electrifies me. All I ever wanted to be was a classroom teacher."

**"I get my energy from teaching; it electrifies me. All I ever wanted to be was a classroom teacher."**

Eight years later, after graduating from the University of North Carolina in Greensboro, Jackie got a master's degree in reading and language arts from East Carolina University. She was certified to teach kindergarten through the fifth grade as well as social studies through ninth grade. Throughout her 32-year career (and prior to her undergraduate education), Jackie has lived within 30 miles of Greenville in the eastern part of the state. She's taught third and fourth grades in two rural Pitt County communities—24 years in Bethel (population 1,800) and 8 years in Stokes (population less than 500).

Jackie's game plan was to retire in her early 50s, collect her pension, and teach part-time because it would not affect her pension status. When she retired in June 2002, Jackie was making nearly $50,000 a year, the top of the pay scale.

It was difficult for Jackie to retire. "I don't play bridge or do things like that. I've always worked. I'm happy when I'm busy. I hoped when I retired that I would teach part-time, but I was called back to teach full-time in Stokes." A temporary change in state law actually permitted Jackie to return to the classroom as a full-time teacher. North Carolina, like most states, has a teacher shortage, and it sweetened the pot to attract veteran teachers. Almost six months to the day after she retired and received her pension, Jackie was back in the classroom as a paid teacher.

"Sure, I'm double-dipping. I'm being paid to teach, and I also get my pension. But there's a shortage of teachers. I can double-dip for another year. Then I'll lose that eligibility. By then, I expect the state will change the ruling again due to the continuing lack of qualified teachers." Besides earning more than $85,000 in combined pension and teaching salary, Jackie is eligible for paid vacation, sick leave, and a bonus.

Even before her current full-time teaching assignment started, Jackie, then retired, was working twice a week as a volunteer remedial teacher at Bethel Elementary School, helping below-level students improve their reading and math skills. She also taught without pay for a friend who was on leave from her classroom following her husband's death. "These were the best three weeks of teaching in my life. I had no meetings, no clubs, or any other duties. Just teach the kids. That's why I went into teaching."

A North Carolina Education Association activist, Jackie has attended 25 National Education Association conventions. It gave her a chance to travel because her husband, Kenneth, doesn't enjoy it. Jackie also conducts training sessions for other state NEA affiliates. "There's no pay, but I get reimbursed for expenses. It's a chance to interact with teachers from other states."

She's been a delegate to the 1992 and 1996 Democratic National Conventions. Early on in Jackie's "retirement," she considered running for the state house of representatives. She decided against it due to the amount of money needed to run for the position. "I was also concerned about the length of the legislative session and decided that I didn't want to commit that much time to politics." However, she has continued her political and community involvement as Bethel's precinct chair and for two years as vice chair of the Pitt County Democratic Party.

Jackie's enthusiasm for her profession seems to have influenced her twin sons, who have both set their immediate postcollege sights on teaching. Brent and Allen, recent graduates of the University of North Carolina in Chapel Hill, teach social studies as well as coach football, basketball, and baseball at North Pitt High School, which they had attended. So ultimately, Jackie's love of teaching is being carried on by both of her sons.

> **It was difficult for Jackie to retire. "I don't play bridge or do things like that. I've always worked. I'm happy when I'm busy."**

## RETURNS TO FLYING
### Arthur (Bud) Eisberg
#### *After an Idle Year, Takes a Pilot's Job*

For commercial airline pilots, one rule remains constant. The Federal Aviation Authority maintains a

**In some ways, Bud's career was based on a series of events created by the Vietnam War.**

mandatory retirement age of 60 for national and regional commercial airline pilots. Though there's talk that the age limit might be raised, the FAA's policy affected Arthur (Bud) Eisberg's flying status in 2002.

In some ways, Bud's career was based on a series of events created by the Vietnam War. Raised in Leonia, New Jersey, Bud graduated from Colgate University in 1965. "I went to work for Ford. The draft board left me alone since Ford was a defense contractor. I left Ford, and returned to Colgate for a master's degree. My goal was a job in college administration."

By 1967, Vietnam was beginning to heat up and so was the draft. "I didn't want to become a foot soldier. Six months earlier, I had taken a navy test for OCS (officer's candidate school) and was accepted. By the time I would have been drafted, I went into the navy, then flight training, and spent some time flying intelligence missions in Vietnam."

Five years later, Bud had met his contractual naval service obligation. By now he was smitten with flying. He thought that his navy experience in flying the equivalent of the four-engine Lockheed Electra would land him a job as a commercial airline pilot. He was mistaken. "There were not many available jobs. Over the next 12 years, I worked for eight different airlines. I went with American Airlines in my early 40s after American bought Air Cal (California). " Living south of San Francisco in easy driving distance of the airport, Bud flew as a first pilot on domestic flights. The years passed and Bud, like many of his contemporaries in corporate America, became concerned with the airline's long-term viability. How would this affect his benefits package? Adding to this concern was the looming FAA retirement barrier.

Rather than wait until he was 60, coupled with the financial uncertainties facing American Airlines, Bud decided to retire at age 59. "This was a quick decision; it came upon us suddenly. My wife (Lynn, a nurse) and I attended retirement seminars put on for pilots. None dealt with the turmoil and consequences that were occurring in the industry at the time. Looking back, I was not prepared mentally and in other ways for retirement. And not having a paycheck deposited twice a month was unsettling."

The first year after leaving American Airlines presented other challenges. A late marriage meant that he still had two sons in high school looking forward to a college education. He could anticipate incurring college expenses until he was in his late 60s. "When I retired, Lynn and I never considered any immediate lifestyle changes. Any talk of cruising in the Caribbean was way into the future. The dust began to settle. It made sense to go back to work. By the time I made this decision, my FAA qualifications had expired. I quickly found out how unimpressed employers were with my 35 years' experience."

Some matters were in Bud's favor. I was fortunate to take my retirement in a lump sum. That opportunity would have gone away if American Airlines went into bankruptcy. "This was a key factor in my early retirement decision. Invested at 10 percent, it gives me about 40 percent of my former pay." Bud receives some additional income based on 22 years in the navy reserve and the rank of commander. It also qualifies him to receive medical benefits as a backup to the American Airlines retirement plan.

A year after retiring, Bud was back in the pilot's seat flying a corporate jet for a Texas-based company. He lives a split monthly schedule—two weeks flying from his Texas base and the other two at home in California.

"I fly the equivalent of a 737 to Europe, Mexico, Hong Kong, Korea, and all over the United States. I agree it's too much time away from home." He earns about 40 percent of his American Airlines salary. Because there is no age limitation for noncommercial pilots, Bud hopes to fly indefinitely, or at least to when he's an empty nester.

Looking back, Bud ponders the career decisions he made in his 20s. "Remember, I had a year with Ford Motor. I made the decision to become a commercial pilot, and I never looked back. However, I have to

"Looking back, I was not prepared mentally and in other ways for retirement. And not having a paycheck deposited twice a month was unsettling."

admit, if I was making the same decision today, I might very well have gone into college administration."

## TAKES JOB WITH A DIFFERENT TWIST
### William Francis
*Early Retirement After 30 Years*

William Francis worked for one company for 30 years before taking an early retirement package when he was only in his mid-50s.

"I left GTE (which several years later merged into what is now Verizon) earlier than I ever expected since I got a good deal," says William Francis. "One of the last things I did before leaving GTE was to head its Y2000 operations. I spent New Year's Eve in a bunker."

Bill is from Erie, Pennsylvania, and is a graduate of Gannon University, located in that city, with both bachelor's and master's degrees in business. After completing military service in the late 1960s, he joined GTE, followed by a series of line and staff positions. "Over the next 30 years, I moved 13 times to places like Indianapolis; Stamford, Connecticut; Durham, and Dallas."

His career was, by corporate standards, a success. He moved up GTE's ladder, and for nine years starting in 1985, he was the general manager of the company's North Carolina operations. He then moved to corporate headquarters in Irving, Texas, for several years just prior to retiring as director of new products planning.

Bill retired years before he ever anticipated. The Francis family—wife, Rae Ellen, and a college-age daughter—left Texas and returned to Durham. He didn't do too much of anything the first year, while the family faced a larger problem. His wife had cancer, which was treated successfully.

Bill decided to put his general experience and know-how in telecommunications to work. He had two options: find another job or start his own company.

He opted for the latter, resulting in Pilot Consulting, a company that was involved in performance software, a process that combines strategic planning and the setting of operational goals. "I decided to get out of the business when I realized it wasn't as much fun as I thought it would be. There was a slow start-up curve to get started. Our clients were mostly in this area, but to grow the business would require much more travel than I wanted to do."

During this time span, Bill also considered another option: buying a house and moving to the North Carolina coast. He already owned a 37-foot sailboat and was licensed by the Coast Guard. "If that had happened, I planned on continuing consulting from the beach."

The scenario changed. Bill wasn't looking for a new job, but he met someone who was about to retire. This person thought that Bill had the necessary skills for the job, and he recommended him to be business manager of the Trinity School in Durham. It was a job somewhat different from those he had with GTE. Bill asked himself whether he would be able to make the transition after 30 years with one large company.

As business manager, Bill's job encompasses Trinity's human resources, finances, and administration, which require a range of skills akin to the ones he used at GTE.

Part of Bill's challenge is to get the school ready for its anticipated growth in terms of the number of students and its physical facilities. Since its mid-1990s start-up, enrollment has grown to about 350 kindergarten through eighth grade students. Starting in 2006, plans call for Trinity to add a high school class each year until it's a four-year high school by 2010.

Like many other early retirees reentering the job market, Bill finds that he poses little risk to other staffers at the school. "I'm not seeking to become the school's director or a classroom teacher. I don't worry about being promoted since my job is the only one of its type at the school." Nor was salary a prime factor in taking the job, considering he was already benefiting from GTE's early retirement package.

**Bill decided to put his general experience and know-how in telecommunications to work.**

> ## "I don't worry about being promoted since my job is the only one of its type at the school."

"The prime motivating factor in taking the Trinity position was the excellent fit of my business experiences and skills with Trinity's needs. The smaller operation and minimal bureaucracy was also appealing."

After a few months on the job, Bill says he's adjusting to the different work routine. Above all, he finds the work much less stressful than previous jobs and a whole lot more rewarding.

---

## TAKING THE PLUNGE WITH EYES SHUT
### Jeanne and Larry Hervey
### *As Novices, They Operated a B&B*

Jeanne and Larry Hervey were looking for the good life. Larry had just retired at age 60 as a district supervisor with the Prince George County school system in Maryland. Jeanne, nine years younger, had raised five children and was an elementary school teacher in the same county system.

The Herveys wanted to change lifestyles and move away from their rural Maryland home into a smaller house.

Being somewhat adventuresome, they drove the mid-South coastal areas looking for a suitable community and a place to live. What happened was hardly in their retirement script.

They visited New Bern and Edenton, both historic smaller communities in eastern North Carolina. They literally stumbled across Washington, a city of 10,000 residents on the Tar River and its junction with Pamlico Sound. It seemed like love at first sight. Unlike so many southern coastal towns, Washington was spared the torch of General Sherman's troops on their 1865 march through Georgia and the Carolinas. As a result, Washington had a number of pre–Civil War homes.

The Herveys found a house that was considerably larger than what they needed. The real estate agent told them that they could set it up as a two-family house with two apartments, or they could convert it into a bed and breakfast inn. Washington at the time had no other B&Bs or equivalent hotel accommodations. "Frankly," says Jeanne, "owning and operating a B&B or any type of business was furthest from our minds."

"In some ways it appealed to Larry," says Jeanne, "because he's the type of guy who needs a project. We sold our house in Maryland, made money on it, and had the cash to buy the house in Washington and convert into a B&B. When we mentioned that we were selling our house and moving to Washington, friends presumed that we were moving into Washington, D.C." (Prince George County borders Washington, D.C.'s eastern boundary).

Along with a local contractor and Larry in his "like-to-keep-busy mode," they converted the two-story 1906 Colonial Revival home into a four-bedroom/private bath B&B. Called the Pamlico House, it retained the widow's walk and a wraparound first-floor porch. The Herveys carved out part of the first floor as their apartment.

Obtaining local approval, says Jeanne, called for overcoming some neighborhood opposition and receiving a special-use zoning permit.

By restoring an early 20th century home, they became eligible for National Historical Preservation status, which gave them some tax credits and added another structure in the city's historic district.

During this process, they violated a number of cardinal business rules. They knew little about B&B operations or the hospitality field. They opted against attending how-to workshops conducted for B&B hopefuls, and as educators they could hardly fall back on any related workplace experience. They were novices. Drawbacks notwithstanding, they decided to learn their B&B lessons by trial and error.

They opened, however, on an auspicious note on April 15, 1988, with broadcaster Charles Kuralt as their first guest. Kuralt, an eastern North Carolina native, was in Washington doing a program on the area's tulip festival.

> "Frankly," says Jeanne, "owning and operating a B&B or any type of business was furthest from our minds."

Their customer base was not the usual tourists. Being located in the county seat, some guests were doing business with county government and the courts. They also received guests from two residential communities being built in the area. The builders provided prospective homeowners with one night of free lodging.

Operating a B&B with only four guest rooms has its drawbacks. The staff is limited. When the cleaning people did not show up, "Larry and I changed linen, cleaned rooms, and swabbed toilets. Otherwise we shared chores. We got up seven days a week at 6 and did breakfast together for our guests. Larry's specialty was pancakes and mine was muffins." Larry gave himself an extra duty driving visitors around town as an unofficial tour guide.

Furnishing Pamlico House was no problem. Besides furniture and fixtures from their Maryland home, eastern North Carolina is a treasure chest of antique shops and flea markets stocked with the types of goods that complement a 100-year-old restoration.

Nine years later, the Herveys decided to sell. "We liked running a B&B, but at times we found it confining. We had few vacations or time away from the place. It was a year-round inn, and we began to tire of it." And, as Jeanne admits, they owned it twice as long as most other B&B proprietors do.

They sold Pamlico House in March 1997. Larry was then 70. The inn was now profitable, and they made money on the sale. The new owner continued to operate Pamlico House until it was sold in 2004, and it reverted to a private home. "Looking back," says Jeanne, "we realized that running a B&B is a job, not retirement."

## POINTS TO REMEMBER

- **Boredom is an important factor** that draws the 50-plus set back to work.
- **Many retirees miss the challenge, competition, and collegiality** of the workplace.
- **There's stiff competition** to get part-time or interim management jobs.
- **Avoid obsolescence.** Upgrade your skills before looking for employment.
- **Be willing to accept a lower salary.**
- **Learn new ways to "sell" yourself** to a prospective employer.

# How Will You Foot the Bills?

**Appendix**

**T**he primary thrust of this book is to help you answer this question: What will I do if I retire? Questions that may be looming equally large in your mind are: How much money will I need to live in retirement? Do I have enough? Where is it going to come from? While whole books have been written on these subjects, this isn't one of them. This book would be the perfect companion to a book on financial planning for retirement and to one on managing your investments to meet your goals. We recommend some appropriate resources in the box on page 25 in Chapter 1. Of course, you've gotten at least a glimpse of how each person profiled in this book is financing his or her "retirement."

That said, this section will help you begin to assess the current and future status of your nest egg and the income it will provide you in retirement. You may realize that the funds you've accumulated for retirement are, in fact, enough and you can devote your energies to developing your new life in "retirement." Maybe you can afford to retire early and devote yourself to an unpaid labor of love or to work for the sheer joy of it, without regard to income. Perhaps accepting a buyout offer will provide the funds necessary to supercharge your retirement nest egg, allowing you ultimately to retire early, if not immediately. You may realize that if you just hang on for another few years and increase your rate of saving and investing, you can afford the travel for which you had always hoped. You may learn that you're going to need to work after you retire, though maybe not the 50-hour weeks you've been putting in for the past 15 or 20 years.

## The Income You Will Need

No two individual or family budgets are the same. What one family calls "just getting by" is luxurious living for someone else. However, one common rule of thumb is that you will need 85 percent of your preretirement income to maintain your "standard of living" after your regular paychecks stop. Some people may be able to do what they want on 75 percent or 80 percent, but unless you're looking forward to a more spartan life than before, aim for the higher figure to help ensure that you'll achieve your retirement lifestyle dream.

### How Much Income Will You Need?

First calculate your income goal at retirement. Multiply your current salary by a future growth factor from the table shown later in this Appendix. For example, use 4 percent estimated annual inflation and add that to the amount you expect your salary to rise each year, say 3 percent, for a total of 7 percent. If you want to retire early in ten years, look where 7 percent intersects ten years and you find the multiplier 1.97. Multiplying that by your current salary—say, $50,000—tells you what you'll be earning ($98,500 in this example) at the point you want to retire. Figure on needing 85 percent

---

**AN EARLY-RETIREMENT WORKSHEET**

If you want to retire early, as many of the people profiled in this book did, you'll have to figure out not only how much of a nest egg you will have by the time you want to leave but also how much of it will be available to you then. The information below will help you with your planning.

of that amount once you retire, and you arrive at an annual income goal after early retirement of $83,725.

A. $_____ × _____ × 0.85 = $ _____

<small>Your current income    Multiplier from future-growth factor table    Equals your goal</small>

Example: $50,000 × 1.97 = $98,500 × 0.85 = $83,725

# Accounting for Future Dollars

The 85 percent of your income that you will need annually in the future isn't 85 percent of your income today. It's 85 percent of your income at the point when you are ready to retire, whether that's a year away, or 5, 10, or 15 years from now. The further out you're looking, the more your income is likely to grow from raises and cost-of-living increases, and the less your purchasing power will be due to inflation. All of this adds up to the need for a bigger nest egg than you might think. But you don't have to panic. The same forces that make your needs grow will help your nest egg grow, too.

# How Long Will You Live?

Knowing how much money you will need in retirement also depends on how long you're going to need it—10 years, 20, 30, or even 40? Life expectancy is on the rise; the average woman retiring today at age 65 is expected to live another 19.5 years, and the average man can look forward to another 16.6 years. Those who have just entered the 50-plus crowd can expect to live even longer.

# Assessing Your Resources

The cornerstone of your retirement nest egg is likely to be your pension (or other employer-provided defined-benefit plan) or a 401(k) or 403(b) (or other defined-contribution plan), together with Social Security. The rest of the gap between pre-

## AVERAGE REMAINING LIFETIME

### AVERAGE NUMBER OF YEARS OF LIFE REMAINING

| AGE | MALE | FEMALE | AGE | MALE | FEMALE |
|-----|------|--------|-----|------|--------|
| 40  | 37.0 | 41.4   | 65  | 16.6 | 19.5   |
| 45  | 32.6 | 36.7   | 70  | 13.2 | 15.8   |
| 50  | 28.3 | 32.2   | 75  | 10.3 | 12.4   |
| 55  | 24.1 | 27.7   | 80  | 7.8  | 9.4    |
| 60  | 20.2 | 23.5   | 85  | 5.7  | 6.9    |

Source: Centers for Disease Control and Prevention/Division of Vital Statistics, *Deaths: Final Data for 2002*, National Vital Statistics Reports, vol. 53, no. 5, October 12, 2004. The year 2002 is the most recent year for which final data are available.

retirement and postretirement income will be filled in by your own savings and investments, and from other resources such as profit from the sale of your home. If you're close to normal retirement age, you've probably accumulated a substantial chunk of your retirement savings. You may know precisely what you can expect from your pension and Social Security, but you may not be fully aware of all the resources available to you, or even how to figure out how long you can expect your nest egg to last. If you're just 50-plus, you've probably got a retirement savings plan under way and you just need time as your ally to fill it up and out. This section will show you what a difference you can make.

### Your Pension

The traditional defined-benefit pension plan is becoming increasingly rare. Many companies have switched to cash balance plans, which combine the protections of a traditional pension with the portability of a 401(k) plan. Under such plans, each year an amount equal to a percentage of your salary—say 5 percent—goes into the account. The money is guaranteed to earn a predetermined interest rate, usually tied to an index such as the consumer price index or the Treasury bill rate. If plan investments earn less than the

## AN EARLY RETIREMENT WORKSHEET

**Anticipated Resources at Crucial Ages**
One of the obstacles to early retirement is that you can't count on all your long-term savings and investments to kick in with income right from the start. You also won't be eligible for Medicare until you're 65 and will have to find some way to cover your health insurance needs, including prescription drug costs, until then.

The worksheet below reflects the fact that employer pension benefits are rarely available before age 55, Social Security benefits can't start before age 62, and IRA funds, except contributions made to a Roth IRA, are generally tied up until age 59½. (Regular IRA funds can be tapped earlier if the money is taken via roughly equal installments based on your life expectancy. To use this loophole, you must stick with the lifetime payout schedule for at least five consecutive years and until you're at least 59½. For more information, consult IRS publications #590, *Individual Retirement Accounts,* and #575, *Pension and Annuity Income.*)

To determine whether you can live on the investment income (before pension and Social Security payments and certain retirement-fund money become available) without depleting capital, multiply your assets by the percent you believe they can earn each year—the example below assumes an 8 percent earnings rate.

| | | TARGET AGE | | | |
| --- | --- | --- | --- | --- | --- |
| | | **50–54** | **55–59** | **60–62** | **62-PLUS** |
| 1. Savings | $_____ × 0.08 = | $_____ | $_____ | $_____ | $_____ |
| 2. Home equity | $_____ × 0.08 = | $_____ | $_____ | $_____ | $_____ |
| 3. IRAs* | $_____ × 0.08 = | $ N/A | $ N/A | $_____ | $_____ |
| 4. Keoghs | $_____ × 0.08 = | $ N/A | $_____ | $_____ | $_____ |
| 5. 401(k)s | $_____ × 0.08 = | $ N/A | $_____ | $_____ | $_____ |
| 6. Pension** | $_____ = | $ N/A | $_____ | $_____ | $_____ |
| 7. Social Security** | $_____ = | $ N/A | $ N/A | $ N/A | $_____ |
| B. Column totals | | $_____ | $_____ | $_____ | $_____ |
| C. Shortfall (A minus B) | | $_____ | $_____ | $_____ | $_____ |

\* You can withdraw your own contributions to the new Roth IRA penalty free anytime before age 59½.
\*\* When they become available, your pension and Social Security benefits form the cornerstone of your retirement income. It's assumed you will not be investing them.

promised interest rate, the employer must make up the difference. If they earn more, the excess counts toward the next year's contribution and reduces the employer's out-of-pocket cost. Because the employer's contribution is based on a percentage of your current salary, benefits in a cash balance plan grow more evenly over the years than those in a traditional pension plan, in which benefits are weighted more heavily toward your last years on the job. When employees leave the job, they can take a lump-sum payout of the account balance and roll it into an IRA. If they are of retirement age, it can be made into an annuity.

Traditional defined-benefit plans guarantee to pay you a specified amount when you retire based on your salary, age, and years of service. Chances are that if your company still has a traditional defined-benefit plan or you've been contemplating leaving early, you've already received an estimate of your monthly pension benefit from your company's pension administrator. If you haven't yet received this information, you might be interested in knowing how a traditional defined-benefit pension is typically calculated. The formula looks like this:

Final average monthly earnings × 1.5%
× Years of service (the benefit accrual rate)
= Monthly benefit due

Final average monthly earnings might be the average of the five consecutive years you earned the most—that will probably be your last five (add income for each of the five years and divide by 60 months).

For example, if you have worked for 30 years, your benefit accrual rate is 45 percent. If your final average monthly earnings are $5,000, then you would get $2,250 per month.

What percentage of your preretirement income will your pension likely replace? The answer varies greatly by employer, but a typical benefit is 50 percent of income at retirement minus 50 percent of Social Security, which works out to 37 percent of income for a 30-year worker retiring at a salary level of $50,000. Usually the longer you stay on at work, the greater the percentage of replacement, though there is generally a maximum period of service allowed for the computation.

To receive the maximum pension, most plans require that you work at the company for 30 years and wait until "full retirement age," which is usually 62 or 65. (Note that your company's definition of "full retirement age" may differ from Social Security's.) Some companies use a point system that lets you retire at full benefits once your age plus years of service total a certain number of points. An early retiree would probably see benefits reduced, depending on his or her age.

### Social Security

In 2006, you can begin collecting your full Social Security benefits at age 65 and 8 months. Full retirement age will continue to increase until it reaches 67 in 2027 (see the box below). For an estimate of your Social Security benefit based on your earnings history, request a personalized benefits estimate from the Social Security Administration (SSA). Call 800-772-1213 and ask for Form SSA-7004, "Request for Social Security Statement." You should receive your estimate in about two to four weeks. The estimate you receive will be based on you retiring at age 62, retiring at full retirement age, and waiting to retire at age 70. (The SSA has begun automatically sending the benefits estimate annually to everyone age 25 and over.) You may also log on to *www.ssa.gov* to request your statement or use online tools to create estimates based on your earnings.

The soonest you can begin collecting monthly Social Security checks is age 62, but if you do, your benefits will be reduced by as much as 30 percent for life. Using the table on page 247, you can calcu-

## WHEN YOU CAN RECEIVE FULL BENEFITS

| AGE YEAR OF BIRTH | YEARS | PLUS MONTHS |
|---|---|---|
| 1941 | 65 | 8 |
| 1942 | 65 | 10 |
| 1943–54 | 66 | 0 |
| 1955 | 66 | 2 |
| 1956 | 66 | 4 |
| 1957 | 66 | 6 |
| 1958 | 66 | 8 |
| 1959 | 66 | 10 |
| 1960 and later | 67 | 0 |

late your reduced benefit. Multiply your estimated benefit at full retirement age by the reduction percentage for the number of months that you plan to retire early. (On the other hand, if you expect to delay retirement, see the discussion later in the Appendix.)

Once you begin receiving Social Security benefits, your spouse can also receive benefits based on your record, even if he or she never worked in a job covered by Social Security. A nonworking spouse is eligible to begin receiving benefits at age 62. At your full retirement age, you will together receive 150 percent of what you would receive on your own.

If your spouse works, he or she will receive a benefit based on his or her actual earnings or 50 percent of your benefit, whichever is more, assuming that you're the first one to retire.

## Other Current Savings

Add up what you've got socked away in any of the following, whether yours or your spouse's:

- Profit-sharing or any other company-sponsored defined-benefit plans
- 401(k) or 403(b) plans
- Individual retirement accounts (IRAs)
- Keogh plans
- Other retirement savings

## Your Home

Don't forget to include your house. If you own a house and plan to use the equity in it to help finance your retirement, you're further along to your goal. Of course, for a realistic picture, you'll need to subtract from your home's market value any mortgage you expect to still owe at retirement, sales commissions and closing costs, and any part of proceeds of the sale of the home you'll use for the down payment on a retirement home. Thanks to a provision in the Tax Act of 1997, chances are you won't have to pay a dime in taxes on the profit when you sell so anything remaining can be added to your nest egg.

## Figuring the Gap

L et's say that you're age 63 in 2006 and you plan to retire from your employer of 32 years at age 66. Your spouse, a late-blooming professional five years younger than you, expects to continue working for four years after that.

Your current salary is $75,000, and you expect a 4 percent cost-of-living increase for each of the next three years ($3,000 in year one, $3,120 in year two, and $3,245 in year three), putting your preretirement income at $84,365.

Your spouse's current income is $50,000 per year. Between merit raises and cost-of-living increases, you think that he or she can reasonably expect an average income increase of 7 percent for each of the eight years until he or she reaches retirement, setting his or her

### HOW EARLY RETIREMENT WILL REDUCE YOUR BENEFITS

| MONTHS EARLY | % OF FULL BENEFIT | MONTHS EARLY | % OF FULL BENEFIT |
|---|---|---|---|
| 2 | 98.9% | 32 | 82.2% |
| 4 | 97.8 | 34 | 81.1 |
| 6 | 96.7 | 36 | 80.0 |
| 8 | 95.6 | 38* | 79.2 |
| 10 | 94.4 | 40* | 78.3 |
| 12 | 93.3 | 42* | 77.5 |
| 14 | 92.2 | 44* | 76.7 |
| 16 | 91.1 | 46* | 75.8 |
| 18 | 90.0 | 48* | 75.0 |
| 20 | 88.9 | 50* | 74.2 |
| 22 | 87.8 | 52* | 73.3 |
| 24 | 86.7 | 54* | 72.5 |
| 26 | 85.6 | 56* | 71.7 |
| 28 | 84.4 | 58* | 70.8 |
| 30 | 83.3 | 60* | 70.0 |

* As full retirement age rises to age 67, these early retirement percentages will apply.

preretirement income at $85,909. For the first five years of your retirement, you will need to replace 85 percent of your annual preretirement income, or $71,710 per year ($84,365 × .85) and in the following 20 years, 85 percent of your and your spouse's preretirement income, or $144,733 per year ([$84,365 + $85,909] × .85) Now, where's that money going to come from?

## Social Security and Pension Benefits

**THE FIRST FIVE YEARS.** Per our calculations using the quick estimate feature at the Social Security Web site, your annual Social Security benefit will be $23,280 ($1,940 a month × 12; for the purposes of this example only, the monthly figure is based on estimated Social Security benefits for the year 2006).

You know that your annual pension benefit will come to $30,542 (50 percent of preretirement income minus 50 percent of Social Security; [.50 × $84,365] − [.50 × $23,280]).

Between what you will get from your pension and Social Security, you will have accounted for $53,822 per year, which is short by $17,888 of your estimated need of $71,710.

**THE NEXT 20 YEARS.** Now your spouse retires and claims his or her Social Security benefit; he or she doesn't have a traditional defined-benefit plan, but we'll account for the value of his or her deferred profit sharing later.

When your spouse retires, he or she will also be considered a higher-than-average wage earner and qualifies for an annual benefit of $27,600 ($2,300 × 12).

Your and your spouse's combined annual income from Social Security and your pension benefit thereafter will be $81,422 ($23,280 + $30,542 + 27,600). That leaves you with a $63,311 gap between your needs and what your defined benefits will provide ($144,733 − $81,422).

## Your Retirement Savings and Investments

How will you fill that gap? Let's look at the retirement savings and investments that will be available following your retirement:

- *Deferred profit sharing.* You estimate that account at retirement will hold $298,000. You plan to take the money and reinvest it.
- *Your individual retirement account.* By the time you retire, your IRA will be worth $30,000.
- *Investment portfolio.* Over the years, you've invested in blue-chip stocks and bonds currently valued at

## HOW A LUMP SUM WILL GROW

This table is useful for anticipating how money you've already accumulated will grow over various lengths of time at various rates of return, compounded annually. Choose the appropriate number of years from the left-hand column and the assumed rate of return from across the top, and mul-

tiply the starting amount by the factor that's shown where the two columns intersect. For example, say that you have $20,000 in a mutual fund that you expect will pay 10 percent per year for the next eight years. At the end of that time, you'll have $42,800 ($20,000 × 2.14).

### FUTURE GROWTH FACTOR

| YEAR | 3% | 4% | 5% | 6% | 7% | 8% | 9% | 10% | 11% | 12% | 13% | 14% | 15% |
|---|---|---|---|---|---|---|---|---|---|---|---|---|---|
| 1 | 1.03 | 1.04 | 1.05 | 1.06 | 1.07 | 1.08 | 1.09 | 1.10 | 1.11 | 1.12 | 1.13 | 1.14 | 1.15 |
| 2 | 1.06 | 1.08 | 1.10 | 1.12 | 1.14 | 1.17 | 1.19 | 1.21 | 1.23 | 1.25 | 1.28 | 1.30 | 1.32 |
| 3 | 1.09 | 1.12 | 1.16 | 1.19 | 1.22 | 1.26 | 1.29 | 1.33 | 1.37 | 1.40 | 1.44 | 1.48 | 1.52 |
| 4 | 1.12 | 1.17 | 1.22 | 1.26 | 1.31 | 1.36 | 1.41 | 1.46 | 1.52 | 1.57 | 1.63 | 1.69 | 1.75 |
| 5 | 1.16 | 1.22 | 1.28 | 1.34 | 1.40 | 1.47 | 1.54 | 1.61 | 1.69 | 1.76 | 1.84 | 1.93 | 2.01 |
| 6 | 1.19 | 1.26 | 1.34 | 1.42 | 1.50 | 1.59 | 1.68 | 1.77 | 1.87 | 1.97 | 2.08 | 2.19 | 2.31 |
| 7 | 1.23 | 1.32 | 1.41 | 1.50 | 1.61 | 1.71 | 1.83 | 1.95 | 2.08 | 2.21 | 2.35 | 2.50 | 2.66 |
| 8 | 1.27 | 1.37 | 1.48 | 1.59 | 1.72 | 1.85 | 1.99 | 2.14 | 2.30 | 2.48 | 2.66 | 2.85 | 3.06 |
| 9 | 1.30 | 1.42 | 1.55 | 1.69 | 1.84 | 2.00 | 2.17 | 2.36 | 2.56 | 2.77 | 3.00 | 3.25 | 3.52 |
| 10 | 1.34 | 1.48 | 1.63 | 1.79 | 1.97 | 2.16 | 2.37 | 2.59 | 2.84 | 3.11 | 3.39 | 3.71 | 4.05 |
| 15 | 1.56 | 1.80 | 2.08 | 2.40 | 2.76 | 3.17 | 3.64 | 4.18 | 4.78 | 5.40 | 6.25 | 7.14 | 8.14 |
| 20 | 1.81 | 2.19 | 2.65 | 3.21 | 3.87 | 4.66 | 5.60 | 6.73 | 8.06 | 9.65 | 11.52 | 13.74 | 16.37 |
| 25 | 2.09 | 2.66 | 3.39 | 4.29 | 5.43 | 6.85 | 8.62 | 10.83 | 13.59 | 17.00 | 21.23 | 26.46 | 32.92 |
| 30 | 2.43 | 3.24 | 4.32 | 5.74 | 7.61 | 10.06 | 13.27 | 17.45 | 22.89 | 29.96 | 39.12 | 50.95 | 66.21 |

$350,000. At an 8 percent rate of growth, you estimate that your portfolio will be worth $441,000 in three years ($350,000 × 1.26; see the table in the box below for an explanation of how to figure money growth).

That gives you a lump sum of $769,000. Off the top you draw about $90,000 to cover the annual income gap of $17,888 you'll have the first five years and put it in a money market IRA. You leave the rest to cook until your spouse's retirement; at 8 percent per year for five years, you'll end up with $998,130 ($679,000 × 1.47).

**THE NEXT 20 YEARS.** You estimate that when your spouse retires, he or she will have $145,400 in his or her 401(k) plan and $40,000 in an IRA, making your total assets $1,183,530.

## Your Home

Finally, let's consider one more resource: your home. When your spouse retires, you are planning to sell your suburban home and move back to your hometown. Your home's current value is $400,000, and you believe you can expect a 3 percent average rate of appreciation each of the next eight years. By the time you're ready to sell, the house should be worth about $508,000 ($400,000 × 1.27 [for money-growth factors, see the table on page 249]). Your mortgage is paid off. Thanks to the 1997 tax act, which exempts from taxation $500,000 in profit from the sale of a home for those filing joint returns ($250,000 is tax-free for those who file single returns), you'll pocket the whole sales price, except for commissions and other sales expenses. That's $465,168 ($508,000 sales price minus $42,832 for commissions and other expenses). You know that you can purchase the home you want in your hometown for $210,000 in cash. That leaves you $255,168 to pad your investment portfolio.

# The Final Tally: How Long Will It Last?

You now have a grand total of $1,438,698. Will it generate the income that isn't covered by Social Security and your pension? And how long will it last? You can use the table in the box on page 253 to figure that out.

You know that you need to come up with $63,311 a year ($5,276 per month) for 20 years. You expect that your nest egg will continue to earn 8 percent annually. The point where 20 years and 8 percent intersect is $119,550. That's the amount needed to produce $1,000 in income per month for 20 years. (The $1,000 will be exhausted at the end of the period.) Because your monthly requirement is 5.28 times that amount ($5,276 ÷ $1,000 rounded up to 2 decimal points), multiply $119,550 by 5.28 and you get a total nest egg requirement of $631,224. You have more than twice that!

But wait: Before you assume that you're on easy street, keep in mind that you need to account for what inflation will do to your nest egg over those 20 years. A safe rule of thumb is to add 25 percent to 40 percent to your total nest egg as an inflation cushion. In this example, that would bring the total required nest egg to between $789,030 and $883,714 [$631,224 × 1.25 = $789,030); $631,224 × 1.40 = $883,714]. So, even with inflation, your nest egg is more than sufficient.

Taxes will also take a bite out of your retirement income. The taxes you pay will depend upon many variables including: your tax bracket in retirement; the extent to which your Social Security benefits will be subject to income tax; the share of your income that comes from savings that have already been taxed; and how long you postpone withdrawing funds from tax-deferred accounts, such as 401(k)s and IRAs. In the early part of your retirement, you and your spouse might depend on your investment portfolio, on which you've paid income tax right along. If you delay tapping your IRAs and deferred profit sharing for as long as possible—or until age 70½, when you must begin to withdraw the money—those accounts can continue growing tax-deferred, and you put off the inevitable tax bill. (If you start a Roth IRA, or convert a traditional IRA to a Roth, you avoid the tax bill altogether, and there is no requirement to begin withdrawals at age 70½.)

Regardless, you're lucky. You've got some options. Maybe you would like to retire now rather than later. Maybe your spouse would like to retire earlier than planned. Maybe you'll be able to do things in retirement that you hadn't imagined. You could give more to your favorite charities or leave more to the kids. Bottom line, you don't have to worry if you live longer than expected.

## Ways to Fill In a Gap

The couple in our example won't have any financial worries, but what if you end up with a gap that you must fill?

■ **You can retire anyway and seek a new work arrangement.** Look for a situation that offers some of the satisfactions of retirement—say, a more flexible schedule—as well as income. This book is filled with examples of people happily pursuing this strategy, whether they have started a business, become consultants (in some cases selling their services back to their former employer), chosen to work part-time, turned volunteer interests into paid positions, or created other options.

■ **You can postpone leaving your current employer beyond your hoped-for retirement age.** This option will allow you to contribute more to your savings and investments for as long as necessary, and while you're at it be thinking about and planning for what you will do next.

■ **You can retire anyway and lower your postretirement standard of living.** Some in the 50-plus set may take certain steps in this direction anyway by simplifying their lives. For example, some whose kids are out of the house may trade in their larger, high-maintenance home for a smaller, lower-maintenance one. From their point of view, they're not lowering their standard of living but improving it.

■ **You can gamble that higher-risk investments will provide you with higher returns, not losses.** This isn't a smart idea if you don't have plenty of time to recoup a loss. This advice applies to business start-ups, too (see Chapter 7).

■ **You can wait to cash in on Social Security.** Social Security now offers a bonus, the delayed-retirement credit (shown in the table later in this Appendix), for each year that you continue working or delay applying for Social Security past your full retirement age. This can mean significantly larger monthly checks when you do decide to call it quits or cash in. Of course, the longer you work, the larger the wage base that your benefit will be calculated on to begin with. Plus, for every year you wait to collect your benefit, the bonus is compounded; that is, each year's bonus percentage is applied to the base benefit plus any previous years' bonuses that you've already earned. And that's on top of cost-of-living increases in Social Security, if any. A financial planner, accountant, or the Social Security Administration can help you figure out how waiting will boost the size of your nest egg.

## HOW BIG A NEST EGG YOU NEED TO COVER AN INCOME GAP

### SAVINGS NEEDED TO PERMIT MONTHLY WITHDRAWALS OF $1,000 AT EACH RATE OF RETURN

| YEARS IN RETIREMENT | 5% | 6% | 7% | 8% | 9% | 10% | 12% | 14% |
|---|---|---|---|---|---|---|---|---|
| 5 | $52,990 | $51,730 | $50,500 | $49,320 | $48,170 | $47,060 | $44,960 | $42,980 |
| 10 | 94,280 | 90,070 | 86,130 | 82,420 | 78,940 | 75,670 | 69,700 | 64,410 |
| 15 | 126,460 | 118,500 | 111,250 | 104,640 | 98,590 | 93,060 | 83,320 | 75,090 |
| 20 | 151,530 | 139,580 | 128,980 | 119,550 | 111,140 | 103,620 | 90,820 | 80,420 |
| 25 | 171,060 | 155,210 | 141,490 | 129,560 | 119,160 | 110,050 | 94,950 | 83,070 |
| 30 | 186,280 | 166,790 | 150,310 | 136,280 | 124,280 | 113,950 | 97,220 | 84,400 |

## If You Work and Collect Social Security

Until you reach full retirement age (65 and 8 months in 2006), if you work and collect Social Security, the government takes away some of your Social Security benefits if your earned income exceeds certain limits. In 2006, if you're age 62 through the year before you reach full retirement age, the government reclaims $1 of benefits for every $2 you earn over $12,480; if you reach full retirement age in 2006, the limit is $33,240. In the year up to the month in which you reach full retirement age, the government deducts $1 of every $3 you earn. In the month that you reach full retirement age you will receive full benefits no matter how much you earn. If you are collecting Social Security, or soon will be, you won't be alone if you view that as an unfair "tax" on top of your regular income taxes. You'll find that many Social Security beneficiaries profiled in this book have limited their paid work to avoid being "shorted" on the money they're due. But believe it or not, the final effect of the earnings limit isn't as bad as most people think it is. That's because it's offset by the delayed-retirement credit, described above, and something called automatic benefit recomputation.

Let's say you're 63 and you earned $50,000 in 2006 from a consulting job. That's enough to eliminate all $15,700 of your Social Security benefits ($50,000 – $15,700 = $34,300; $34,300 ÷ 2 = $17,150). But because you didn't get any benefits, the government treats you as if you had delayed applying for Social Security by one year, and your future benefits will be hiked by 5 percent (see the table on page 255). That would add about $785 a year ($15,700 × .05)—plus future cost-of-living increases on that amount—to your benefits for the rest of your life. This will apply each year that your benefits are withheld before you reach age 70.

Even so, this bonus doesn't entirely make up for the loss of benefits you'll incur. Assuming an average

| THE LATE-RETIREMENT BONUS | |
|---|---|
| **YEAR YOU WERE BORN** | **ANNUAL BONUS FOR WORKING BEYOND FULL RETIREMENT AGE** |
| 1929–30 | 4.5% |
| 1931–32 | 5.0 |
| 1933–34 | 5.5 |
| 1935–36 | 6.0 |
| 1937–38 | 6.5 |
| 1939–40 | 7.0 |
| 1941–42 | 7.5 |
| 1943 or later | 8.0 |

lifespan, the higher benefits resulting from the credit will pay back just over half of what you lose to the earnings test. As you can see from the table in the box below, the situation will improve over the years for younger members of the 50-plus set, with the credit rising to 8 percent for those retiring in 2008.

The practice of automatic benefit recomputation helps if, in a year when you lose benefits, your annual earnings exceed the lowest yearly income (adjusted for inflation) originally used to figure your monthly benefit. Plugging a higher number into the formula pays off in a higher level of benefits. That can be particularly valuable if you have fewer than 35 years of employment. In that case, your earnings after retirement would replace a year without earnings earlier in your life.

While you may want to review your income-producing plans with a financial advisor, your choice on this issue may ultimately come down to principle: You'll have to decide which means more to you— working for pay or collecting the full amount of the Social Security you're due. It's up to you.

# Using the Equity in Your Home

The Tax Act of 1997 included a wonderful break for homeowners. It excludes up to $500,000 of profit on the sale of every principal residence you own—provided you've occupied it for at least two of the last five years prior to the sale—if you file a joint return ($250,000 is tax-free if you file a single return). Until that new law was enacted, those over age 55 had a one-time opportunity to take the first $125,000 of profit on the sale tax-free. And there were other restrictions as well.

If you own your home outright, another way to get at your equity in it is a reverse mortgage. A lending institution sends you a monthly check against the equity in your home. The older you are when you apply for a reverse mortgage, the more money you're likely to get, because you won't be around as long to collect the monthly checks. When you sell, move, or die, the loan comes due. The lender repays itself the balance of your loan plus interest from the proceeds of the sale of your home. The disadvantages of reverse mortgages are the costs associated with getting one and the relatively high interest rate. That's why it's wise to compare the pros and cons of a reverse mortgage with those of a home-equity loan or a second mortgage. However, it can be a good alternative for people with little monthly income who would probably not qualify for a home equity loan. And if you do get a reverse mortgage, you'll want to make use of it for long enough (say, not less than five years) to lessen the impact of its costs and maximize its benefits. For more information, contact AARP. The information booklet *Home-Made Money: A Consumer's Guide to Reverse Mortgages* (#D15601) is available online at its Web site *(www.aarp.org/revmort)* or you can order the booklet by calling 888-687-2277. You can also call the Department of Housing and Urban Development or check its Web site for free information about reverse mortgages (800-217-6970; *www.hud.gov/buying/rvrsmort .cfm*).

# Index

# Share the message!

### Bulk discounts
Discounts start at only 10 copies and range from 30% to 55% off retail price based on quantity.

### Custom publishing
Private label a cover with your organization's name and logo. Or, tailor information to your needs with a custom pamphlet that highlights specific chapters.

### Ancillaries
Workshop outlines, videos, and other products are available on select titles.

### Dynamic speakers
Engaging authors are available to share their expertise and insight at your event.

**Call Kaplan Publishing Corporate Sales at
1-800-621-9621, ext. 4444,
or e-mail kaplanpubsales@kaplan.com**